the book of the burren

TírEolas

We would like to gratefully acknowledge the generous assistance of those whose names are found below in helping to make this book a reality.

Jim and Mary Barr, Dunguaire Thatched Cottages.
Douglas and Sarah Culligan, Whitethorn Restaurant & Crafts.
Peter and Moira Haden, Gregan's Castle Hotel.
Roger and Susan Johnston, Aillwee Caves.
The Galway County Development Team.

the book of the burren

by   John Feehan
     Cilian Roden
     Gordon D'Arcy
     John Waddell
     Paul Gosling
     D. L. Swan
     J. W. O'Connell
     Lelia Doolan
     Caoilte Breatnach
     Charlie Piggott
     Anne Korff
     Patrick F. Sheeran

Editors   J. W. O'Connell
          A. Korff

Published by   Tír Eolas

First published in 1991 by Tír Eolas,
Newtownlynch Kinvara Co. Galway.
© **Tir Eolas**

2nd edition 2001 © Tír Eolas

Text Editor: Jeff O'Connell
Visual Editor: Anne Korff

Editorial Policy
Given the complexity of place-name studies
and the successive layers of meaning incorporated in their Irish and English versions,
our policy has been to allow a certain freedom
to the different authors in how they choose to
present them in their chapters. With such a
diversity of contributors, we have preferred to
allow this to come across in the individual
chapters, firmly believing that it imparts a
variety and a spontaneity that would suffer
were we to impose an absolute uniformity.

ISBN 1 873821 15 8 PAPERBACK
ISBN 1 873821 16 6 HARD COVERS

Layout and design: Anne Korff
Typesetting: Johan Hofsteenge
Printed by Colour Books

Foreword

I have had a love affair with the Burren since I was a student of archaeology at University College, Galway over twenty years ago. I cannot think of anywhere else in Ireland that equals this varied and rich concentration of stone monuments, particularly wedge tombs, cashels, twelfth to fifteenth century churches and tower houses. The terraced karsts of the Burren give the impression of a white grey stone wilderness; however, it is anything but as the excellent grazing and unique botanical survivals show.

Although the geological and botanical credentials of the Burren are of international significance, it is as an archaeologist that I can really commend it. Could I suggest that in addition to the better-known destinations like Corcomroe, Poulnabrone, Newtown, Leamaneh and Kilfenora that the extra effort necessary to visit sites like Oughtmama and Cahercommaun will more than repay your efforts and give you some healthy exercise into the bargain.

I commend and welcome this book and I congratulate Anne Korff, Jeff O'Connell and their distinguished team of contributors on the production of what I know to have been a labour of love, a worthy tribute to the spare majesty of the Burren and its treasures. The book is the culmination of years of dedication by Anne and Jeff; their pictorial guides and maps have already become indispensable to motorists, cyclists and pedestrians getting to grips with the area.

This work will be treasured both in the field and later, as a souvenir. It will help a new generation to discover and cherish the Burren in the way that the knowledge and enthusiasm of Westropp, Duignan and Killanin, De Valera and O Nualláin, Cunningham, Harbison, Rynne, Brother McNamara (a native son) and Vin Butler in their different ways have done for me.

It is essential that neither the monuments nor the environment suffers in any way as a result of the greater discovery of the Burren and the influx of additional visitors. The scale, economy and nature of the area will ultimately be best served by small seriously motivated groups (e.g. families!) rather than by busloads flushing through this sensitive part of our heritage thinking they've "done" the Burren. You only have to look up at the faces of the clerics on one of the carved capitals of the east window in Kilfenora cathedral to see what real Burren folk feel about vulgarisation! On a personal note, I hope that the relevant local authority will have replaced the access to Corcomroe with a more bicycle-friendly surface in time for what I am sure will be a prompt second edition of this welcome work.

Patrick F. Wallace
May 1991

Contents

Burrens of the Mind, Landscapes of the Imagination

"...Burren's hilly grey expanse of jagged peaks and slippery steeps, a country nevertheless flowing with milk and yielding luscious grass."

Caithreim Thoirdhealbhaign (The Triumphs of Turlough) c.1345-1360

Let's begin with a story. A few years ago Paul Gosling, one of the contributors to this book, found himself in Lisdoonvarna for the weekend. On the Sunday morning, Paul went into a local supermarket to get the papers. It was after Mass and there was a crowd bunched around the check-out counter. Amidst all the shoppers - both locals and visitors - Paul noticed one man who was trying to attract the attention of the girl at the cash register. Eventually, after she had dealt with most of the customers lined up at the counter, the poor man succeeded in catching her eye.

"I wonder could you help me", he inquired, his accent unmistakably proclaiming him a Dubliner, "I'm trying to get directions". The check-out girl sighed and asked him, "Where are you looking for?" The Dubliner replied, "I'm trying to find the Burren. Where exactly is it?" Quite unperturbed by the question, the girl got down to basics. "How did you get here?" "I came through Bally-vaughan", he told her. "Well," she declared, "You've been driving through it all the way". By now thoroughly confused, the poor man ventured another question, "What is the Burren, then?"

Paul didn't tell me how the young girl fielded this one. A pity, for it would be interesting to know her answer. Maybe she referred him to one of the guide books that were on sale in the shop. Or, less likely, perhaps she told him to go see one of the locals and ask him. But what sort of answer would he have received from that quarter?

This little story neatly sums up the experience of many people visiting this particular part of North Clare. And it illustrates something else as well - questions are sometimes even more interesting than answers. Why? Well, it's not simply that they stimulate inquiry, though that's certainly important. It is, rather, that a good question starts a debate, a to-ing and fro-ing of opinion, speculation and imaginative exploration. Paul's confused Dubliner had asked two of the basic questions that would occur to anyone coming to the Burren: Where is it? and, What is it?

So, as this is an introduction to a book "of the Burren", it would seem a good idea to take a look at how these two questions have been approached by the contributors.

I

The name itself is not a great deal of help. It does, though, provide just a glimpse of a partial answer. Burren is derived from "bhoireann", which means "a stony place". The stone in question is mainly carboniferous limestone, the porous qualities of which, brought into contact with the moulding and, later, melting Pleistocene ice-sheets, have resulted, on the surface, in the characteristic bare, fissured pavements that are such a typical feature of this weirdly beautiful land-scape, while an intricate cave-system exists underground. John Feehan describes the lengthy process through which this distinctive landscape was formed, but he would certainly admit that the Burren is more than just "a stony place".

Anyone with eyes can see at once there's something unusual about the geology of the place. But what does the naturalist have to say? Cilian Roden, carefully examining the abundant plant life, describes how gradually an image of the Burren as "an extraordinary place where arctic and mediterranean plants co-mingled" fastened itself on the minds of a small but growing number of naturalists throughout the 19th century. Today the gentian, for example, has become almost a symbol of the Burren. For a botanist, the Burren is its flowers.

Gordon D'Arcy, approaching the Burren through the variety of its wildlife, fixes his attention on what we could call the "hidden" Burren. He shows how the careful eye of the naturalist reveals the rich splendours of a delicately balanced ecological hierarchy, from the tiniest insects to the different mammals that range through glens, over rocky hills and through the few remaining forests found here.

So our first three contributors would answer the second of our questions - What is the Burren? - as follows: The Burren is a geologically distinctive landscape, the habitat of a rich and even unique variety of flora and fauna.

Our first question - Where is the Burren? - would prompt a more complex answer. Most people ordinarily think of the Burren as a more or less clearly defined geographical area, bounded on the north east by a range of mountains stretching from Abbey Hill to Mullaghmore, extending west from Corofin to the Cliffs of Moher, and taking the sea as a natural limit along the north west and north east coastlines.

But each of our first three contributors would argue that the "real" Burren extends, for example, as far as Ballindereen and the Gort lowlands to the east, and that a spot as seemingly securely within the "conventional" Burren as Kilfenora is cannot really be described as Burren landscape at all. Furthermore, they would all agree that if we are to be strictly accurate, the Aran Islands are as much a part of the Burren as, say, Slieve Elva.

One of the tough things about being an editor is having to restrain the enthusiasms of your authors. While agreeing with and accepting the solid arguments for extending and contracting precisely "where" the Burren is, there are also good reasons for taking, with a respectful nod in the direction of the geologist and the natural historian, the more conventional location as practically useful. In truth, landscape is indifferent to boundaries. It is rare to find abrupt limits in nature. We can all recognise that one particular type of landscape

shades off gradually into another.

And, in any case, the natural landscape has received over countless centuries an equally important human dimension. As well as a natural history, the Burren has a human history.

II

The people who inhabit a place give it an identity, at once unmistakable and yet sometimes frustratingly indefinable. For several thousand years, man has been laying down an almost bewildering succession of human meanings in the Burren, with important consequences for the natural landscape. At the same time, the evolving natural landscape has also delicately affected those who have made their homes here, from Neolithic times to the present day. It was the naturalist W.H. Hudson who expressed the importance of this reciprocal relationship:

"The nature of the soil we live on, the absence or presence of running water, of hills, rocks, woods, open spaces; every feature of the landscape, the vegetative and animal life - everything in fact that we see, hear, smell and feel - enters not into the body only, but the soul, and helps to shape and colour it".

John Waddell tells us "the human story of the Burren may have commenced as long as ten thousand years ago", and the impressive remains of prehistoric burial monuments like Poulnabrone and Poulawack, not to mention the extraordinary concentration of wedge-shaped gallery graves, are testimony to an age and a people far removed from us not only in time but in modes of thought and behaviour.

9

"Looking at Poulnabrone", he tells us, " it is easy to imagine simpler ways of disposing of the dead". Who built these imposing tombs remains a mystery. Their ordinary dwellings have vanished. The names of the gods and goddesses they worshipped have disappeared with them. Yet these primordial Burren people settled here, raised families, worked the land, watched over their herds of cattle and sheep. Why did they choose this place?

For choose it they did. And named it. As Paul Gosling shows, one of the earliest references to this place is found in the Dindshenchas, an 11th - 12th century collection of stories, prose and verse about the names of noteworthy places. There, in the story of "Liamun", we hear first the descriptive phrase "Boirenn in Corcumruad" - the "stony place belonging to the people of Mruad". From this "people" or tribe we derive the name "Corcomroe", still used today because the Normans adopted it as the name of the administrative unit they called a barony.

The coming of Christianity brought yet another defining dimension to the Burren. And as Leo Swan demonstrates, the number of ecclesiastical sites in the Burren is quite exceptional, a point taken up, as we will see, in another context by Patrick Sheeran. With Kilfenora (not part of the "true" Burren, remember, for the geologist and natural historian) as the episcopal focus, churches and monastic settlements spread across the landscape, shaping the sensibilities of the people in ways too numerous and too subtle to mention.

From the Middle Ages - another term with a meaning as impossible to strictly define as that of the landscape itself - to the present day, families such as the O'Briens, the O'Loughlins, the O'Connors, the Dalys and many others added their marks to the Burren, whether as chieftains and landlords or simple farmers. Paul Gosling and I have tried to provide a descriptive and narrative account of this period of history. And in doing so, we see once again how history is the human country, and that castles and "big houses", thatched cabins and cottages, stone walls and cultivated fields are the typical response Burren people have made to this unique landscape.

Another response is that embodied in folklore. Professional historians love the written word, for it gives them a tangible hold on the past. But there is an entire oral tradition, passed on from father and mother to son and daughter, that expresses the voice of the ordinary people. It is this that Lelia Doolan and Caoilte Breatnach deal with, taking as examples from out of the vast amount of material carefully recorded by folklorists, traditions about cures, holy wells and the life of the shepherd. Only a small sample of the rich heritage of an otherwise "silent" population.

Not far removed from folklore is what Charlie Piggott calls the "Bardic Connection" - the story of music and song in the Burren. Today this tradition has made places like Doolin world-famous. There is, once again, something altogether distinctive about the music made in the Burren, a quality that undoubtedly comes from receiving the "strange floating sounds" heard in the wind, in the waves, and caught with the inner ear from around the corners of castles and ring-forts.

Of course the spectacular visual panorama has inspired artists over the centuries. And Anne Korff has assembled a unique representative selection of artistic responses to the beauty and strangeness of the Burren, from George Petrie's romanticised vision of St. Bridget's Well to contemporary works by Brian Bourke and Derek Hill.

Finally, in the most unusual contribution to this book, Patrick Sheeran has explored the tradition of the Burren as a spiritual focus. Taking the name of the Cistercian Abbey of Corcomroe, Sancta Maria de Petra Fertilis - Saint Mary of the Fertile Rock, he examines the fruitful paradox of a place both fertile and barren, and relates it to the tradition of "desert" spirituality developed among the early Christian Church Fathers.

The Burren certainly has an identity, but it is one which requires us to take account of both the natural and the human dimensions. From the rocks that give it its name and the plants that draw visitors from all over the world, to the people who have lived here and given it a distinctive human quality through their labour, their spirituality, their traditions, and their music, the Burren is as much a landscape of the imagination as it is the province of the scholar and the historian.

III

With such a unique place as the Burren there is always the question of just how we get to know it. Today tourism is one of the most important aspects of the Irish economy. In such a situation, places like the Burren are obvious attractions. But, as everyone can recognise, tourism is a two-edged sword. Almost fifty years ago the poet Robert Graves, who had gone to live on the unspoiled island of Majorca and found a way of life that had changed very little in centuries, drew attention to the paradox of tourism.

Modern means of transport have put virtually every spot on earth no more than a plane ride away. Whereas in the past, most people lacked the means and the leisure to travel to distant and unspoiled places, nowadays there are few people who cannot afford to set off for the four corners of the earth. Many go out of an entirely blameless and even praiseworthy curiosity. Cliché though it has become, there is still truth in the saying that travel broadens the mind, though it is equally true that what you derive from visiting new places depends to a large extent on what you bring with you. And we are not referring simply to guide books and expensive cameras.

The paradox Graves pointed to can be put quite simply. People in today's busy, crowded and increasingly polluted world are drawn irresistibly to unspoiled places. Yet it too frequently happens that the large numbers of people travelling to these places tend eventually to destroy the very things that have drawn them there in the first place.

The Burren has only recently begun to attract large numbers of tourists. It is still too early to say how this fragile landscape will cope with the increasing numbers that can be expected in the years to come. If the experience of other unspoiled landscapes is anything to go by, there are certainly grounds for concern. Already enormous tour buses plow down roads never built to handle them. More and more people tramp the delicate landscape, clambering over stone walls. "Invasion" may be too strong a word to use, but there is a serious question as to how many people the Burren can handle and still remain the special place it is.

As there is no question of preventing people from visiting the Burren, perhaps a more fruitful way to approach matters is to consider the best way to visit it. There is an interesting parallel between those concerned about the present situation in the Burren and the situation faced a hundred and fifty years ago by someone who loved another unspoiled landscape.

In the summer of 1844, a new company was formed with the intention of bringing a railway line from Kendal to Windermere in the Lake District of England. One of those who strongly opposed the scheme was William Wordsworth, the native-born poet who had drawn his spiritual nourishment from the districts' lakes and mountains, its low sheltered valleys and its quiet villages. His poetry was rooted in the traditions of the people of the Lake District - their stories, their music, their folktales. Like many today who love the Burren, Wordsworth feared the effects of an increasing number of people on all of those things that made the Lakes special.

While much of his objection to the scheme was based on the actual destruction of the landscape that would attend the construction of the railway line, at the heart of the two letters he sent to the editor of The Morning Post lies an idea that will find a responsive echo in the minds of many of those concerned to preserve the Burren as a "special" place.

Briefly, Wordsworth argues that a landscape like that of the Lake District is one that needs to be carefully approached and gradually experienced. Railways bringing large crowds directly into the heart of what was in effect a wilderness were not, he argued, the proper means of introducing people to a quiet and hidden beauty. Rather, he says, those coming to the Lakes should approach it at a distance, slowly taking in aspects of the larger scene. And then they ought to be prepared to spend time observing, without haste, the minute beauties. Only in this way, Wordsworth concludes, can the landscape work its magic, and only in this way can the visitor gain anything more than a fleeting and ultimately unsatisfactory impression.

The parallels I referred to are clear. How many times have we encountered people who, travelling as part of a large party on a bus that makes certain pre-arranged stops for brief periods, express disappointment or bewilderment at the Burren. Is not the reason obvious? You need time to allow this landscape to enter you. And you need to explore it, ideally, by yourself.

Part of the pleasure of visiting a place like the Burren is the element of exploration. There is also the additional pleasure, which can still be a genuine experience, of feeling as if you are discovering something for the first time. Too many signs, too much explanation beforehand, too much imposition of the latest technology, however well-intentioned, can destroy all of this. A landscape can be "used up". The Burren is not a "theme park".

There are plenty of people in the Burren who can share Wordsworth's feelings about his own "wilderness". For them the Burren is a "special" place, even a sacred place. It is the responsibility of those who love the Burren to ensure that it retains the quality of uniqueness. But, of course, anyone who loves a place wants to share it with others who don't know it. Perhaps - and if it seems a bit abrupt to propose it in this final paragraph, I can only say I certainly haven't much idea how it could be developed - what we really need is an "ethics of tourism". But that, as they say, is for another time.

J.W. O'Connell

Photograph: Thomas Quinn

The Rocks and Landforms of the Burren

John Feehan

The first chapter in the story of any place is that which can be read in the rocks hidden below the surface. It is also one of the most exciting and important chapters in the whole story, opening windows through which we can catch glimpses of the vanished worlds in which our little corner of the earth took shape.

There is no part of Ireland where rock so obviously dominates the landscape as it does in the north-west corner of County Clare. This is the Barony of Burren, and the name could not be more appropriate, because boireann in Irish means a place of rocks.

Here in the Burren the bare. exposed limestone, which is up to 780m in thickness, covers an area of 250 square kilometres: great slabs of

1.2

Pavements are characteristic of dense, pure, massively-bedded limestone. They originate as bedding surfaces: the tops of layers of soft limey sediment laid down in the ancient Carboniferous sea. However, rain and weather quickly go to work on the naked limestone once it is exposed to the air, etching it away and sculpturing it into a microlandscape of runnels, grooves and pits. In time the beds will altogether disintegrate, and many limestone surfaces are littered with the ruin of the beds which lay on top of them.

rock which are almost as flat and undisturbed as they were when they were formed in the warm, shallow seas of the Carboniferous ocean 340 millions years ago.

On the floor of this shallow sea, lime-rich debris accumulated - mainly derived from the skeletons of the plants and animals which lived in the warm waters, as well as small amounts of mud brought in by rivers.

The limestone is pale-grey to greyish-blue in colour, and never seems to vary much from place to place. Yet no two sequences of beds in the limestone are identical, because that great thickness of rock took hundreds of millions of years to accumulate on the sea floor. During all that time the creatures of the sea were changing, evolving slowly, so that the fossils which are found at each level in the limestone are slightly different from those above and below.

The most striking aspect of the Burren landscape is the way it is sculptured into flat, bare terraces, criss-crossed by joints, each terrace abruptly separated from the next by a cliff, so that the whole landscape looks like a fantastic, series of stairs, the steps of which you can sometimes follow for miles if you want.

The reason for this terrace and cliff topography is that this vast thickness of limestone wasn't laid down continuously, without a break.

There were long pauses during which the seas retreated and the ocean floor was exposed for a time to the air, before once more being submerged. The major terrace surfaces in the Burren represent these periods when the Carboniferous ocean had retreated, and the young limestone sea-floor was briefly exposed to the atmosphere.

One of the most characteristic features of the limestone pavements is the way in which they are broken up by three sets of vertical cracks or joints. These joints are important for many reasons, most obviously because weathering of the rock is concentrated on the joints, which widen out to give the characteristic grykes of the Burren, but also because later in their geological history these joints acted as passageways for the movement of mineral-bearing fluids from deep in the earth's crust. As a consequence, joints are often mineralised, and these joint veins were extensively worked in the past for the minerals in them. On Aillwee Mountain, for instance, lead-silver ore was mined, and the calcite veins on Moneen Mountain and elsewhere were worked in the 19th and 20th centuries.

The pavement surface has been moulded and sculptured into a variety of solutional features - pits, hollows, rills and channels, for which the generic term is karren. Some of the most

1.3

A simplified geological map of the Burren. The main feature to note is the boundary between the Carboniferous Limestone and the Clare Shales. Notice how caves and potholes in the Western Burren are concentrated along this boundary, whereas the older caves and potholes in the Eastern Burren are a long way from it - but when these caves were active, the limestone-shale boundary was much closer to them.

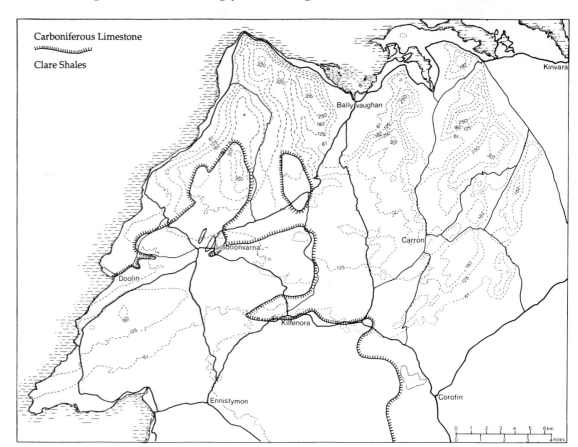

remarkable and diverse karren assemblages can be seen along the shore, where marine influences come into play, producing a landscape in miniature, a microcosm all of its own with complex networks of pinnacles and precipices, depressions and gorges in whose shaping the life forms which live on the limestone, both in the water and on land, all play their part.

The uppermost surface of the limestone represents an important break in the middle of the Carboniferous. For this is the actual land surface of that remote time. We can still walk on parts of this exhumed ancient surface in some parts of the Burren, where the overlying shales have just been stripped away to expose it.

The limestones of the Burren were laid down at the end of the Lower Carboniferous period, and at the very end of Lower Carboniferous time, when there were dramatic changes in the ocean. Where previously limestones had been formed by the accumulation of myriads of creatures living in those clear, warm seas, with very little sediment being washed in by the rivers, now vast amounts of dark mud and sand were washed into the sea from an area of land which lay somewhere out to the west.

For millions of years these sands and muds poured in, totally altering the life of the seas, and in time these new sediments on top of the limestones also hardened to shale and sandstone. These younger Upper Carboniferous rocks reach a thickness of over 330 metres here in North Clare, and nowhere in Ireland are they more breathtakingly exposed than in the Cliffs of Moher. The shales with which the Upper Carboniferous sequence begins are called the Clare Shales, and the overlying sandstones are generally referred to as the Millstone Grit.

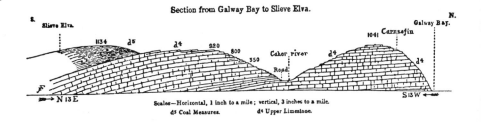

Section from Galway Bay to Slieve Elva.

1.4

Two sections across the Burren to show the overall geological structure. The Coal Measures are the Upper Carboniferous rocks, so called because these are the rocks in which coal occurs. The seams of coal which occur in the Upper Carboniferous rocks of Clare are thin and not very extensive, but they were formerly mined on a small scale. The numbers are heights above sea level (in feet).

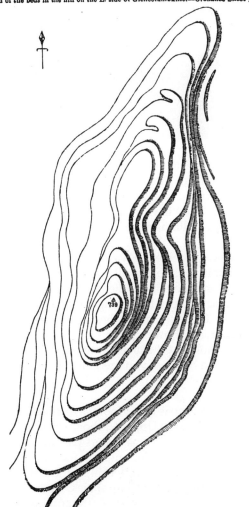

Plan of the beds in the hill on the E. side of Glencolumbkille.—Ordnance Sheet 5.

Scale—6 inches to a mile.

1.5

The step-like succession of cliffs and terraces of bare limestone so characteristic of the Burren is nowhere more magnificently displayed than on the hills on the eastern side of Glencolmcille, shown in this bird's eye view.

17

1.6

The gently-dipping limestone pavement is broken by a system of very regular and closely-spaced cracks or joints. Once the bedding surfaces are exposed at the surface, the sensitive scalpel of weathering quickly identifies these lines of weakness in the rock, and they become the target for subsequent erosion, deepening to form gullies and runnels, and eventually becoming deep grykes. The most prominent set of joints runs approximately north-south, and individual joints can sometimes be followed for miles.

Joints like these are sometimes mistakenly interpreted by the non-geologist as glacial striae. Striae only affect the very surface of the rock, and so they quickly disappear once they are stripped of their protective blanket of glacial drift. Good places to search for striae include Finnevarra, Poulsallagh and Ballyallaban.

At one time, the sandstones and shales we see in the cliffs of Clare also covered the limestone of the Burren, and indeed of the rest of Ireland as well. They have long ago been stripped away by millions of years of erosion.

However, on Slieve Elva a last patch of Upper Carboniferous rocks still blankets the limestone, and there is another at Poulacapple in the area between Ballyvaughan and Lisdoonvarna. The fact that patches still remain is an indication of how recently - in geological terms - the whole of the Burren limestone was protected by these younger, impermeable rocks.

The famous spas at Lisdoonvarna owe their properties to the Upper Carboniferous rocks through which the spa waters pass on their way to the town. The sulphur and iron in the waters come from the decomposition of the iron sulphide in the Clare shales. There are two main kinds of "waters": the sulphur wells, and the iron spas, which are situated mainly in the deep ravines of the Aille River south of Lisdoonvarna and along the Kilmoon Stream - on waters which had a long journey over and through the shales.

Unlike the limestones, the shales are impermeable, which means they don't let water pass through them. When the rains from the Atlantic sweep across Slieve Elva, the ground can't soak up the water the way it does on the limestone. So the acid water comes pouring down the slopes of Slieve Elva, but as soon as it hits the limestone it disappears beneath the surface through a series of swallow holes, and down beneath, within the limestone, the waters have hollowed out one of Ireland's most remarkable underworlds. The peculiar landscape which results from solution of limestone and underground water circulation is called karst - and the Burren is Ireland's most famous karst area.

The largest cave system in the Burren is the Poulnagollum-Pollelva complex, which is the longest explored cave system in the country, with over 11km of galleries. There are two main entrances to this complicated cave system, the enormous gaping potholes of Pollnagollum and Pollelva, as well as at least 40 other small swallets and potholes, all strung out along the limestone-shale boundary on the east side of Slieve Elva. Poulnagollum is something like 25m deep and 40m across. Pollelva is even deeper, 30m straight down.

The surface waters entering the Poulnagollum-Pollelva complex run underground through the Main Stream Passage, and its many tributaries, and rise again to the surface south of Poulnagollum, at the Killeaney Rising. In dry weather this is a gentle stream, but following heavy rainfall the waters gush forth and inundate the surrounding country.

The waters from Killeaney flow for a while at the surface as the Oweentoberlea Stream before ducking into the limestone again. They make their final escape to the surface at St. Brendan's Well. Most of the caves drain away to the south, following the slope of the limestone.

Some of the most famous caves are at Kilcorney, 10km south of Ballyvaughan. Here the Cave of the Wild Horses, like many other caves in the Burren, discharges floods over the surrounding countryside in Winter, and these can build up extensive alluvial deposits. The name of the cave derives from a story that after one such flood a herd of wild horse came out of the cave and overran the country.

Another famous cave is Poll Gorm, which is said to communicate with the sea at Muckinish. The story is told how sheep-killing dogs were thrown into this hole, and that the dead bodies were sometimes found floating in the sea off Muckinish.

It is hardly surprising then that this land of bare, thirsty limestone has only one or two permanent surface streams, and even these are little more than trickles. There are several dry valleys - like the Ballyvaughan and Turlough Valleys, formed in the remote past by rivers long since swallowed by the limestone.

The broad, shallow valleys west of Poulacapple are the remnants of pre-glacial river valleys, once occupied by streams which flowed off the shale-covered uplands, but which now disappear underground at the shale-limestone boundary. These are especially conspicuous on the west side of Slieve Elva. The valleys that run north from Kilfenora to Kilcorney, and between Lough Aleenaun and Carran, are also ghostly remnants, modified over many tens of thou-

1.7

sands of years by glacial and postglacial remoulding of the landscape, of the original Tertiary rivers which flowed across the Burren when the limestone was still protected under its blanket of Upper Carboniferous strata. The Tertiary was the period of earth history which preceded the Ice Age, and it lasted from 65 to around 1 million years ago.

Something like 100 closed depressions of various sizes occur in the Burren. They are closed in the sense that they have no surface outlets, although valleys, or traces of valleys, lead into all of them. The smaller depressions, of which Poulavallan and Poulelva are fine examples, are dolines, more or less circular hollows formed by cavern collapse, and these may be as much as 18m deep and 180m across.

The larger closed depressions are more frequent, and indeed they are among the most distinctive features of the eastern part of the Burren. Four depressions are particularly

In the normal course of events the Burren upland should not be there at all: such a fragile rock formation should have simply dissolved away long ago. Part of the reason it has survived so long is that it was protected by its covering of Upper Carboniferous rocks into the Tertiary period of earth history. The other reason is that the limestone lies on a hidden cushion of granite which imparts stability. But towards the edge of the cushion, the limestone has been distorted by tectonic forces at work in neighbouring regions. This is well seen on Mullaghmore, where the limestone is gently folded because of its proximity to the unstable Fergus Shear Zone to the east.

1.8

The vertical cliffs of the Upper Carboniferous rocks are one of the most impressive sights in Ireland. They are made up of alternating shales and flagstones; the shales are easily eroded, but what makes the cliffs so spectacular is that the rocks are traversed by great vertical joints which break them up in readiness for the sea, making the onslaught of the waves all the more devastating.

1.9 Entrance to the underworld

Pollnagollum pot, seen here in a splendid photograph taken in 1952, is the entrance to the Burren's most extensive cave system. Potholes are formed at the edge of the limestone by streams flowing off the shale uplands of Slieve Elva. Pollnagollum is no longer an active pothole: it is now some way from the shale-limestone boundary and no longer receives a stream. The Main Stream Passage is some 30m below the entrance to Pollnagollum pot, and is fed by dozens of small active potholes located along the geological boundary.

prominent. From east to west these are: Kilcorney, Poulawillan, Caherconnell and Carran. These depressions mark the places where the ancient Tertiary river systems of the Burren, which flowed on a surface which was still underlain by Upper Carboniferous sandstones and shales, first disappeared underground and began to eat at the limestone below. As time went by, continuing solution of the limestone by acid water draining off the surrounding land to the north widened and deepened these initially small windows into the buried limestone.

The biggest of the large closed depressions (which are sometimes called poljes, which is the word used for similar features in the classical karst area of Yugoslavia) is the Carran depression, which is more than 2 miles long, up to a mile across and over 200 feet deep. They are only found in the east and central Burren, and they are elongated north-east - south-west, along the fold axes.

Ice over the Burren

Another event in the geological history of the Burren which profoundly influenced the shape of the modern landscape we see today was the Ice Age. During the Ice Age, which started around a million years ago, glaciers swept several times across the Burren, stripping away anything they could prise loose, including much of the remaining protective Upper

Carboniferous cover.

There is clear evidence for two episodes of glaciation in the Burren. There were undoubtedly many glacial advances, but the last two have stripped away any evidence for earlier events. The earlier glaciation brought south-moving ice across Galway Bay from Connemara, and covered the whole of the Burren, leaving erratics of Galway granite strewn over the surface as the tell-tale proof of its place of origin.

The final advance was weaker, only covering the eastern Burren, where it replaced the granite of the earlier glaciation with its own limestone erratics. Today the erratics of granite are found mainly on the hill summits in the northern part of the Burren. During this final episode, glacial ice moved south-westwards from a centre of build-up between Athlone and Galway, across towards the Burren over the Slieve Aughty hills, and then south towards Kilkee, where the ice front lay.

Towards the very end of the Ice Age, the ice front stood for a time at Fanore. Long before this though, the Burren had begun to shed some of its ice. Slieve Elva and neighbouring Knockauns Mountain to the south-west stood above the surrounding glacial sea as islands of frozen land standing above the snowfields. Such islands are known by the Eskimo word for them - they are nunataks.

The ice carried boulders of limestone up to 300m on the northern slopes of Slieve Elva and to 240m on the southern slopes. Limestone erratics are never found above this level, because the ice didn't reach any higher. It streamed round Slieve Elva, cutting a sharp edge into the north-eastern side of the mountain. This 45m-high scarp is still a well-defined feature in today's landscape. The three main

wide valleys which face Galway Bay were greatly widened by the earlier ice moving southwards from Connemara. The valley between Slieve Elva and Knockauns Mountain is a spillway which drained off meltwater from the ice trapped between the mountains and the glacier for a brief period before the receding ice found an easier way round the hills. Glacial meltwater also carved out the gorge of the Glencolmcille Valley.

The ice rounded and smoothed the shoulders of the hillsides as it ground its way slowly forward; in most places the smooth profile has been much altered since the Ice Age, but it can still be seen on Gleninagh Mountain, to the north of Carran village, and south-east of Murrough.

Evidence of glacial scouring and plucking is seen in many places, notably on the east side of Ballyvaughan Valley at about 75m, on the eastern slopes of Slieve Carran and 180m and south-west of Moneen Mountains.

In the wake of the Ice Age, materials deposited by the melting ice covered much of the surface, and choked up the old sinkholes and cave systems which had been in existence before the coming of the Ice.

Patches of moraine were left in the valley bottoms, with more pronounced drumlin-like deposits in some places such as the

1.10

Erratics abound all over the limestone pavements of the Burren. Stranded by the retreating ice, they often rest on a little pedestal of limestone which is protected from erosion by the weight of the boulder on top. The height of the pedestal is an indication of the rate of erosion since the erratic was deposited on the surface. Most of the erratics are of limestone, though granite erratics brought across from Connemara during the penultimate ice advance are quite common in the north-west corner of the Burren.

Glencolmcille Valley. A large fan of outwash sand and gravel was left behind at the northern end of the valley. Further west, deep moraine choked the Cahir Valley and piled up against the west flanks of Slieve Elva. Because the limestone was now once again protected by something on top, streams flowed on the surface of the post-glacial Burren for a while - and in one case still does.

There is a small group of drumlins south-east of Slieve Elva, but most of the Clare drumlins lie on the sandstone and shale country to the south. These were moulded in a NE-SW direction by the south-west moving ice.

Just north of Doolin strand, near Poulsallagh, the glaciated pavement is gradually being exposed by the wearing away of its glacial drift cover, and the striated surface can be clearly seen before it wears off, and karren formation begins.

The Legacy for Man

When the last of the ice had melted away, the polished and striated pavements were covered with a blanket of boulder clay or till, the rocky debris which the glacier had picked up on its journey, and now had to leave behind at its final halting place, a mixture of everything from clay to enormous boulders. The biting winds of postglacial Ireland whipped this protective cover from the exposed higher west-facing slopes, but the returning vegetation soon stabilised it over most of the Burren, and as climate steadily improved, forests of hazel, yew and pine spread over the area.

This was the paradise which the first human communities saw as they moved along the fringe of the prolific sea in Mesolithic time, and whose destruction began when the first farmers moved into the Burren in the Neolithic 5000

1.11

One of the streams in Lisdoonvarna. Here the Clare Shales can be seen directly overlying the limestone. A phosphate band occurs in the Clare Shales: these thin bedded phosphorites in the shales have only been known since 1925, and they were quarried on a small scale for use as fertilisers during the Second World War.

1.12

One of the resurgence springs at Saint Brendan's Well.

years ago, attracted by the prospect of all-year-round grazing, and initiating a long regime of deforestation, overgrazing and soil erosion which brought ever increasing areas of bare pavement to the surface. A palimpeset of skeletal monuments, fashioned of the ever-present stone at every period of human exploitation of the Burren, now litter the stripped and abandoned pavements, one of the starkest reminders in the Irish landscape of how dramatically we can alter it and deplete its precious resources, when we do not understand or take adequate account of the forces that interact to maintain its delicate balance.

The Burren Underworld

John Feehan

The limestone which makes up half of Ireland's rocky skeleton was formed on the floor of the ancient Carboniferous sea, 340 million years ago. But as soon as it is exposed to the atmosphere, limestone is quickly eaten away by the forces of erosion. For limestone more than for other rocks, rainwater is the most corrosive of these forces, because it is almost completely made up of a single chemical substance, calcium carbonate, which comes from the skeletons of the plants and animals which lived in the warm Carboniferous sea. Carbonate simply dissolves in acid; rain is a dilute solution of carbonic acid, and so it eats away slowly at limestone wherever it is exposed at the earth's surface, concentrating on lines of weakness such as bedding planes, cracks and joints.

In most landscapes water falling on the surface flows away in streams, which coalesce to form bigger streams, which eventually become rivers and enter the sea. But when limestone is exposed at or near the surface, water can only flow above ground for a short time before it disappears into the limestone to follow a new course below ground, reappearing at the surface further on. With some streams in limestone country this may happen several times before they find their way eventually to the sea.

Because of this subterranean circulation, limestone landscapes have a unique underworld geography. The special landscape which results from the solution of limestone and underground water circulation is called Karst (after the region in north of Yugoslavia where it is most classically developed): and the Burren is Ireland's finest and most famous karst area. Here the limestone is honeycombed by an extensive system of caves which is still far from fully explored.

Tens of millions of years ago, the Upper Carboniferous sandstones and shales which are so splendidly exposed in the Cliffs of Moher and all along the south-west coast of Clare covered the entire Burren - and indeed the rest of Ireland as well. Millions of years of erosion have stripped them away from most of the country, but they haven't been eroded away entirely from the Burren. On Slieve Elva one last area of Upper Carboniferous shales still blankets the limestone, and there is another smaller patch at Poulacapple between Ballyvaughan and Lisdoonvarna.

That is the key to much of what is happening today in the Burren landscape. These shales are impermeable, which means they don't let water soak through them. After heavy rain, acid water pours down the slopes of Slieve Elva until it reaches the edge of the shales, where it eats its way into the limestone. The burrows it makes in the rock are called swallow holes. Once below ground the streams continue their journey, carving out subterranean channels in the limestone and dissolving out the very heart of the rock.

The caves in the Burren fall into two categories: those which are still active, which is to say they are still occupied by the streams which shape them, and those which are not - they have been abandoned by the streams they once contained. The critical feature in the formation of caves is the proximity of the overlying shales. The active caves are all concentrated along the shale-limestone boundary in the western Burren, mainly around Slieve Elva and Poula-capple. Extensive cave systems occur also around the inliers of limestone which occur as windows in the shales further south (the Doolin and Coolagh systems). The limestone-shale boundary retreats as the shale continues to erode, and new lines of sinkholes form along the advancing edge of the limestone, to be abandoned in their turn as the retreat continues.

The active caves of the western Burren have all formed since the Ice Age, although some parts of the larger systems here are older. For instance, many of the main entrance sinks to Pollnagollum-Pollelva are now some way back from the critical geological boundary, and there are sediments in these and other cave systems which were probably laid down during an interglacial episode.

The caves have a dendritic pattern comprising miles of dark twisting passages and canyons. They are wonderful places, full of marvels and mysteries, branching in the way streams do at the surface (Illus. 1.13). These underground canyons are sometimes wide and spacious, up to 8 m in height and 3 m wide, but in other places the walls are so close together you can hardly squeeze through, and the roof is often so low that you can only proceed by crawling, perhaps up to your nose in water, and not infrequently underwater altogether. Stretches of caves which are completely water-filled are called sumps, and although they bring the exploration of the casual cave visitor to a disappointed end, they merely raise the level of challenge for the true caveman or woman, who will don scuba gear wherever necessary.

You have to be prepared to swim if you want to experience the marvels of the Doolin and Coolagh River cave systems for instance. Doolin has the distinction of being one of the few caves to run underneath a river, the Aille. At one point the river seeps down through a rift in the cave roof, the cascading warmer surface water steaming like a shower as it meets the colder air and water of the cave. More often than not however the shower is turned off, because the leaky Aille river only holds water after heavy rain.

1.13

Geology and Caves, North County Clare.
A. *Pollnagollum*
B. *Pollelva*
C. *Pollcragreagh*
D. *Killeany Rising*
E. *St. Brendan's Well*
F. *Cullaun Series*
G. *Gragan West*
H. *Pollaphouca*
J. *Faunarooska*
K. *Polldubh-Pollballiny*
L. *Pollnagree*
M. *Pollomega*
N. *Coolagh River Cave*
O. *Poll an Ionian*
P. *Doolin Cave System*

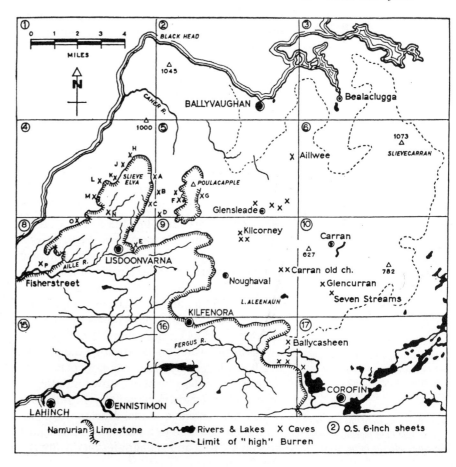

25

The main entrance to Doolin Cave is Fisher-street Pot, a classical steep-sided pothole 12 m deep; its providential location so close to Gussy's Pub has often been remarked on by thirsty cavers emerging from the underworld. The cave resurges - that is, it reappears again at the surface - below high water on Doolin Strand. Other older caves have their resurgences much further out to sea; these sea caves - known as the Green Holes to rival the Blue Holes of the Bahamas - are fascinating, exciting and dangerous places to explore, and are one of the main areas of interest for serious cavers at the present time. They are also especially interesting because they must have formed at a time when sea level was much lower than it is at present.

Another cave with a sea connection of a different sort is Poll Gorm, which is south-east of Moneen Mountain, and which may be partly artificial. This cave is said to connect with the sea at Muckinish; the story is told how sheep-killing dogs were formerly thrown into it, and the dead bodies were sometimes found floating in the sea off Muckinish.

Many caves are completely filled with water at an early stage in their formation. Such caves are said to be phreatic, and one indication of a phreatic cave is that it has a more or less tubular cross-section, as do many Burren caves. Stalactites and stalagmites, and all the other wonderful formations found in caves, can only form when the water-filled tube drains as the water breaks through the bottom to a lower level, and water can now percolate through the limestone above down into the cave. Calcite (calcium carbonate, the mineral of which limestone is made) precipitates from solution in the lime-rich water, forming stalactites on the roof and stalagmites on the floor,

and mantling the walls with flowstone formations. Every cave in the Burren is different and wonderful, and many are places of extraordinary beauty; most of these are difficult of access, which is just as well, because cave formations are extremely fragile, and would not survive for long if they could be easily reached. The most spectacular single cave formation in the Burren is the 7m long stalactite in Poll an Ionian, said to be the longest free-hanging stalactite in Europe (Illus. 1.14).

The largest of the Burren caves is the Pollnagollum-Pollelva complex, which is known to extend for more than 13 km (Fig.). Pollnagollum - poll na gcolm, the pigeon cave - is a common name for caves in different parts of the country, where they were formerly the haunt of rock doves (Columba livia - colm is the Irish word for a pigeon; Pollnagollum is also the old name for Fisherstreet Pot, but to avoid confusion it is not often so called). The most dramatic of its more than 40 entrances is the great sinkhole of Pollnagollum Pot, which lead into one of the loveliest stretches of reasonably accessible cave in the Burren, a main stream passage which meanders along for 3 km through a wonderland of cave formations, an unforgettable experience where all around the water thunders over subterranean waterfalls and into rock pools. Beyond this the going gets tougher, and in the section appropriately known as the Maze it is very difficult to find a way at all. A semi-artificial passage now connects Pollnagollum with the Pollelva cave system; Pollelva itself is a magnificent pothole more than 30 m deep which, like Pollnagollum, is some distance back from the shale-limestone boundary.

The waters from the Pollnagollum and Pollelva cave systems eventually join together and flow

1.14

"Scrambling over large boulders we stood speechless in a large chamber of ample width, length and impressive height. As our lamps circled this great hall we picked out a gigantic stalactite over thirty feet in length, the only formation in the chamber, and set proudly in the middle. It is really majestic and poised like a veritable sword of Damocles". In these awestruck words, Craven Potholing Club described their discovery in 1952 of the magnificent stalactite in Poll an Ionain, said to be the longest free-hanging stalactite in the world.

southwards through the limestone, emerging to the surface at the Killeany Rising. Below Killeaney there is a surface stream called the Owentoberlea, which flows for 1 km or so before dodging underground again; its course thereafter is marked by a dry valley as far as St. Brendan's Well, where it finally comes up for breath again and stays on the surface. The junction between the shales and the limestone is especially well seen and easy of access here and is well worth an expedition - especially after heavy rain, when the rising waters which have rushed through subterranean conduits down from Slieve Elva spout impressively through the open joints in the limestone floor of the stream bed.

The Pollnagollum-Pollelva caves were the first Burren caves to be thoroughly explored. The geologist W.H. Stackpoole Westropp, writing in 1870, described how

Some foolhardy individuals attempted to explore them (the Burren caves), after having fortified their nerves with liberal allowances of whiskey; under the influence of the potent spirit they beheld, while in the caves, divers strange sights and visions, the description of which has quite deterred the natives from following their example.

Systematic exploration of the caves began early this century, and important new discoveries were still being made in the 1950's.

The older caves of the High Burren

The caves of the High Burren are very different, silent now except for the drip of percolating water, abandoned by the streams which formed them. They are often remnants of once larger cave systems formed when the shale-limestone boundary was close at hand.

Among the most accessible of these old caves are Poulcarran, Glencurran - the Cave of the Wild Horses - at Kilcorney. Kilcorney is by far the best known because of the legend from which it takes its name, which tells how a herd of mythical wild horses which had their stable in the cave emerged every year to ravage the plains of Ireland. The entrance to the cave is at the base of an impressive cliff on the south of the Kilcorney depression, not far from the old graveyard; higher up in the cliff face are two other cave entrances. The entrance cavern is low, but after crawling over boulders you find yourself in a widening passage. Although the cave is still semi-active, the water which floods out of it after heavy rain is not runoff from the shales.

1.15

The narrow streamway passage of the Coolagh River Cave.

28

The gaping entrance to Glencurran cave is in a crag near Cashlaungar, west of the Killinaboy to Castletown Road. Beyond the entrance is a fine stream-deserted gallery which can be explored for 70 m or so with little difficulty. The cave at Poulcarran is located in a crag to the east of the old church at Carran. Here the former stream passage can be followed for some 25 m from the entrance cave.

Vanished caves

In time, erosion and decay will lead to the disappearance of these old caves, and there are places in the Burren where the final stages of disintegration can be seen. One fascinating corner of the Burren where you can see the relics of a vanished cave is the Glen of Clab, which is about 3 km north of Carran; at the western end of this little glen is a sort of crater known as Pollavallan. Here, scattered on the surface, are great boulders of sandstone, completely out of their proper geological context. The Glen of Clab is actually an un-roofed, collapsed cave passage, and Pollavallan is an old doline or swallow hole. The alien sandstone boulders are part of the original roof of the cavern, which collapsed before the blanket of Upper Carboniferous rocks was stripped away from this part of the Burren. So this quiet valley was once part of the Burren underworld, but the teeth of erosion have eaten their way into it. Few places in the Burren demonstrate so well the relentless, ongoing decay of the limestone. Another series of abandoned swallow holes, and a dry ravine formed as a result of the collapse of the roof of another vanished cave, can be seen east of the pass at Mam Chatha (3 km south-east of Ballyvaughan). These ancient cave features date from a time when the shale covering over the Burren was very much more extensive than it is today.

The caves are an important part of the natural history of the Burren for another reason also: they provide homes for several different kinds of animals. Although badgers are widely distributed in the ravines and glens of the Burren, they are especially common along the shale-limestone boundary, where the swallow holes provide ideal setts. Some of the caves are also home to one of the rarest of Ireland's bats, the lesser horseshoe bat. Several smaller animals are even more characteristic, most notably the cave spider (Meta menardi) and the cave moth (Tephrosia crepuscularia).

Caves also occur in the Burren Lowlands south of Corofin, where lakes and turloughs occupy ice-hollowed basins in the limestone, which has plenty of water here because the water table is very near the surface. In this area surface streams have the enchanting habit of disappearing underground and bubbling back to the surface somewhere else. One of the few explorable caves of emergence occurs in this area: Ballycasheen Cave near the head of the River Fergus, which gathers its waters from the High Burren.

New discoveries
New caves are still being discovered. One recent discovery is the entrance on Knockaun Mountain to one of the deepest, longest and most difficult cave systems in Ireland; this entrance has been aptly named Poll na gCeim, the stepped pothole, because it plunges down for 75 m in four stepped vertical pitches. Another exciting discovery is the old dry river cave near Doolin mentioned earlier, which can only be entered through one of the caves in the sea floor - the Green Holes - and is filled by the sea at its downstream end. These sea caves are perhaps the wildest and most remote places in a landscape filled with wonders. They will be forever out of reach of most of us, but even a brief foray through any of the entrances to the Burren's dark underworld will give you something of the magic.

1.16

The ancient phreatic tube of the cave at Kilcorney 2.

Aillwee Cave

About two miles north of Ballyvaughan is Aillwee Cave, discovered in 1944 by Jack McGann. As a young man, McGann developed a great interest in Aillwee Hill and the ancient remains to be found around Ballyvaughan. Working much of his life as a herdsman, he was fascinated by the traces of previous occupation he came across while looking after cattle on Aillwee Hill. His curiosity prompted him to examine 19th century herdsmens huts and other structures connected with a vanishing way of life and he sent a number of his finds, most notably a small bronze bracelet dated to the Bronze Age, to the National Museum in Dublin.

In 1944 Jack was up on Aillwee Hill and his dog caught sight of a rabbit. Jack followed the dog and was surprised to see him vanish into a hole in the side of the mountain. With a candle Jack went inside and explored as far as he dared. Not until 1973, however, were the 210 metres of passages and caverns fully surveyed by a team from Bristol University. In 1976 Aillwee Cave was opened to the public for the first time. And in 1977 a further 1,034 metres was discovered.

Aillwee Cave is a typical example of the many caves found throughout the region. Originally formed as a result of an underground river cutting its way through limestone, after the retreat of the Ice Age, the waters retreated and the cave became a hibernation site for bears. Today Aillwee Cave, with its spectacular stalactites, caverns and underground rivers, provides a very enjoyable introduction to the caves of the Burren. The beautiful access building - a fine example of a modern development working with the character of the surrounding landscape - was designed by Andrzej and Danuta Wejchert and awarded the EEC Europe Nostra Prize.

(Editor)

Acknowledgements for illustrations

Illus. 1.1	Photo, John Feehan	Illus. 1.8	Photo, Anne Korff
Illus. 1.2	Photo, John Feehan	Illus. 1.9	Photo, Irish Press 1952
Illus. 1.3	After O.S. Map	Illus. 1.10	Photo, John Feehan
Illus. 1.4	Drawing, from the Geological Survey Memoir	Illus. 1.11	Photo, David Drew
Illus. 1.5	Drawing, from the Geological Survey Memoir	Illus. 1.12	Photo, David Drew
		Illus. 1.13	Map, after Coleman
Illus. 1.6	Photo, John Feehan	Illus. 1.14	Photo, Tim Fogg
Illus. 1.7	Photo, John Feehan	Illus. 1.15	Photo, David Drew
		Illus. 1.16	Photo, David Drew

2.1. Hazel scrub and limestone pavement along the road from Clooncoose to Mullaghmore in the south east of the Burren. It appears that the hazel is presently colonizing the bare pavement and patches of woodland, such as those visible on the terraces of Mullaghmore, are more frequent now than a hundred years ago.

The Burren Flora

Cilian Roden

The repute of the wildflowers of the Burren is today so well established as to be almost cliché. The flowers of the Burren are now included along with Connemara, New Grange and Georgian Dublin, as part of Ireland's heritage. Any threat to this strange flora is material for the national media and readily accepted as yet another attack on our increasingly disturbed and fragile environment. Indeed, so established has this favourable view of the Burren become, that academia has not been able to resist the temptations of revisionism. Certain ecologists and other scientists, for example, have suggested "that a more detailed and critical examination of the evidence would show that the Burren has been intensely and catastrophically affected by human activity".[1] In short, what once was typical Irish forest is now reduced to bare crags and rock plants, probably thanks to our ancestors.

A Rich and Rare Variety

Yet, to the naturalist, especially the botanist,

the Burren is fascinating in the present - regardless of its ecological derivation. Over a very large area - at least 300 km^2 - rare and spectacular plants occur in an abundance normally associated with daisies or thistles. Nowhere else in Ireland, Britain or even north west Europe can such quantities of the blue Spring Gentian *(Gentiana verna)*, cream Mountain Avens *(Dryas octopetala)* or yellow Shrubby Cinquefoil *(Potentilla fructicosa)* be encountered. Yet these are only conspicious members of a very distinctive flora consisting of perhaps twenty or more lime loving plants otherwise rare in Ireland. Perplexingly, these plants have very different habitats abroad. Mountain Avens is more usually found on high mountains of Europe and beyond, while Maidenhair Fern *(Adiantum capillus-veneris)* grows in damp hollows along the Mediterranean and the warm Atlantic coasts of south west Europe. Shrubby Cinquefoil is scattered across the colder parts of continental Europe and Asia, while the Dense Flowered Orchid *(Neotinea maculata)* is almost confined to the Mediterranean basin. Nowhere else in the world is this precise mixture of plants found growing together.

However, the interest of the Burren is not confined to this rather exotic and conspicious group. Many plants rare in Ireland generally have also a few stations in the region. The list is long and varied: Pyrimidal Bugle *(Ajuga pyramidalis)* at Poulsallagh. Wintergreen *(Pyrola media)* on top of the hills, Irish Saxifrage *(Saxifraga rosacea)* around Black Head, Fly Orchids near Mullaghmore, Welsh Poppy *(Meconopsis cambrica)* above the Cliffs at Deelin Mor... to list but a few examples. Besides rarities, many plants with local or narrow distributions in Ireland occur most commonly here. High up on Black Head one can walk across Juniper *(Juniperus communis)* and Bearberry heath *(Arctostaphylos uva-ursi)*, while all over the Burren, Water Avens *(Geum rivale)* and Hawkweeds *(Hieracium)* grow in sheltered cliffs beside ferns and Blue Moor Grass *(Sesleria albicans)*. Orchids are everywhere, 23 of the 27 Irish species are to be found. Not only that, but some specialists recognise distinctive forms specific to the Burren; for example *Dactylorhiza fuchsii spp. okellyi*, a white flowered form of the Common Spotted Orchid.

So many botanists have visited the Burren that many difficult and ill defined species have been recorded that may well occur elsewhere in other less frequented regions. No less than 24 different species of dandelion *(Taraxacum)*, including 2 types practically unique to the Burren have been recorded. Equally, a type of grass with the interesting name of *Festuca indigesta* was seen by a German botanist in 1949 - it has never been refound - possibly because Irish botanists are totally unfamiliar with the distinctive features of this plant otherwise only found in south west Europe.

The most interesting of the controversial plants must be *Arenaria norvegica* - this white flowered cushion plant is typically found in the arctic with rare stations in Scotland. It was found once in 1961 somewhere in the hills south of Black Head - a specimen was collected for confirmation, but no one has succeeded in rediscovering it.

The affinity of rare or unusual plants for the Burren was best illustrated for me during a walk on the west side of Moneen Mountain. Round a spring I found a colony of large Flowered Butterwort *(Pinguicula grandiflora)* - regarded by Praeger as the most beautiful member of the Irish flora, but best known as a member of the "Lusitanian" flora (those plants only found in Ireland and northern Iberia), and more or less confined to acidic habitats in West Cork and Kerry. Here it was, growing happily in alkaline water, high up on the Burren limestone. It had been discovered on Cappanawalla in 1949. This second station confirmed for me that not only was the Burren home to a recognisable group of lime loving plants, but it also seems to hold populations whose presence was totally unexpected and that even after 150 years of exploration, further surprises are still in store.

There are two further reasons why the Burren attracts naturalists. Firstly, it is one of the few limestone regions that sit on the very edge of the European Atlantic coast with all this implies in terms of unusual climate by continental standards, isolation and maritime influences. Secondly and sadly, with so much environmental destruction in lowland Europe, the absence of pollution and the striking scenery of the karst, the Burren would still be a most attractive place for naturalists even if Gentians hadn't grown here since the last glaciation.

Botanists in the Burren

Botanical knowledge of the Burren has gradually developed over the last 350 years. Mountain Avens and Spring Gentian were described as very plentiful as early as 1650. Obviously these flowers were well known to the local inhabitants long before this as the Gaelic names of many of the Burren flowers testify, (Leaithin for example is Irish for Mountain Avens, Dúchosach for Maidenhair Fern).

Linnaeus' classification of flowering plants in 1753 laid the foundation for systematic recording of species and in the first half of the 19th Century, many of the most conspicious plants were first recorded, mainly by Dublin based or English botanists. Wade, for example, found Shrubby Cinquefoil near Killinaboy by 1804. Dropwort *(Filipendula vulgaris)* was recorded as early as 1735.

After 1850 (and incidently the great famine which must have made a large difference to the landscape) the idea of the Burren as a centre for rare flowers becomes firmly established. A Dublin clergyman, Rev. T. O'Mahony addressed a paper to the Dublin Natural History Society on a botanical ramble in Clare in 1852. Ten years later F.J. Foot, a professional geologist, presented a paper to the Royal Irish Academy "On the distribution of plants in the Burren District County of Clare".[2] He opens on a now familiar note "the rocky tract of limestone hills occupy the N.W. corner of the country of Clare known as "Burren" or "the Burren" possess a flora probably the most remarkable for the extent of district, in the United Kingdom". Reading this paper 130 years later, one is struck by how little the flora has changed since.

Foot's account lists 114 species together with their distributions. He deals with most of the major attractions in the flora, Gentian, Mountain Avens, Rockrose *(Helianthemum canum)*, Bloody Cranesbill *(Geranium sanguineum)*, Pyrimidal Bugle and so on. In many ways most subsequent botanical work in the Burren has been an amplification and refinement of Foot's original description. Many new plants have been found since, but these are either very local, such as Water Germander *(Teucrium scordium)* in one turlough or taxonomically difficult: the Dandelions or Hawkweeds.

2.2.   In the Burren rare plants can be as common as daisies: Mountain Avens (Dryas octopetala) flower in May.

2.3. Bloody Cranesbill (Geranium sanguineum) in a gryke or crack in the limestone pavement. Note the long fruits - hence the name - cranesbill.

2.4. Spring Sandwort (Minuartia verna) growing on limestone pavement. A plant in Ireland confined to the Burren and the Basalts of Antrim and Derry.

Foot omits a now common plant, the Hazel *(Corylus avellana)*, and he refers to the Ash only as a dwarf form. Nowhere in the paper does he mention hazel scrub or woodland. Bugle *(Ajuga reptans)*, now a frequent plant in hazel scrub is recorded at only one place, Corkscrew Hill, and there rare. Reading between the lines it seems that the now common hazel scrub was far less conspicuous in 1860 - the suspicion is proved when one reads that the old dry stems of Mountain Avens were a common fuel! Only in a country devoid of any standing timber would these stringy centimetre thick stems appear an easy means of warmth.

In Foot's time, many of the people were Gaelic speakers. Two of his comments hint at a folk knowledge of plants now forgotten. On Shrubby Cinquefoil - "the peasantry have a superstition that it formerly grew to a great height and bore thorns; and that from it the crown of thorns of the crucifixion were made, ever since which time it has been under a curse, lost its thorns and became stunted in growth".

On Dropwort (in Ireland confined to the eastern side of the Burren) "it is well known to many of the peasantry the Irish name being "Fillyfindillaun" (I could not ascertain the correct orthography of this word) and is much used when boiled in new milk, as a remedy for diseases of kidneys".

Another visitor, T.H. Corry from Belfast, was in the Burren nearly twenty years later in July 1879. He gave a talk to the Belfast Naturalists Field Club about his journey.[3] By now, the Burren's reputation had become well known, even though it was thought to be a remote region, difficult of access. Corry calls Poulsallagh - site of Pyrimidal Bugle - "Classic ground" and the Burren as a whole is "the botanists happy hunting ground". Well known though it might be, Corry succeeded in adding the Dense Flowered Orchid to the list of rarities. Amongst botanists, this is, perhaps, the most famous of the Burren's plants. Again the Burren is stark and bare, so much so, that tinted glasses are felt necessary; a visit to Eagle's Rock on Slieve Carran includes no mention of trees, now one of the best developed woods is found here including not only Hazel but mature Ash *(Fraxinus excelsior)* also.

After 1895 no one could doubt that the Burren was a magnet for naturalists. On the morning of Saturday July 13th of that year the Galway Bay Steamboat Company's S.S. Duras arrived in Ballyvaughan from Galway city carrying no less than a hundred visitors.[4] These were members of field clubs in Belfast, Dublin, Cork and Limerick attending the first Irish Field Club Union conference held at Galway, and had crossed the bay to spend a day in the Burren. This immense party did not intend to discover new plants but rather to view rarities whose presence was long established. In this they were very successful and returned to Galway at 5.30 p.m. some having seen Maidenhair Fern towards Black Head along with Irish Saxifrage and Lesser Meadow Rue *(Thalictrum minus)*. Others had climbed Cappanawalla to see Wintergreen and marveled at the endless grey slabs of limestone. Everyone saw Gentians, Mountain Avens, Bearberry, Bloody

Cranesbill. The Dense Flowered Orchid was still a recent discovery and then regarded as extremely rare (present records suggest it is quite common in fact). But perhaps the greatest rarity they encountered was in the person of Mr. P.B. O'Kelly - a botanist who actually was a native of the Burren (his house is marked on Tim Robinson's map south of Ballyvaughan village). Perhaps because of his very uniqueness O'Kelly is treated with reserve by some naturalists, but he knew the Burren well and made several interesting discoveries, including, according to Praeger,[5] the rare Mudwort (*Limosella aquatica*). He seems to have been a "free enterprise" man and ran a commercial nursery which sold a variety of native plants apparently relying on the Burren's fame to boost sales.

This huge excursion was organised by a man whose contribution to Irish Botany was equally large - Robert L. Praeger.

When Praeger published his definitive account of Irish plant distributions - Irish Topographical Botany , in 1901 - he felt that the flora of north Clare was so well known that he hardly bothered to visit this area at all. However, his description in *The Botanist in Ireland* is still an excellent summary.[6] He published a note on the south east Burren around Mullaghmore in 1906 where he found some additional plants. He also reported that Hazel was widespread.

And so, by 1910 the concept of the Burren as an extraordinary place where arctic and mediterranean plants co-mingled was established. But only established amongst the scientists, naturalists and that section of the public generally interested in natural history. In the Ireland of 1910 this group was largely unionist in sympathy. Amusingly, both Foot and Corry saw in the blue Gentian, white Mountain Avens and red Bloody Cranesbills on a Burren hillside, a marvellous reflection of England's red, white and blue on the western extremity of the United Kingdom.

After 1922, the influence and interests of this group declined. For much of the twentieth Century, Irish intellectual life centred on literature and history. Most of the 19th Century field clubs disappeared, natural history retreated into the universities and the studies of isolated individuals. It was in this very period that the science of ecology matured - the study that attempts to explain the mutual influence of organism and environment. Sadly, the Burren, so clearly bristling with ecological problems, was bypassed as suitable subject for investigation. Some famous continental ecologists paid a brief visit in 1949, but their influence hardly extended to the general public. As late as the 1960's even the most authoritative guidebooks hardly mentioned the Burren's flora concentrating instead on Corcomroe Abbey and Poulnabrone Tomb.

By then, the tide had turned. From 1960 the universities initiated a whole series of studies on the flora and ecology of the Burren, this work culminated in the first full book on the subject - *The Flora of Connemara and the Burren* by D.A. Webb and M.J.P. Scannell, which is essential reading for any true botanical visitor.[7] Equally, ecologists had at last made some attempts to explain how the Burren came into existence and why it was so strange. Their first results based on analysis of fossil pollen and present day plant communities suggest that the karst and bare landscape is not a natural wonder, but a by product of man's culture - a strange reflection for those drawn by the Burren's apparent isolation and freedom from pollution!

Alongside this revival in biological studies, the Burren's uniqueness has, at last, percolated through to the general population. As a recent arcticle in an English botanical magazine stated "almost everyone in Ireland seems to know about the Burren". It is not easy to explain this revival, obvious causes are better education, more time and money for travel, the rise of the television documentary, an intellectual life less exclusively focused on the humanities. More subtle influences might be the writings of R.L. Praeger which link this generation of naturalists to their 19th Century predecessors, the popularity of County Clare in musical circles and the endless stream of student visitors to Doolin!

The Original Landscape?

Now, in 1991, our idea of the Burren flora is informed by three different and perhaps contradictory chains of evidence. Our own eyes confirm the picture described by Foot over a century ago. The Burren is a wild rock garden resplendent with rare and striking plants set in amongst extraordinary bare hills. The arctic alpine nature of some of these plants makes it easy to accept the view of many botanists that "It is certainly no accident that the Burren Region of County Clare harbours such a peculiar flora.... this curious largely treeless vegetation of the Irish limestone must be a direct descendant of the late glacial vegetation of ten thousand years ago. It is an odd corner of N.W. Europe over which the forest has never completely closed nor acid blanket bog developed".[8] Or is it? Pollen analysis from the south east Burren shows that late glacial vegetation was followed by Pine and even Oak forest, much as in other parts of

Ireland, to be followed about 5,000 years ago by extensive forest clearance, by man one presumes.

This conflict is of somewhat more than theoretical interest, for if we wish to conserve the Burren we must have some idea about what the "natural" state of the region might be. It is common for Irish naturalists to regret the vanished ancient forests, especially as their passing was almost certainly due to man's destructiveness and short sighted mismanagement. For many this forest was the "natural" vegetation of the island, but in ecology the idea of a natural climax vegetation specially suited to a region is now very suspect. It must be remembered that all the vegetation of western Europe is but a remnant of a much richer flora destroyed by the natural catastrophe of the ice age. Ireland itself was only 15,000 years ago covered by ice, whose trace is still to be seen in the Burren. The plants that reached the Burren were determined as much by accidents of migration and history as by an exact ecological suitability. Nor do we know how these plants migrated, when individual species arrived and how often chance extinction removed them once again. We do know that some present day plants were present in the late glacial before forests formed. For example, Mountain Avens, Rock Rose, Meadow Rue, Burnet Rose (*Rosa pimpinellifolia*), Juniper, were found in deposits near Mullaghmore, but these were soon replaced by shrubs and trees such as Hazel. Later Pine and Yew (*Taxus baccata*) were very common. As agriculture expanded, woodland declined until, by the 19th Century as we saw, the stems of Mountain Avens were prized as fuel.

But this process of forest growth and clearance is found throughout western Europe. The

2.5. Early Purple Orchid (Orchis mascula). This is one of the first orchids to flower, it is common everywhere.

2.6. Spring Gentians (Gentiana verna) growing on the slopes of Abbey Hill in May. This is the most spectacular of the Burren flowers but the intense blue of the petals cannot be reproduced in illustrations.

2.7. Red Broomrape (Orobanche alba) a plant parasitic on common thyme and consequently lacking green leaves. North Clare is one of the few places in the British Isles where it is common.

2.8. Dark Red Helleborine (Epipactis atrorubens). In Ireland this striking orchid is almost confined to the Burren. It is quite frequent on the higher hills and flowers in July. It is unlikely to be found by the road-bound traveller, but amply justifies the climb to the summit plateaux of any of the northern hills.

Burren flora is not. To regard all the present day vegetation as a secondary growth only made possible by man's activities begs too many other questions. Where did the Mountain Avens and Gentian come from if not always present since the glacial period? How could plants on the retreat throughout Europe, compete with the grasses and herbs that succeeded the forests in other places. It is, perhaps, stated too often that the Burren flora extends unchanged from the hill tops to sea level. This is not strictly true. On the higher slopes of the north western hills, a very interesting community of dwarf shrubs is found (the *Arctostaphylos uva-ursi - Dryas octopetala* nodum of Ivimey-Cook and Proctor). This vegetation is dominated by mountain shrubs including Mountain Avens, Juniper, Bearberry, Crowberry and seems to be a richer limestone version of heath found on the Twelve Bens in Connemara and other Irish mountains. This seems to be a vegetation never colonised by trees, mainly due to exposure to fierce winter gales which prevent tree growth. Many characteristic Burren plants grow here. Indeed, Black Head and the adjacent west coast, the most exposed regions, harbour the richest flora of the area. While it cannot be proved, at present it seems likely that this north western area has always been a refuge for early post glacial vegetation. Equally, the many cliffs and lakeshores would never be smothered by trees

2.9. Woodsage (Teucrium scorodonia). This plant is extremely common on limestone pavement. In no way rare throughout Ireland, it is one of the few plants to grow on dry, almost soil-less bare pavement.

2.10. Cat's Foot (Antennaria dioica). This flower often grows in the company of the Mountain Avens and other characteristic Burren plants. It is however widely distributed throughout Ireland and Europe.

and would retain an earlier flora.

Unlike many rare plants at the limits of their range, the Burren flowers show no evidence of declining populations (other than through habitat destruction by man) or other signs of stress or obvious genetic peculiarities. On the contrary, they appear adapted to their present habitat and reproduce successfully. It is possible that the normal succession from herbs and shrubs to closed forest is less assured on the Western limestones than in most of Europe, some environmental factors may retard the growth of trees. Possible examples are the lack of deep mineral soils due to glacial scouring, some of the strongest winds in western Europe and a remote location, only reached by a fraction of the European tree flora. Usually succession is accompanied by a reduction in the liminess of the soil, a factor which harms the colonising plants: The Burren with its massive beds of pure limestone, is obviously more buffered against this change than many other areas. At present, grazing must play some role in retarding tree growth but when grazing first started in the Burren is perhaps an open question.

The presence of southern plants such as Maidenhair Fern or Dense Flowered Orchid is paralleled by the presence of southern sea-weeds along the adjacent coast. While the ranges of these algae, *Bifucaria bifurcata* for example, are continuous along the west European coast, their presence reflects the warm winter temperatures of the Atlantic and the marine fauna and flora of the west of Ireland is usually regarded as having a southern rather than a northern aspect. To explain the presence of southern European species immediately after the last glaciation calls for a lot of special pleading. But we know very little about migration of plants across water - except that it happens - and it is possible that the

whole problem of plant migration to Ireland is misconceived. Modern work on biogeography interprets an island's flora in terms of a continuous process of chance migration balanced by an equally random extinction - a very different view than the traditional, once and for all, emigration across a transient land bridge.

But at this point we are dealing in almost pure speculation. It is better to say we simply don't know the origins of the flora we see. For me, however, the Burren is best seen as a remote and unusual habitat but recently colonised and then subject to man's domination long before a "natural" equilibrium or climax could evolve. The future task for the botanist is not to discover yet more rarities, although they may well exist. Instead, we should try to understand more clearly topics such as the interplay of plants and grazers, the occupation of new ground by plants, how existing communities renew themselves, then we could replace speculation by something more solid and have some guidance in the conservation choices that inevitably lie ahead of us.

The Burren Flora and Man

Man arrived in Ireland at least 9,000 years ago, not much later than the broad leaved trees and possibly by means of a land connection, rather than over sea. However, his livelihood was that of hunting rather than agriculture and his impact on the developing vegetation was slight. Still, it is an interesting reflection that prehistoric men were witnesses to the expansion of the broadleafed forest and much later to the developing boglands.

However, even primitive farming can have a startling impact on vegetation, especially in areas where soil or soil nutrients are in short supply. Huge areas of the Burren are now bare limestone with no surface soil except in the deep fissures or grykes. The vegetation is confined to these cracks and is difficult to classify as it seems to represent a whole variety of fragments from woodland, grassland and fen. There are no species peculiar to the pavement and, contrary to what is often written, bare pavement is not the place to seek the Burren flora - areas of thin rocky soil or lakes, fens and turloughs are far more rewarding. In the last fifty years, the bare pavement has been invaded very successfully by a dandelion like plant called Wall Lettuce (*Mycelis muralis*). A fragmentary vegetation and susceptibility to invasion by weeds, probably indicates a severely disturbed habitat. When we also notice in many places, now ungrazed, hazel scrub re-invading the pavement, it seems probable that much of the pavement was formed by excessive grazing or agriculture in prehistoric times removing both trees and whatever thin soil covering existed. This idea is supported by pollen analysis in the eastern Burren. It would be pushing the argument too far to say that all pavement is artificially derived. If *Arenaria norvegica* is ever refound on the limestone pavement 800 ft up on the south slope of Gleninagh Mountain, as recorded in 1961, it will prove very difficult to reconcile the presence of a plant from the arctic with the possibility of a former woodland cover.

In the period which culminated in the Famine of 1846 - 1850, a mixture of poverty, mis-government and rapid population growth made the Ireland of 150 years ago very similar to many third world countries today. The impact on the environment was equally severe, with complete deafforestation and an attempt to cultivate even the poorest of land. 30 years later there are plenty of comments in T.H. Corry's account, which indicate that extreme poverty was still a commonplace background for botanical exploration. This was possibly the period in recorded history when human affairs most threatened the Burren flora. Even now it is worth remembering that some degree of prosperity in the community is an essential prerequisite for a successful conservation policy.

We've no evidence that man has driven any plant to extinction in the Burren.
Now, however, our increased knowledge of agriculture and our capacity to generate vast quantities of pollutants could endanger the relatively satisfactory *status quo*. These dangers include excess use of nitrate fertilizer which allows agricultural grasses to replace the present flora and contaminates the ground water, affecting both people and plants that use it. Land reclamation, using mechanized vehicles, makes it possible to place a thin skin of soil over rock and thus produce pasture, but it also eradicates all the plants that went before. Drainage schemes as always, threaten all fen and lakeshore plants, while the absence of SO_2 scrubbers from the Moneypoint coal fired power station means that a watch must be maintained for signs of acid rain problems.

Of the ten thousand years of the post glacial era man has farmed the Burren for perhaps five or six, his claims to be a natural part of the environment cannot be disregarded. But we have now arrived at a point where the future of any of our landscapes must be the subject of conscious decisions rather than relying, as in the past, on Nature's ability to look after itself. There are many reasons for conserving the Burren flora: its beauty, its scientific interest, its link with the vanished vegetation of the early post glacial era.

Perhaps the best reason is the most obvious - because many, many people value and love this flora and this wonderful landscape.

Interlude: Along the Burren Shoreline

Cilian Roden

To the west of the Burren is the Atlantic Ocean. This sea has a profound influence on the natural history of the region, and especially on it's climate. Many people in Ireland attribute our mild, wet winters to the Gulf Stream, picturing perhaps a jet-like flow of warm water from the Caribbean, lapping against the headlands of Munster and Connacht and avoiding the less fortunate coasts of our Scottish, English or French neighbours. But this is too simplistic a view. There is a wind-driven movement of Atlantic water from the south and west that tempers the climate of Western Europe from North Cape to Galicia, Ireland included, but very recently oceanographers have suggested that the exceptional warmth of this water reflects a vast northerly movement of water from the Mediterranean rather than the Caribbean.

On many European coasts, this ocean water is separated from land by a band of less salty coastal water formed by the major rivers of the continent, which insulate the land from a direct contact with the ocean. But Ireland stands well to the west of the European mainland and is surrounded by the sea, so coastal waters are not well developed in contrast, for example, to the North Sea. This is particularly true in the case of the Burren. Water circulation in Galway Bay is anti-clockwise, so Atlantic water moves by Black Head and then east to Kinvara and Galway, while the outflow of the Corrib flows west along the coast of Iar Connacht. This oceanic influence is very obvious in winter. Water temperatures at New Quay in the last four years have rarely fallen below 8°C.

Indeed, on cold winter days, mist can be seen rising off the water as cold and warm elements meet. In summer, water temperatures are moderate, rarely exceeding 16°C, except in the almost land-locked bays of Aughinish and Muckinish.

This moderate temperature range has allowed a basically warm temperate flora and fauna to develop along the shores of Co. Clare, which bears comparison with that of Brittany and, to a lesser degree, North West Spain. Many animals and plants occur which are only found in the extreme south and west of the British Isles - such as the purple sea urchin (*Paracentrotus lividus*) and a brown seaweed (*Bifucaria bifurcata*). Both occur in rock pools, the former in spectacular abundance at Fanore where it burrows into the limestone flags. The latter can be seen at Black Head, although its appreciation is perhaps more of an acquired taste! The plant and animal communities of the shore do not contain the strange geographical mixture so characteristic of the terrestrial communities. Instead, they reflect the position and environment in which they are found. This difference underscores an essential aspect of the natural history of Ireland. Marine communities are rich in species. Land communities are poor in species, isolated from the mainland, and show many peculiar characteristics, nowhere more so than in the Burren.

There are a great variety of shores along the coast of the Burren, although major estuaries are absent. In the north east, the two bays of Aughinish and Muckinish are almost enclosed and strong tidal currents occur at their entrances, while within there is more shelter. Both bays contain natural oyster beds and these are now being redeveloped after almost complete extinction due to overfishing. The entrance narrows have shingle shores but rich communities of seaweeds, sea anemones and - in Muckinish - corralline algae *(Lithothamnion sp.)* are found in shallow water.

The shore around Ballyvaughan is a mixture of sand, shingle and rock outcrops but is overshadowed by the magnificent coastline that stretches around Black Head and south to Doolin. Here the limestone beds form cliffs and terraces that descend to the sea. A marvellous variety of animals and plants are to be found - too many, unfortunately, to list - ranging from the brown seaweeds - *Laminaria* sp. and *Alaria esculenta* - to tiny limpets, mussels and squat lobsters. This diversity is only the fringe of an even greater variety of plants and animals that occur beneath the sea, only accessible to divers. Recently divers have discovered that caves - so much a part of the Burren - open to the surface below sea level and contain a most interesting and as yet little-known community of marine animals.

Unlike the terrestrial flora, the Burren marine life did not attract the attention of many 19th Century naturalists. However, one great naturalist in the recent past spent much of her time studying the seaweeds of the Burren - Professor Mairin DeValera (1912 - 1984) of University College Galway. In particular, she studied the algae of the reef called Carrigh Fhada, just west of New Quay, which runs out from the Flaggy Shore. Consequently a very detailed knowledge of the seaweed flora now exists. A small residential field station was built for University College Galway beside

Carrig Fhada by Clare County Council, but in recent years it has not been much used - a symbol perhaps for our relative lack of interest in sea life compared to terrestrial and the knowledge that still awaits discovery.

Acknowledgements for illustrations

Illus. 2.1 to 2.11, photographs, Cilian Roden

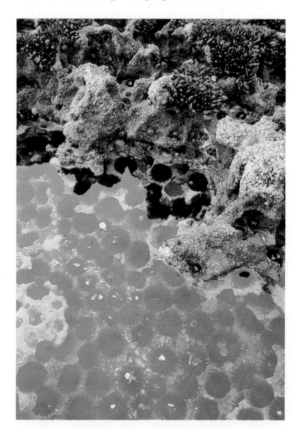

2.11. *The purple sea urchin (Paracentrotus lividus) is a southern species abundant in the limestone rock pools from Black Head to Doolin. It occurs along much of the Atlantic coast of Ireland, but is very rare in Britain and Northern Europe.*

43

Some Naturalists' Impressions of the Burren

"Looking south from the Connemara shore across Galway Bay, the hills of Burren are seen rising gaunt and bare. Although their skyline is undulating and unbroken, the face of the hills is ruled with parallel horizontal bands, as if painted with streaks of grey of varying shades"
(*R. L. Praeger, 1934*)

"A morning of driving mist found the naturalists embarked on board the SS "Duras" at nine o'clock, which in now way lightened as the steamer passed down the river and set her course for Ballyvaughan, on the southern side of Galway Bay. However the cheerful predictions of the conductors were duly fulfilled, for as the destination was approached the clouds broke and the sun shone out, lighting up gloriously the strange bare slopes of the Burren mountains and the great masses of vapour that still hung over the higher summits . . ."
(*R. L. Praeger, 1895*)

"The view from the summits of these hills is very extensive; far to the southward stretches a country almost entirely covered with grey crags, so as to have quite a strange and weird appearance, and amid which neither road nor habitations can be distinguished, the desolate character of the country being only relieved here and there by little lakelets, and the trees of Rockforest in the distance. This country is really as desolate as it looks, very sparingly inhabited; most of the roads were made at the time of the relief works for the great famine. Coming down from the summit along a fence we came upon the white flowers of the purging Buckthorn and when we did arrive in safety at the base we knew not whither to turn, for an aspect of sameness prevailed, and how or in what direction, the road lay we could not discover. I should therefore strongly advise anyone visiting a desolate crag country to provide himself with a good pocket compass, and to make use of it. Skirting the edge of a lake we picked up Northern Bedstraw, and shortly afterwards came upon a sheep, which we judged to be a sign of civilization and followed its track accordingly."
(T. H. Corry, 1880)

"At a distance these bare rocky hills seem thoroughly devoid of vegetation, and the desert like aspect thus imparted to the landscape has been compared to that of parts of Arabia Petraea. But on a closer inspection, it will be found that all the chinks and crevices, caused by the above mentioned joints, and the action of the rain, are the nurseries of plants innumerable, the disintegration of the rock producing a soil, than which none is more productive. So rich and fattening is the pasture in the valleys, and often in the barest looking crags, that high rents are paid for tracts for grazing, that a stranger en passant would hardly value at two pence an acre."
(*F. J. Foot, 1862*)

"Other who ascended to the flat summit of Cappanawalla brought back strange accounts of the vast stretches of bare grey limestone that extend on the higher grounds."
(*R. L. Praeger, 1895*)

A Climín at Bell Harbour
A raft of seaweed being brought to mainland for manuring soil.
At low tide the man walks to the islands, where he builds his
raft around his feet, the real skill being in the way the weed is
tied. He poles it to the quayside with the incoming tide.
Photo Irish Press, 1952, Clare County Library.

Young Seal.
Photo, T. Quinn.

3.1   *PINE MARTEN*
       (Martes martes)

People who are lucky enough to have watched a pine marten go about its business in some quiet spot in the Burren, are unanimous in praise of its beauty. Having cat-like proportions though with a dog-like head, this carnivore is endowed with luxuriantly thick and soft fur, and with equally appealing character to boot. Though not to deny its predatory instincts - it will kill chickens like a fox should it be permitted access to a coop - its main preoccupation is with smaller fare such as field mice, rats, birds and a range of wild fruits and fungi. In captivity, a pine marten will become quite docile if handled carefully, while maintaining its essential wildness.

The Wildlife of the Burren

Gordon D'Arcy

The term "wildlife" is both hackneyed and vague in describing living organisms. It is often used in a restricted sense to describe wild animals or fauna, flora being considered separately (as in this book). The term is, however, unsatisfactory in another sense: unlike "natural history" it refers to the contemporary rather than alluding to the changes wrought by time.

The history of nature in the Burren is closely bound up with that of man and his activities, and the wildlife existing there today does so both as a consequence of, and despite, these activities. The familiar frog, for instance, is known to have been introduced into this

47

country, albeit hundreds of years ago. The pine marten, on the other hand, has doubtless survived in the Burren since before the arrival of man. Much has been learned about the ancient plantlife from analysis of pollen diagrams which have been developed from core samples of sediments in Burren lake beds. Information relating to the ancient fauna has been extracted from post-glacial deposits in caves and other final resting places of animals.

The original entombment occurred in the rock itself (then the muddy bed of a tropical sea) for, contained within the carboniferous limestone are the fossil traces of countless marine animals, the original "wildlife" of the Burren. This 300 million year old fauna in its diversity and concealment is a worthy metaphor for the wildlife inhabiting the Burren today.

Insects and Other Invertebrates

Take, for example, the butterflies - most showy of all the insects. Of the thirty or so species found in Ireland, only two are absent from the Burren and the majority are abundant there. Some, like the butter-coloured brimstone *(Gonepteryx rhamni)* and the common blue *(Polyommatus icarus)* are conspicious, but many, like the dingy skipper *(Erynnis tages)* are cryptically marked and difficult to see clearly in the field. The grayling butterfly *(Hipparchia semele)* has an underwing pattern which matches perfectly the lichen-covered limestone on which it normally rests, allowing it to melt visually into the background. A couple of the butterflies are regional specialities. The brown hairstreak *(Thecla betulae)* and the pearl-bordered fritillary *(Boloria euphrosyne)* are more or less confined in Ireland to the Burren and its hinterland.

The diversity and abundance of the butterflies indicates the richness of the flora and fauna, generally, for they are an integral link in the natural food chain (they pollinate plants in the process of feeding on nectar, but fall victim themselves to other invertebrate predators and birds). Were the Burren to be artificially fertilized on a widespread basis, butterflies would be much scarcer than at present. They are therefore living representatives of the region's environmental equilibrium - indicators of the Burren's quality as an all round wildlife habitat.

While the butterfly species are counted in tens, their close relatives, the moths, are numbered in hundreds. Some are either absent or distinctly rare outside the region. One, the Burren green *(Calamia tridens o.)* is found nowhere else in Ireland or Britain. Its grass green colour enables this moth to remain undetected during the day; it becomes active only after dark. The majority of the Burren's moths are nocturnal and therefore difficult to locate. A wide variety, however, have been identified using a mercury vapour light which attracts them at night.

A few of the moths are diurnal (day flying) some of which are as brightly coloured as our most gorgeous butterflies. Prominent amongst them are the burnets *(Zygaenidae)* which are easily recognised by their glossy black, red-spotted wings. They are, however, shunned by predators due to their capacity to manufacture a poisonous compound (cyanide) in their body juices. Most of the day-flying moths are elusive little insects, difficult to locate and identify. A number of the moths occurring in the Burren have the disarming capacity to look like something else. The bee hawk moth *(Hemaris tityus)* for instance, looks more like a bee than a moth, while the humming bird

3.3 BURREN GREEN MOTH
(Calamia tridens o.)

This rather noticeable moth remained unknown in Ireland and Britain until it was discovered in the Burren in 1949. Since then it has been found to be fairly widespread in the region. The greenish brown, black spotted caterpillars feed on grasses including the limestone-loving blue moor grass and hatch out into the adult moth in August and September. A member of the Noctuid family of moths, the Burren Green flies at night, hiding up during the day in low vegetation. Burren green moth (centre); burnet moth (top); bee hawk moth (bottom).

3.2 GRAYLING BUTTERFLY
(Hipparchia semele)

What the grayling butterfly lacks in glamour it makes up for in character. No other butterfly blends in so totally with its background: the intricate pattern of bars, blotches and irregular markings on the underwings is virtually indistinguishable from the lichen-covered limestone rocks on which it normally settles. The grayling will adjust its position in relation to the sun in order to avoid casting its shadow on the rock - a 'give-away' to a potential predator. The caterpillars feed on grasses and the adult butterfly flies in July and August.

49

hawk moth (*Macroglossum stellatarum*), a scarce visitor from Mediterranean countries, looks for all the world like a tiny humming bird as it hovers, feeding on the nectar from the wild flowers.

With such an abundance of nectar bearing plants in the Burren, bees are naturally widespread. Honey bees *(Apis mellifera)*, escapees from hives, have become naturalized in places by setting up their own hives in limestone crevices. They are, however, much less common than their truly wild counterparts, the bumble bees *(Bombus spp.)*. Cuckoo wasps, and bees which resemble their unwilling hosts, parasitise their hives by laying their own eggs within them. Solitary bees and wasps, on the other hand, live nomadic lives wandering from plant to plant, feeding on nectar and pollinating them in the process. One species of solitary wasp is the primary pollinator of the remarkable fly orchid whose insect-mimicking flower heads have evolved to fool wasps.

While the open country is abuzz with the activities of these insect pollinators, the damsel and dragonflies are patrolling the marshy borders of the turloughs and lakes, feeding on midges, mosquitoes and their kind. Beneath the water surface, the dragonfly nymphs (dragonfly larvae) indulge their aggressive predatory characteristics, feeding on any small, underwater creatures that they can catch. Here they co-exist with strange aquatic invertebrates with equally strange names like water boatmen *(Corixidae)*, and the sinister-looking water scorpion *(Nepa cinerea)*.

One of the best places to observe the underwater survival drama of these interesting creatures is in the holy wells, of which the Burren has many (Tobar Phadraic on Abbey Hill, for example), or in the puddles remaining as the turloughs retreat down the swallow holes in Spring. In places, the dried beds of the seasonally flooded wetlands reveal depositions of freshwater snails (mainly of the genus *Lymnaea*) with their delicately spiralled thin shells. A variety of shrimp-like crustaceans are also revealed in these conditions, including the rare fairy shrimp *(Tanymastix stagnalis)* which is confined to turloughs. Before the turloughs dry out completely and the shrimps die off, eggs are laid which survive the summer drought in the soil of the dried out bed. Reflooding stimulates the eggs to hatch and develop quickly into adults.

Though primarily limestone bedrock, the Burren is in places, lightly mantled with an organically rich lime soil known as rendzina. This is the habitat for many of the terrestrial invertebrates. These comprise insect larvae, ants, beetles, woodlice and myriad others. Many constitute the primary food source for other invertebrates like spiders, harvestmen and centipedes. Snails, (particularly the attractive banded snail *Helix nemoralis*), and slugs are the 'micro cattle' of the region, grazing as they do on algae and on other plants. They are especially in evidence after wet weather. Fragmented shells, scattered around in quiet secluded places, show that the snails do not have it all their own way. Song thrushes *(Turdus philomelos)* exploit the hapless molluscs by bashing open their shells on convenient rocks.

Coastal Invertebrates

With the exception of the Fanore dune system and the Rine saltmarsh, the Burren coastline is, for the most part, rocky. The high tidal fluctuation typical of the west of Ireland attains an intertidal range of 5 metres (and more) at the period of spring tides. This is a good time to look at the wonderful rock pools around Black Head which abound in marine invertebrates. Shelled creatures, molluscs, like mussels, cockles, limpets and winkles; crustaceans, like crabs, shrimps and barnacles; echinoderms, like starfish and sea urchins, are easy to find in these habitats. Red and green sea anemones and types of sponges are also found in the pools. Many of the molluscs filter feed (i.e. extract plankton food from the sea water), while the dog whelks *(Nucella lapillus)* and starfish *(Asterias rubens)* raid their colonies like marauding wolf packs. Both specialize in feeding on the molluscs: the dog whelks by boring a tiny hole in the mussel shell, injecting a fluid allowing the mussel to be extracted; the starfish by using the suckers beneath its legs to actually prise open the shells, allowing the starfish to extend its jaws into the gap to feed on the mussel within. Just offshore beyond the kelp beds are the lobster pots of local fishermen - the rocky shelf providing sanctuary to these massive slate-blue crustaceans. Skulking in the submarine clefts and caves is the squat lobster *(Galathea strigosa)*. In contrast to its more eagerly sought relative, the squat lobster is red brown in colour but with an electric blue flash on its back.

At the Flaggy shore near New Quay, an extensive limestone reef is exposed at low spring tides which supports a remarkable variety of marine creatures. Crabs are especially common. Besides the familiar shore crab *(Carcinus maenas)* and the pinkish coloured edible crab *(Cancer pagurus)*, the velvet crab *(Macropipus puber)* and porcelain crabs *(Porcellana spp.)* also occur. In the shallows, the strange looking sea 'Hare' (a large blackish sea slug) *(Aplysia punctata)* can be observed going casually about its business.

Fish

The fact that international angling contests are regularly held along the Burren coastline is testimony to the wealth of fish life to be found there. Indeed, inshore species like mackerel *(Scomber scombrus)*, pollack *(Pollachius pollachius)*, lesser spotted dogfish *(Scyliorhinus canicula)*, ballan wrasse *(Labrus bergylta)*, and conger *(Conger conger)* are common and are readily caught. Others, like bass *(Dicentrarchus labrax)* and certain flatfish can still be caught from the beach at Fanore. Occasionally the shark-like tope *(Galeorhinus galeus)* is caught off Black Head, but it is the unusual which draws most attention - like the basking shark *(Cetorhinus maximus)* which was seen drifting along the Burren coast in the summer of 1988.

The North Atlantic Drift has brought many other strange creatures to the Burren coast, like the "by-the-wind" sailor *(Velella velella)*, a kind of miniature jellyfish with a sail! It has turned up, on occasions, in hundreds.

With the exception of the Caher river which empties into the sea at Fanore, there is an absence of flowing surface water in the region. Consequently, freshwater fish are scarce. Small trout *(Salmo trutta)* live in the Caher, and eels *(Anguilla anguilla)* and sticklebacks *(Gasterosteus aculeatus)* are to be expected wherever there is running water. The lake system between Corofin and Boston - the source of the river Fergus - holds a variety of coarse fish, notably pike *(Esox lucius)*, perch *(Perca fluviatilis)*, rudd *(Scardinius erythrophthalmus)*, and bream *(Abramis brama)*, but tench *(Tinca tinca)* have been introduced there as well.

3.4 WATER SCORPION
(Nepa cinerea)

The common name (water scorpion) for this aquatic insect is misleading for, though it bears a vague resemblance to the scorpion, it is quite unrelated. While the tail of the true scorpion sports a lethal sting, that of the water scorpion functions as a hollow breathing tube. The strange tail is most conveniently observed when in the act of stocking up on air which it does by penetrating the water meniscus from beneath the surface like a syringe. The water scorpion is a ferocious hunter catching its prey in its grasping forelegs. It feeds on any invertebrate it can catch - occasionally even on small fish like sticklebacks.

3.5 SNAIL ON FERN
(Cepaea sp.)

With such an abundance of calcium available for their shells, limestone country is ideal for snails. Indeed the Burren has dozens of different species - most of which have only obscure Latin names. The genus Cepaea, the banded snails, are found in a variety of colours including delicate pink: they have distinctive concentric black bands around their surface. By grazing on a wide variety of plants, snails act as important controllers of plant proliferation. They are intolerant of dry conditions, however, and will retreat into the cool dampness of the grykes in warm summer weather.

Amphibians & Reptiles

Both the frog *(Rana temporaria)* and the newt *(Triturus vulgaris)* are common in the Burren's wet places. Remarkably, the frog can also be found in the driest parts, as on the plateau of Turloughmore hill far from any water source. A favoured locality for the newt is in turlough swallow holes or in wells where it can be viewed with comparative ease. Both the frog and the newt hibernate in a torpid state, the former in mud in or around pools, the latter beneath stones, sometimes well away from water (at the base of stone walls, for instance).

Our only native reptile, the common lizard *(Lacerta vivipara)* is probably easier to observe in the rocky Burren landscape than elsewhere in Ireland. Due to its dependency on the sun's warmth to become active and the scarcity of its invertebrate food in winter, the lizard too has to hibernate. In summer it likes to bask in heat traps, out of the wind. Favourite places are on walls or in the enclosures of the stone cahers (as in Caher Dun Irguis on Black Head). The cryptic colouration and pattern on their scaly bodies render lizards invisible to most predators. The keen-eyed kestrel, however, can often be seen in the summer sky on the lookout for such reptilian delicacies.

The common lizard is not the only reptile to be found in the Burren. In recent years sighting of 'snakes' near the Clare/Galway border have turned out to be slow worms *(Anguis fragilis)* - legless lizards up to 0.5 m long, resembling small, bronze coloured snakes. They are doubtless the progeny of introductions from outside Ireland for they are not considered to be native here. The origins of a colony of green lizards *(Lacerta viridis)* is better established. These were discovered in the Burren in 1958 but were definite introductions from their natural habitat - the much warmer countries surrounding the Mediterranean. Though one was seen in 1962, it is highly unlikely that they still survive in the Burren today.

Birds

The limestone country, though well populated with common birds, is not a particularly outstanding bird habitat in the Irish context. Many summer visitors like wheatears (*Oenanthe oenanthe*), willow and sedge warblers (*Acrocephalus schoenobaenus*), whitethroats (*Sylvia communis*) and cuckoos (*Cuculus canorus*) breed there and there are scarce summer visitors too like the whinchat (*Saxicola rubetra*) and the rarely seen nightjar (*Caprimulgus europaeus*). But the majority of its avian inhabitants are all-year-round residents. Birds like thrushes, finches, pigeons and tits occupy the scrubby areas, while pipits, larks and crows inhabit the open ground. The Burren has lost some of its birds too, at least partly, because of conflict with man's activities; the corncrake (*Crex crex*) and grey partridge (*Perdix perdix*) have disappeared within living memory, their decline hastened by changing agricultural practices. Eagles too, are gone from the Burren for more than a century - shot and poisoned as threats to 19th Century agri-business. Nor are the birds of prey that remain secure. The peregrine (*Falco peregrinus*), hen harrier (*Circus cyaneus*), and the merlin (*Falco columbarius*) remain only as rare nesting birds, their continued survival dependent on intrusive human activity such as quarrying, rock-climbing, afforestation and other developments which constantly threaten their survival. The sparrow hawk (*Accipiter nisus*) and the kestrel (*Falco tinnunculus*) are, however, still widespread and fairly common in the Burren.

In winter, birds are generally much less obvious in the limestone country than in the summer. Though the hazel scrub is tenanted by foraging birds like goldcrests (*Regulus regulus*) and the rocky escarpments echo with the croaks of ravens (*Corvus corax*), it is by no

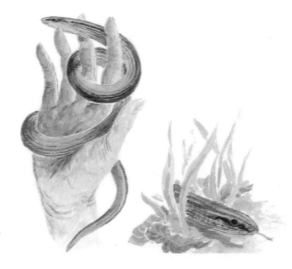

3.7   See page 54.

3.6   *SLOW WORM*
        (Anguis fragilis)
Neither slow nor a worm, this snake-like creature is, in fact, a kind of lizard. As with other lizards, it is capable of detaching itself from its tail when seized by a predator. In the hand (it is quite harmless) it shows other lizard characteristics such as eyelids that blink and a strap-like tongue which it flicks out constantly to scent the air. It is really only in the hand that the beautiful sleekness of the slow-worm's body can be appreciated resembling, as it does, finely varnished wood. The question as to the origins of the colony in the eastern Burren in unresolved but it appears to have been an introduction, perhaps from Britain, in or around the early 1970's.

means unusual to encounter only a dozen or so bird species in the course of a winter walk in the high Burren.

The freshwater wetlands are interesting for birds at all times of the year. In summer the lakes and fens support breeding wildfowl particularly mallard (*Anas platyrhynchos*), moorhens (*Gallinula chloropus*) and coots (*Fulica atra*). Wading birds such as snipe (*Gallinago gallinago*), lapwing (*Vanellus vanellus*), and, to a lesser degree, redshank (*Tringa totanus*) and curlew (*Numenius arquata*), breed in the short wetland pasture. Common sandpipers (*Actitis hypoleucos*) nest regularly on Lough Bunny (and perhaps elsewhere in the Burren). On Lough Bunny too, a variety of waterfowl raise their families. These often include tufted duck (*Athya fuligula*) and little grebes (*Tachybaptus ruficollis*) and occasionally great crested grebes (*Podiceps cristatus*) and red-breasted mergansers (*Mergus serrator*). One of the islands on Lough Bunny is home to a substantial colony, about 300 pairs, of black headed gulls (*Larus ridibundus*).

In winter the turloughs are flooded and they support flocks of wintering wildfowl and wading birds. The largest in the Burren, at Carron, holds two or three hundred surface-feeding ducks, mainly wigeon (*Anas penelope*) and teal (*Anas crecca*) and often small numbers of wild swans and Greenland white-fronted geese (*Anser albifrons f.*). The lake system around Corofin holds hundreds of wildfowl like wigeon, teal and shoveler (*Anas clypeata*) with up to 200 wild swans (Whooper swans and Bewick's swans). Frequently, thousands of golden plover (*Pluvialis apricaria*) and lapwings occur there also.

Scarcer ducks, like goldeneye (*Bucephala clangula*) and gadwall (*Anas streptera*) are found in small numbers on some of the lakes, including Loughs Bunny and Atedaun.

The undrained condition of the freshwater wetlands has an important bearing on the richness of the birdlife. They are highly productive birdwatching habitats. Up to 50 species can be identified there in both summer and winter with occasional rarities besides.

The coastal region is also interesting throughout the year. The cliffs of Moher, though not strictly a part of the Burren, are nevertheless too important to be omitted. They consitute a seabird city supporting about 4,000 pairs of guillemots (*Uria aalge*) with lesser numbers of other auks like razorbills (*Alca torda*) and puffins (*Fratercula arctica*). Thousands of kittiwakes, herring gulls (*Larus argentatus*) and fulmars (*Fulmarus glacialis*) share the cliff ledges, while shags (*Phalacrocorax aristotelis*) and black guillemots (*Cepphus grylle*) occupy the lower rocks. Other interesting birds found at the cliffs of Moher include ravens, choughs (*Pyrrhocorax pyrrhocorax*), rock doves (*Columbia livia*), and their chief predator, the peregrine.

In winter the cliffs are almost devoid of birdlife, the summer occupants having moved off to their wintering quarters in the open Atlantic. Coastline promontaries, particularly at Black Head are good places to watch out for movements of sea birds. From the Head in autumn (stormy weather is the best time to watch), flocks of migrating and storm-blown birds such as auks, gannets (*Sula bassana*), petrels, including storm petrels (*Hydrobates pelagicus*), manx shearwaters (*Puffinus puffinus*) and terns (*Sternidae*) stream past within binocular range. Rare visitors from the far north also turn up at this time and include arctic gulls and phalaropes (*Phalaropidae*).

The north coast of the Burren, incorporating the Rine near Ballyvaughan and the inlets of inner Galway Bay, is an important winter habitat for certain marine water birds including brent geese (*Branta bernicla h.*), long tailed ducks (*Clangula hyemalis*), and divers

3.7 WHEATEAR
(Oenanthe oenanthe)

Of all the summer birds which inhabit the rocky landscape, the wheatear is surely the most typical. From early April until the end of September, wheatears are in evidence from sea level to the rocky heights. And wheatears are ostentatious birds: they invariably perch where they can see and be seen - particularly on top of drystone walls and on boulders. It is not until the wheatear flies, however, that its true distinctiveness can be seen, for its black-tipped tail is dazzlingly white and renders its identification easy, even from a distance. Wheatears make their nests in clefts and cracks in the rocks where they raise their offspring before flying off to winter in Africa.

(Gaviidae). Black throated divers *(Gavia arctica)* are regular winter visitors in small numbers to the north coast of the Burren. They are rare elsewhere in Ireland.

Mammals

There are considerably more mammals than there appear to be in the Burren, but, due to their secretive or nocturnal habits, they are often overlooked. The feral goat herds are the most accessible. Though not truly "wild" (having been released into the region at some time in the past) they nevertheless soon adopt wild herd behaviour - the older billies acting as combatative custodians to the rest of the herd. With their shaggy coats, beards and swept back horns these ancient-looking creatures blend naturally into the rocky wilderness of the Burren. They are in need of protection if they are not to be eliminated by poaching, which has been on the increase recently. The most famous (though least seen) of the Burren's mammals is the pine marten *(Martes martes)* or marten cat, as it is locally known. It is found both in the woodland plantations of the periphery and in the limestone heartland where it feeds on small mammals, birds and berries. The young (kittens) are born in spring but do not fend for themselves in the open until autumn. Few people have been fortunate enough to have had a good view of this chocolate-brown animal with yellowish-white throat patch and long furry tail. Other carnivores like the fox *(Vulpes vulpes)*, the badger *(Meles meles)* and the stoat *(Mustela erminea h.)* are well represented in the region. The stoat is most often seen running along the top of a stone wall, a handy vantage from which this aggressive predator can stalk on the more timid of the mammals on which it preys. The rabbit *(Oryctolagus cuniculus)* is not so common as the Irish hare *(Lepus timidus h.)* which is found throughout, from the sand dunes at Fanore to the high plateau. Though there is a virtual absence of high timber, the red squirrel *(Sciurus vulgaris)* (but not the grey squirrel) is found in the hazel scrub where an abundant food source is available.

Of the smaller mammals, the wood-mouse *(Apodemus sylvaticus)* is most common, finding a ready-made sanctuary in the limestone grykes. Its abundance can be gauged, to an extent, by the widespread caches of hazel buts secreted in the scrub and the frequency of occurrence of its bones in fox droppings. That even smaller creature, the pigmy shrew *(Sorex minutus)*, is also widespread. A good place to look for them is along the high-tide line at dusk where they forage for food. The bats, best known of the night squeakers, are particularly well represented in North Clare, with all seven Irish species being found there. One of these, the lesser-horseshoe bat *(Rhincophus hipposideros)*, is thought to have the bulk of its European population in the west of Ireland. The souterrains of the region's many ring forts act as winter hibernacula (hibernating places) for many of these bats, where they hang from the roof, their wings enclosing their tiny torpid bodies - "Dracula style". In this state they are extremely vulnerable to disturbance and should be left alone where possible.

Not all of the Burren's mammals are terrestrial. The otter *(Lutra lutra)*, normally an animal of rivers and lakes, is found along the Burren's coastline, where it has adapted to the marine environment. Its young are regularly reared in a holt (the otter's underground home) on the Rine point, near Ballyvaughan. Common seals *(Phoca vitulina)* utilize Illaunloo, also off Ballyvaughan, but they may be encountered anywhere along the coastline. Grey seals *(Halichoerus grypus)* are less frequent, favouring the more exposed coastline of Connemara to the comparative shelter of Galway Bay. Porpoises *(Phocoena phocoena)* may be seen off Black Head at any time of the year, but dolphins *(Delphinus delphis)* are more frequent in the summer months. Occasionally other cetaceans (marine

3.8 WOOD MOUSE
(*Apodemus sylvaticus*)

An altogether more appealing little rodent than its dingy house-haunting relative, the wood or field mouse is undoubtedly the Burren's commonest mammal. Its distinguishing features include its tawny fur (white underneath), its large dish-shaped, pinkish ears and its extremely long tail - longer than its body. Its aesthetic characteristics are obviously of lesser importance in the priority ranking of the Burren's predators for it is a significant dietary item for carnivores such as the fox and the stoat.

3.9 OTTER
(*Lutra lutra*)

Otters are adaptable animals. Though essentially aquatic in their lifestyle (as the webbing between the toes of their back feet would testify), they nevertheless spend a great deal of time on land. During the day they rest up in an underground burrow known as a holt and venture out to fish mainly at night but they will go out and about during the day if the occasion demands. Their menu comprises inshore fish of many species and other marine creatures such as crabs. In spring, they venture up the streams to seek out those ponds occupied by breeding frogs - one of their favourite foods.

mammals) like killer whales *(Orcanus orca)* turn up at this time too. During the warm summer of 1984 a small pack of these most striking of marine mammals stayed for a period along the Burren's north coast, sustained, no doubt, by the rich fish stocks and the occasional seal besides.

The hibernation pits and bones of the brown bear *(Ursus arctos)* from the famous Aillwee caves are relics of a now-extinct Burren fauna from the end of the Ice Age - before the coming of man. There is evidence too in the wealth of placenames that both wolves *(Canis lupus)* and deer *(Cervidae)* roamed the Burren while man was establishing his settlements there. (There was a deer park just north of Leamaneh castle). Both animals are now gone, obviously eradicated by man. Gone too are the majestic sea eagles *(Haliaeetus albicilla)* which, up to the mid 19th Century, soared in the updraft at the cliffs of Moher and nested against their craggy face. Such predatory birds and animals were regarded as a threat to developing agriculture and were ruthlessly exterminated as vermin. It is only with the wisdom of hindsight that we can evaluate their former role in the ecosystem and (at our leisure) rue their passing.

The Future

The Burren may have lost most of its spectacular wildlife, but a great deal remains which distinguishes the region as a wildlife haven. A critical stage is approaching, however, where the protectiveness afforded by the ruggedness of the terrain will no longer be enough, where the custody implicit in the wildness of the place is being increasingly violated by developing man. The pressures affecting the continuing proliferation of the exceptional flora are also affecting the wildlife, for they are inter-dependent. Foremost among these are the conflicts associated with modern agriculture. Intensification is the current buzz-word and it is manifest in widespread land clearance

3.10 KESTREL and LIZARD
(Falco tinnunculus) and
(Lacerta vivipara)

The Irish name for the kestrel, Pocaire gaoithe (beater of the wind), is highly descriptive for it is often to be seen hovering in the sky as though suspended from a string, its eyes transfixed on the ground for potential prey. This prey can range from small mammals like the pigmy shrew to a variety of invertebrates like beetles. A favourite prey is lizard which, when basking in the sun on an exposed rocky outcrop, is vulnerable to attack from above. Several pairs of kestrels nest in the Burren, mainly on exposed cliff faces.

Acknowledgements for illustrations
Illus. 3.1 to 3.10, Watercolours, Gordon D'Arcy
Illus 3.11, Photograph, T. Quinn

to accommodate increasing herd sizes. Silage production has increased enormously over the past decade, reducing the area of natural meadow and threatening groundwater pollution.

The larger mammals, particularly the pine marten, the fox and the unfortunate badger are under serious threat due to their alleged conflict with livestock interests. Their bad reputation has resulted more from a mixture of unreliable observation (foxes feeding on still-born lambs), "scape-goating" (badgers and bovine T.B.) and folklore (claw in the tail of the pine marten?), rather than from scientific evidence. Indeed, even if wildlife were to conflict directly with man's interests, its existence in the Burren since before the time of man's arrival entitles it to continued survival.

In these days of espoused maturity in regard to land-use policy, where Ireland's contribution to the European community is a measure not only of its capacity to produce but also of its capacity to conserve, the ultimate question is a simple one. Does Ireland, Europe, the world, need another 150 square miles of agricultural sameness more than it needs a unique wildlife habitat that is the Burren still?

3.11 FERAL GOAT

4.1. *Ballyganner Wedge Tomb.*

The First People
The Prehistoric Burren

John Waddell

It is possible that the human story of the Burren may have commenced as long as ten thousand years ago. Certainly we know that from about 8000 BC parts of the rest of Ireland were occupied by small communities of hunters and foragers who depended on wild pig, red deer, fish and edible plants and nuts for their subsistence. Such hunting and foraging bands may well have existed in the Burren, but, if they did, no traces of their camp sites or their characteristic implements of chert and flint have yet been found.

4.2. The ruined Court Tomb in Teergonean townland now appears at first glance to be a jumble of stones. However, the tall slabs on the left are the remains of a semi-circular fore-court and the lower box-like arrangement on the right is the roof-less remnant of a long rectangular burial chamber. All traces of the long cairn, which once covered this chamber, have disappeared.

4.3. Plan of Teergonean Court Tomb.

Given that a hunting and food gathering economy would probably only permit a population density of about 0.1 person per square kilometre, the few hundred square kilometres of the region might only have supported one or two small hunting communities, possibly no more than one or two dozen people. If this was the case, it is not surprising that their presence - if such there was - has not been detected.

The earliest farming groups have not been identified either. Their existence is not attested until they began to build burial monuments. At the present stage of research it is the funerary record which offers the earliest certain evidence of human occupation. It is a fortunate paradox that these people, while living in impermanent timber houses, preferred to construct durable stone monuments to contain the bones of their ancestors. On present evidence, the first farming communities began to build stone tombs shortly after 4000 BC.

The Burren landscape of 4000 BC which those early tomb-builders confronted would have looked very different from that of today. Open pine forest was widespread. The analysis of pollens preserved in ancient sediments in lakes at Gortlecka and Rinnamona, north-east of Kilnaboy, has revealed that about this time there was considerable woodland cover of pine, elm, and hazel, along with some oak, at least on the margins of the limestone uplands (Watts 1983, 1984). Low percentages of grass pollen indicate some open ground. Similar pollen analysis in the Carron Depression (in the limestone upland area) confirms that here too pine and hazel were the main woodland species (Crabtree 1982). The hazel scrub, pasture and limestone pavement so visible today may not have developed until the early part of the first millenium AD.

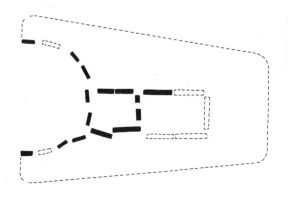

The Tomb Builders

The megalithic or great stone tombs are the most visible testimony to extensive early prehistoric activity. Over seventy tombs occur in the Burren, over half the total from Co. Clare as a whole. A few Portal Tombs and Court Tombs, as they are called, may represent the earliest monuments (from about 3800 BC), many if not all of the Wedge Tombs being somewhat later in time probably belonging to the third millenium BC.

Two Court Tombs, in Ballyganner North near Noughaval and in Teergonean near Doolin, are both very ruined, with roof-stones and covering cairn now gone. A third is recorded in Leamaneh North (O Nualláin 1989). The Ballyganner tomb has been described in detail by De Valera and O Nuallain (1961). This sort of tomb is so called because it had a characteristic stone-built fore-court in front of the burial chamber. At Teergonean, only four stones of this court survive (Illus. 4.2) but the stumps of others can be detected. Originally the forecourt was probably almost semi-circular, the tallest and most imposing of the upright stones flanking the narrow entrance to the long rectangular burial gallery. Only some of its side stones remain and all the roofing stones are gone. Five thousand years ago, however, when in use, a long cairn of stones would probably have covered the tomb. The forecourt would have been open and unroofed and was probably used for ritual purposes. Excavation elsewhere has shown that these tombs normally contain some cremated bone and perhaps a few pieces of flint and some fragments of pottery.

Portal Tombs usually have two imposing portals or entrance stones flanking the front of a relatively small rectangular or sub-rectangular chamber. The capstone, which sometimes rests just on the end stone and on the portal stones, is often very large. Four such monuments occur in Co. Clare, but only two in the Burren. One of these is in Ballycasheen townland north-west of Kilnaboy on the very edge of the region, while the other, situated in the very heart of the Burren at Poulnabrone, is also one of the best-known examples of these monuments in the whole country.

The striking Poulnabrone tomb was excavated by Dr. Ann Lynch of the Office of Public Works in 1986. According to her summary account:

"The excavation of the chamber and part of the surrounding cairn revealed much about the form and structure of the tomb. The orthostats of the chamber were sitting directly on the limestone bedrock, held in place by the weight of the capstone like a house of cards. The sill-stone at the entrance to the chamber was

4.4. *Reconstruction of Teergonean Court Tomb.*
It is generally assumed that the fore-courts of Court Tombs were used for ceremonial purposes but the nature of these rituals is unknown. Funeral rites, ancestor worship, propitiation or initiation rituals, fertility or divination ceremonies, are all possibilities.

4.5. *Poulnabrone Portal Tomb.*

From the chamber deposit and from the grykes running through the chamber and the portico, the unburnt remains - disarticulated and fragmentary - of between 16 and 22 adults and 6 juveniles, including a new born baby, were recovered. It was estimated, on the basis of the meagre demographic data that "the majority of the adults died before reaching the age of 30 while only one lived past 40 years". Of the 8 adults of whom it was possible to determine sex, there was an equal distribution of males and females.

The dental data indicated that these people had a coarse diet suggestive of stone-ground cereals. Studies of vertebral pathology also indicated that these individuals shared a lifestyle characterised by hard physical labour. Only a single weapon - the tip of a flint or chert arrowhead embedded in a hip bone that probably belonged to a male - was found among the remains. "There are no signs of healing having taken place", the excavator noted, "so this wound would have occurred shortly before or even after the time of death. It is unlikely, however, that this injury was the cause of death".

As the remains - apart from those of the infant - consisted of a complete jumble of disarticulated bones, it is likely that bodies were either deliberately defleshed or were initially interred (or left exposed to decay) elsewhere and later transferred to the tomb.

Dr. Lynch concluded:

"The number of individuals interred at Poulnabrone can hardly represent a Neolithic community, so we must regard the tomb as a place for special dead. Objects which must have been of particular significance to these people were placed in the tomb with their remains and included a bone pendant, part of a mushroom-headed bone pin, a polished stone axe, two stone disc-beads, two large quartz crystals, flint and chert scrapers, and projectile points.

sitting in an east-west gryke (a crevice in the limestone pavement) which formed a natural socket. Its original height is impossible to determine since it fractured at some stage in antiquity close to the present floor level, but it may have extended to the underside of the capstone, thereby effectively closing off the burial chamber. At the entrance to the chamber, just outside the sill-stone, three stones had been placed on edge, forming a portico or antechamber which had been backfilled with earth and stones shortly after construction. The function of this feature is unclear, but it neatly delimited the cairn edge at the tomb entrance".

In her report, Dr. Lynch described the cairn as roughly oval in plan and stated that "it seems reasonable to assume that when originally built the cairn at Poulnabrone appeared much as it does today...It would seem that the soaring capstone was designed to be seen".

Over sixty sherds of undecorated coarse pottery were also recovered from the burial deposit".

Some of the human bones from Poulnabrone were submitted for radiocarbon dating and the results suggest that burials took place there between 3800 and 3200 BC. The skeleton of the newborn baby which had been placed in a limestone crevice proved to be a later, Bronze Age, insertion.

The relatively small number of persons found in many (though not all) megalithic tombs and the prodigious amount of labour often involved in their construction are but two of several factors to have prompted the suggestion that these were more than mere burial places. Looking at Poulnabrone, for example, it is easy to imagine more simpler ways of disposing of the dead. It is thought likely that monuments like this must also have had some symbolic role and may have played an integral part in the lives of the community. They may well have contained the bones of special dead, perhaps the remains of revered ancestors who served some function as intermediaries with the gods or spirits who were believed to control the natural world.

These tombs may thus have been the focus of magical or religious ceremonies at certain times of the year, such as autumn or spring, times of particular significance to a farming group. Their imposing size, or even their aura of sanctity, may also have embodied them with special territorial significance and they may have been intended as a very visible expression of a community's rights to the surrounding lands. Poulnabrone, in its day, may have been much more than merely a stone container for human remains.

Most of the tombs in the Burren, over 90% of them, are classified as Wedge Tombs. This is the commonest type of Irish megalithic monument widely distributed in the south-west,

4.6. *A range of stone artifacts found in the burial chamber of Poulnabrone Portal Tomb. They include a miniature polished stone axe, arrowheads and scrapers.*

west and north of the country, and the Burren group is the densest concentration known. These tombs are so named because they have a wedge-shaped ground plan, that is, they are usually narrower (and lower) towards the rear, eastern end. The broader part usually faces roughly south-west to west towards the setting sun. Almost half of them show traces of double-walling, a second line of stones 50 cm. to 1 m. outside the chamber wall itself. The opportunity to use the readily available slabs of limestone gives these structures, particularly the smaller ones, a rather box-like appearance (Illus. 4.8). As with other tombs, the cairns of stones which once surrounded them are invariably denuded, though they were probably round or oval originally.

The fact that the distribution of these tombs is mainly confined to the higher ground of the Burren between 400 and 700 feet above sea-level, where even today there is thriving winter grazing, led De Valera and O Nualláin (1961) to suppose that the tomb builders were mainly

63

pastoralists. "Cattle would appear to have been the principal stock, though sheep and goats could also have played an important role".

Why so many tombs should be clustered in such a relatively small area, however, is a puzzle. There are, for example, no less than eleven examples in or near the townland of Parknabinnia, north of Kilnaboy; they form a rough linear scatter some 200 m. long. It is possible that concentrations like this represent a sequence of tomb building in an area. Excavated examples elsewhere in Ireland suggest that this tomb fashion may have lasted for quite a number of centuries. None of the Burren wedge tombs have been excavated and, therefore, many questions about their date and their builders remain unanswered. Evidence, mainly from the north of Ireland, shows that some of these tomb builders had a knowledge of copper working and the use of these monuments continued well into the early Bronze Age, overlapping with the new burial practices of that period. The time span for wedge tombs as a class (and not necessarily the Burren series) could be a millenium or more, extending from c. 3000 to 2000 BC.

Poulawack

a long sequence of ritual activity

There are a number of prehistoric burial mounds in the Burren. The large round cairns on the summit of Turlough Hill and on Slievecarran are two of the most prominent and striking sites, but there are many smaller examples as well. Dates in the Neolithic and early Bronze Age are probable, but some round mounds with enclosing circular banks could be even later. A number of small cist graves have also been recorded (Coffey 1985).

Certainly one of the most impressive of these burial mounds is the cairn at Poulawack, about

4.7.   Parknabinnia Wedge Tomb.

4.8.   Plan and section of Parknabinnia Wedge Tomb.

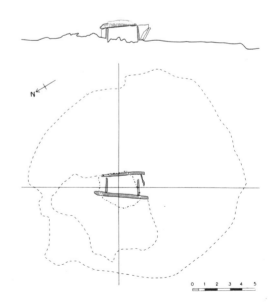

64

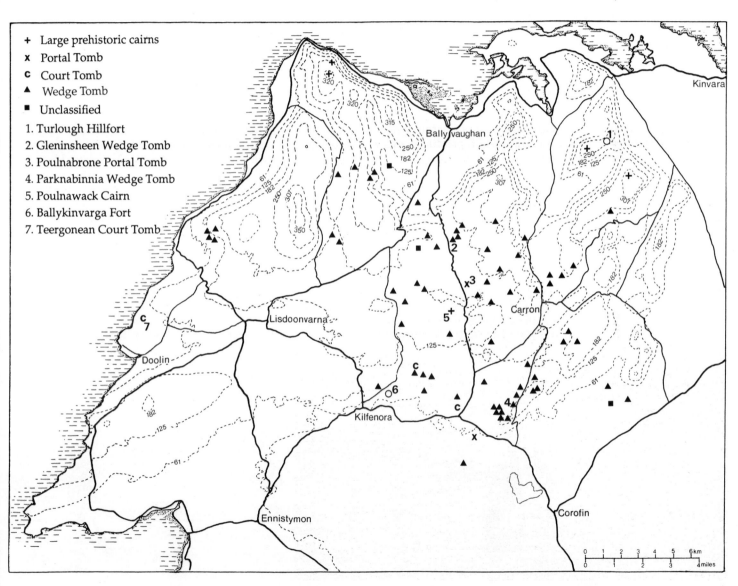

4.9. *Map showing large prehistoric cairns, Portal Tombs, Court Tombs, Wedge Tombs and unclassified tombs.*

+ Large prehistoric cairns
x Portal Tomb
c Court Tomb
▲ Wedge Tomb
■ Unclassified
1. Turlough Hillfort
2. Gleninsheen Wedge Tomb
3. Poulnabrone Portal Tomb
4. Parknabinnia Wedge Tomb
5. Poulnawack Cairn
6. Ballykinvarga Fort
7. Teergonean Court Tomb

4.10. *Large prehistoric cairns occur on several Burren mountain summits including Slievecarran on the left and Turlough Hill on the right. Why so much labour was expended in such high places is unknown but perhaps these great monuments were built not merely to contain burials but also, perhaps, to give prominent expression to a symbol of the power of the Otherworld.*

4.11. *Reconstruction of the primary phase of Poulawack cairn.*
   The first burial structure on this site was a slab-built grave surrounded by a stone wall. This grave and enclosure may have been the focus for magico-religious activity for a period of time before other graves and the large cairn were built.

two miles west of Carron, which was excavated in 1934. It produced a large number of human bones but few dateable artefacts. Because the great majority of the bones were unburnt, however, the excavator assigned the burials to the earlier Bronze Age when unburnt burial was popular. It was clear that a sequence of burials had occurred at Poulawack but the timespan of this activity was uncertain (Hencken 1935).

Recent reassessment of the Poulawack finds, however, now indicates that it had a long and complicated history. The cairn, 20 m. across, was found to contain ten graves with the remains of some sixteen individuals. The central grave was the earliest and the focus for much of the later activity. Numbered 8 and 8A (Ill. 4.13) by the excavator, it was a cist, a slab-built box, of two compartments, surrounded by more slabs leaning inwards. A few unburnt bones, a boar's tusk, two tiny pieces of pottery and a flint scraper were found in one compartment, while the other contained the mixed-up bones of four persons and an oyster shell. The four individuals were a male and female, forty to forty-five years old, a young adult female of about twenty-one, and an infant. (Some of the infant's bones were in the compartment with the boar's tusk and other items).

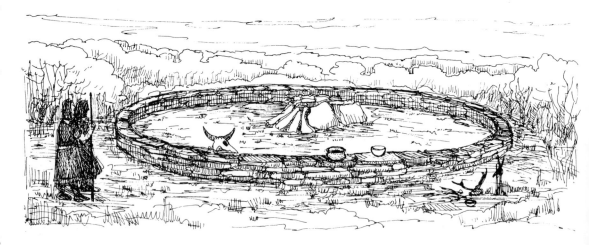

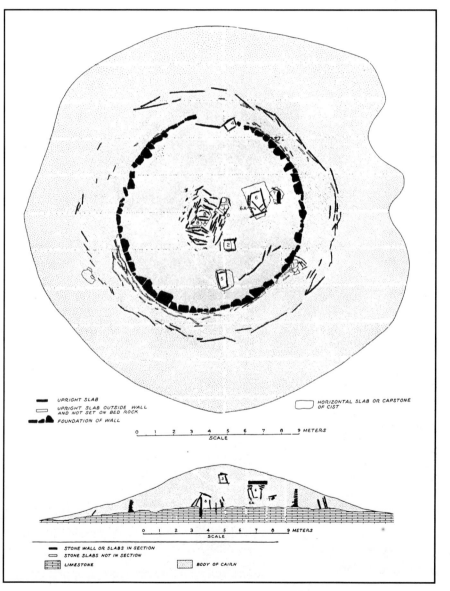

4.12. *Poulawack cairn 1991.*

4.13. *Plan of the burial cairn at Poulawack with a cross-section through the middle of the mound showing the later, secondary position of some graves.*

This sort of irregular cist is now known to be a Neolithic type dating to about 3300 BC, and it is possible that it originally stood exposed in the centre of the walled circular area found beneath the cairn. The wall would presumably have served to separate the sacred precincts of the grave from the world outside. Grave 5, a rectangular cist, was then built on the ground surface a few metres to the south but still within the wall. It contained the unburnt bones of a child and a teenager. A tiny fragment of pottery was all that survived of any grave offering.

It seems as if the cairn was then built and further graves incorporated in it during its construction. Grave 6, for instance, was another cist, placed about halfway up in the body of the mound (Illus. 4.13). It contained burnt as well as unburnt bones, representing four persons altogether. A small piece of decorated pottery suggests this grave dates to about 2300 BC.

Finally, several graves, such as Grave 3 (Illus. 4.13) were actually inserted into the cairn at some later date.

Poulawack, therefore, seems to have had a much more complicated and long drawn-out history than was first thought. Its burials seem to span more than a thousand years. To bury sixteen people within a few generations might be a normal enough sequence of events. But when spread over a very long period of time, it does seem as if those people were very special

UPRIGHT SLAB

UPRIGHT SLAB OUTSIDE WALL AND NOT SET ON BED ROCK

FOUNDATION OF WALL

HORIZONTAL SLAB OR CAPSTONE OF CIST

0 1 2 3 4 5 6 7 8 9 METERS
SCALE

STONE WALL OR SLABS IN SECTION

STONE SLABS NOT IN SECTION

LIMESTONE

BODY OF CAIRN

0 1 2 3 4 5 6 7 8 9 METERS
SCALE

indeed to be accorded the rare privilege of formal burial in this monument.

Settlements, Finds and Other Features

There is abundant other evidence for early settlement in the Burren: enigmatic circles (MacMahon 1982), hut sites, and other enclosures; stone forts and the remains of ancient field systems are common. Unfortunately this evidence is almost all of unknown date, and it is impossible at present to identify the settlements, for example, of the tomb and cairn

4.14. Excavation of fulacht fiadh at Fahee South.

builders. Indeed, many of the settlements and field systems are probably of early Christian or Medieval date.

One intriguing monument - many examples of which are now known to date to the Bronze Age - is the so-called fulacht fiadh or burnt mound. Over 300 of them have now been identified (Coffey 1984). These are usually horse-shoe shaped mounds of burnt stone, often located in wet or marshy areas. Excavation has invariably produced much burnt stone and charcoal, as well as traces of a hearth and a stone-lined or wooden trough.

Stones heated in the fire were dropped into the water-filled trough, eventually bringing the water to the boil. Experiment has shown that meat can be cooked in this fashion (or even roasted by just placing the hot stones around the meat). The mound was formed by the discarded stones, hence the name burnt mound. The absence or scarcity of animal bones from excavated sites has prompted the suggestion that some at least of these sites were not just cooking places but used for some other purposes, perhaps even as bathing places.

The one Burren burnt mound which has been excavated sheds some significant light on this debate. This is a mound at Fahee South, near Carron, excavated by Diarmuid O Drisceoil in 1981 and 1982. (Illus. 4.14). Here, in addition to burnt stones, charcoal and the remains of an oak trough, he also found some animal bone, in particular, five cattle teeth and two fragments, one deer tooth and two deer antlers, one horse mandible and tooth, and 13 teeth and 20 bone fragments unidentifiable as to species. O Drisceoil concluded on the basis of radiocarbon dating that the Fahee South burnt mound was used around 1400 - 1200 BC. Of the class as a whole, he stated that "cooking must still be the most likely primary function even though bathing by immersion or sweating may have been a secondary activity".

Aside from burnt mounds, some further Bronze Age activity is reflected in the casual discovery of the occasional bronze implement or weapon. For instance, part of an early copper axehead was found at a depth of eight feet in a bog in Boghil, near Lisdoonvarna (Harbison 1969, 11) and a fine bronze dagger comes from a sandpit in Gortaclare, north of Carron (Lucas 1970, 150). This dagger is an unusual piece (Illus. 4.16). It originally had a bone or antler handle, probably attached to the blade by six rivets (two of them in rivet notches). This style of attachment and features such as fine grooves near the edges of the blade indicates that it is related to a prestigious

4.15. Burnt mounds or fulachta fiadh seem to have been particularly popular in the second millenium BC. Whether they were generally used as cooking places, as washing and bathing places, or for other purposes demanding hot water is debated. At the moment the cooking hypothesis is favoured.

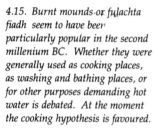

type found in southern England and dated to about 1500 BC. The unknown owner of the Gortaclare dagger was probably a person of considerable status in the community.

A later weapon, possibly dating to about 1000 BC, is a bronze rapier found in a bog in Bally-connoe South, east of Lisdoonvarna (Illus. 4.17). These long slender stabbing weapons represent a development in the fighting arts in later prehistory. Indeed it has been suggested that two-handed combat may have been customary about this time, a short dirk being held in one hand, the longer rapier in the other (Burgess and Gerloff 1981).

Two bronze swords - possibly dating to several centuries later - show that the Burren region continued to follow changing European martial fashions in the later Bronze Age. Swords such as these, with more effective bronze hilts (originally with bone or antler grips rivetted to them) and broad blades, were cutting and thrusting weapons. Part of a sword comes from a bog in Cohy near Noughaval, and a complete but broken ex-ample was found in Nooan townland, north of Kilnaboy (Eogan 1965).

The Gleninsheen Collar

The most extraordinary piece of evidence for a late Bronze Age presence, c. 700 BC, comes from the townland of Gleninsheen. This famous gold collar or gorget (Illus. 4.25, page 70/73) was found by accident in 1932 and its preservation is due in great measure to D.F. Gleeson who published the following account in 1934:

"On 17th January, 1934, when rabbit shooting at Gleninsheen, Ballyvaughan, Co. Clare, a young man named Patrick Nolan, who resides there, told me he had found a "queer looking thing" some time ago and asked if I would care to see it. He said his uncle was of the opinion that it was part of an ancient coffin mounting,

4.16. The Gortaclare bronze dagger was found at a depth of almost two metres in a sandpit. It is a well made weapon 20cm. in length with a stout midrib to strengthen the blade. Finely engraved lines decorate the blade parallel to its edges and form a U-shaped design below the mark of the haft. The haft would have been made of bone or antler fastened to the blade by six rivets, three of which are present. Size 23 cm.

4.17. Bronze rapier from Ballyconnoe South, scale 2 : 5.

and told him not to keep it in the house. He then took the gorget out from behind a wall on the rocky passage to the road from his house, which we were traversing at the time. It was then almost dark and too late to inspect the place where he had found it two years before, so I took it with me, and communicated at once with Dr. Mahr, Keeper of Irish Antiquities, National Museum. Dr. Mahr came to Ennis on the 19th and took charge of the gorget which is now in the Museum. He and I inspected the site where it was originally discovered. It was in a fissure near the base of one of the typical rock formations which abound in the Burren country...it had apparently been hidden there, as it was pushed as far as possible into a very narrow fissure, and a thin flat stone flake was wedged in front of it. It was a pure chance that Nolan looked in the fissure, as his dog had "set" a rabbit in the cavity between the rock and the adjoining one. Investigation of the site produced no further find. When found, and even after being two years thrown on the passage as described, the gorget was intact and in very fine condition".

Mary Cahill of the National Museumdescribes it (1983) as:

"One of the finest achievements of Irish Later Bronze Age goldsmiths. It is one of eight such collars still in existence although historical sources indicate the former existence of several more...Their distribution is very restricted, being confined mainly to Counties Clare, Limerick and Tipperary".

The quality of goldwork of this period from this part of northern Munster raises the distinct possibility of a major settlement (perhaps that of a tribal chieftain) and a manufacturing centre somewhere in the region. If this was so, the Gleninsheen find might suggest that the Burren came within its sphere of influence.

4.18. *A Burren warrior of the Iron Age as he might have looked.*

The Iron Age

There are a few dateable bronze finds which reveal an Iron Age presence in the Burren. It is very probable that some stone forts date to this period too but, in spite of categorical assertions that they are Iron Age monuments, evidence is lacking at the moment. A bronze pendant (Illus. 4.19) found in a bog at Ballyalla, south of Lisdoonvarna, is, however, an incontrovertible Iron Age piece, perhaps dating to the early centuries AD. It is generally accepted that these objects, a distinctively Irish type, were an item of "horse furniture". They are called pendants because it is thought their most likely function was as a decorative piece suspended below a horse's bridle. Occasionally they have been found with bronze bridle bits and the existence of a few matching pairs of both bits and pendants implies paired draught (a pair of horses being yoked to a wheeled vehicle).

One bronze bridle bit was found about ninety years ago in Lough Inchiquin on the southern fringes of the Burren. Unfortunately, it is now lost and known only from an old photograph (Illus. 4.20). It had three links and two side-rings. Items of bronze horse harness such as these were probably highly prized objects and many bits have signs of considerable wear and tear and some show signs of careful and ingenious repairs (Raftery 1983, 1984). A few are intricately decorated and may have been the valuable possessions of the upper orders of society. One such decorated horse bit was found near Corofin about 1925 and was said to have had "scroll-work on it like the ones from Attymon", Co. Galway. Sadly the finder did not realise the significance of his discovery; he used it on his own horses until it broke and then threw the pieces away (Rynne 1982).

One iron spearhead (Illus. 4.21) found near Lough Inchiquin has unusual bronze insets in the blade and traces of geometric decoration on its socket. A spear like this was conceivably part of the weaponry of an aristocratic warrior. The well-dressed Burren warrior of the period was probably an impressive and frightening sight. In addition to spear, short sword and shield, he may well have sported an elaborate hair-style, possibly braided and dyed, a torc or neck-ring, and at least one brooch fastening a great decorative cloak, its size and quality denoting the wearer's status.

Obviously the rather scanty Iron Age material so far recorded from the area tells us rather little about its inhabitants. These elusive people probably buried some of their dead in small and inconspicuous burial mounds of the ring-barrow type. These are so-called because the small low mound is invariably surrounded by a ditch and an external bank. Several are recorded, including a number in Doonagore, near Doolin (Illus. 4.22).

4.22. Ring-barrow in Doonagore, near Doolin.

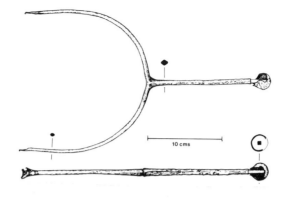

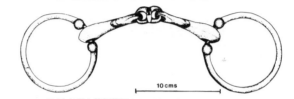

4.19. Bronze horse pendant from Ballyalla.

4.20. Bronze horse bit found in Lough Inchiquin.

4.21. A corroded iron spearhead found in the nineteenth century near Lough Inchiquin. It is 22cm. long and is unusual in having faint traces of some incised or hammered rectilinear ornament on the socket and a pair of oval openings in the blade. These openings each contain an openwork bronze inset, possibly a decorative feature. The iron rivet which once attached the spearhead to a wooden shaft survives in the socket.

71

Ballykinvarga

It is very probable that some of the numerous stone forts found in the Burren date to this prehistoric era, though their use and construction also continued into the early Christian period. Obviously without careful excavation it is impossible to accurately date any of them and it must be stressed that educated guesses as to when they were built are no more than that. Because defended hill-top enclosures are a well-known feature of later prehistory across Europe, such hill sites are often labelled "Iron Age", but any date from the Neolithic onwards is possible. An enclosure of rather irregular plan on top of Turlough Hill, at an elevation of about 800 feet above sea level, is an enigmatic site and, like the many hut circles in its vicinity, is of unknown date. A hill top location by itself can no longer be considered synonymous with "Iron Age".

4.23. Ballykinvarga.

4.24. Only scientific excavation will reveal the date and purpose of the various stone forts and enclosures in the Burren. The great stone fort with chevaux de frise at Ballykinvarga may well prove to be the settlement of an important early 'cattle-baron'. It probably contains the remains of one or more circular stone and timber houses. Nearby enclosures, if contemporary, may contain similar dwellings or may have been built to hold and protect livestock.

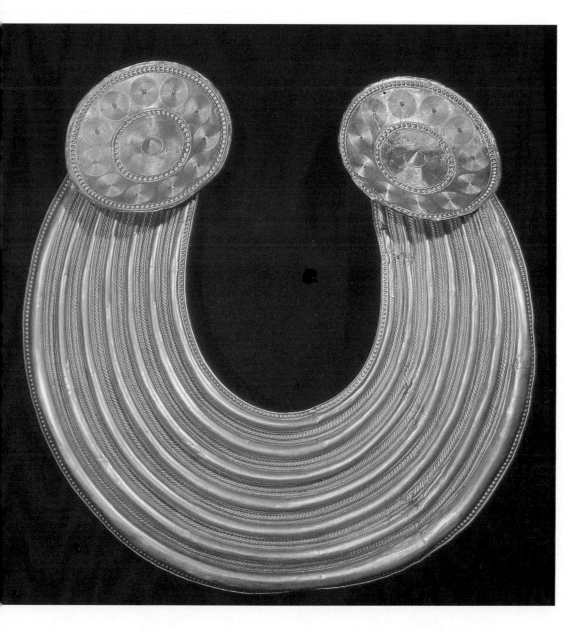

4.25: The Gleninsheen Collar is, according to Mary Cahill's detailed description (1983) "a crescent of sheet gold to which two terminal discs are stitched using twisted gold wire. The collar is formed from a single sheet which expands from 7.4 cm to a maximum width of 10.5 cm at the centre. In order to reinforce and finish the raw edges a narrow strip was rolled over to the front, giving an edge of semi-circular section. Immediately inside the edges is a single row of oval bosses punched from the back. The intervening space is filled by even concentric raised bands which, like the collar itself, widen toward the centre. The area between each pair of raised bands is decorated by three rows of rope-moulding; two narrow cables on either side of a wider one . . .

The construction of the terminal disc is very simple. Two circular plates, one slightly larger than the other, are fitted together by overlapping the edge of the large (back) plate and pressing the two plates together, thus giving a rather unfinished appearance to the front of the terminals.

Both discs are decorated in a similar way. The main feature of the front plates is a large conical boss set in a series of plain concentric circles, bordered by a circle of bosses and two concentric rows of rope-moulding. A band, c. 2 cm wide, is filled with eleven smaller conical bosses, also set in concentric circles. The perimeter of the disc is finished by a circle of bosses contained by a further two circles of rope-moulding . . .

The collar is attached to the terminals by inserting the edges into a slit in the back discs and tacking the two together with a fine twisted gold wire."

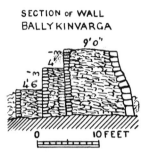

SECTION of WALL
BALLYKINVARGA

9'0"

0   10 FEET

4.26. *Plan and wall section of Ballykinvarga.*

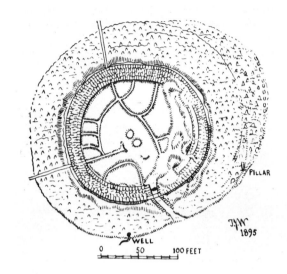

PILLAR

WELL

0   50   100 FEET

In contrast there is still some slim justification for claiming such a date for the celebrated stone fort at Ballykinvarga, near Kilfenora, because it is one of a small number of forts whose defenses include a chevaux de frise, a

term used to describe wooden stakes or upright pointed stones placed in the ground outside a fort to hinder access. The name is said to derive from spikes used by the Frisians to impede enemy cavalry in the latter half of the 17th century. Stone chevaux de frise of supposedly Iron Age date are known in Scotland, Wales and Spain, and their occurrence at sites such as Dun Aengus on Aran and Ballykinvarga has inspired the notion that these forts are Iron Age too.

Ballykinvarga is a visually impressive circular stone fort about 50 metres in diameter. T.J. Westropp published a short account accompanied by a characteristically diminutive sketch-plan in 1897 (Illus. 4.26):

"This very fine fort, possibly the 'Cathair Fhionnabhrach' reserved to the King of Cashel in the 'Book of Rights', appears in O'Brien's Rental, about 1380, as 'baile cin margad'...It is first described by Eugene O'Curry, 1839, as "a very large caher...around which were formerly a great number of stones forming a circle about

4.27. *Ballykinvarga.*

it". S.F. (Ferguson) notices it thus:- "Close to Kilfenora is one of those stone...cyclopean fortresses...Caherflaherty. Its dimensions are not comparable to those of the great Aran citadel, but the arrangement of the ramparts and the distribution of the stone caltrops in the space between the body of the fortress and the outer circumvallation are the same". Lord Dunraven 's description is equally misleading, as he omits any account of its chevaux de frise, monoliths, and hut sites, and says its wall is double and its passage curved, which is not the case; he only calls it "one (fort) near Kilfenora". Mr. T. Foote also alludes to it in a letter to Du Noyer, 1862, "a fort that has pointed stones planted upright all around it".

When perfect it must have been a beautiful specimen; now the vandal country lads, rabbit-hunting and tearing blocks out of its wall, must soon bring it to complete ruin. It is well built of large blocks, 3 feet to 5 feet long, and where most perfect to the east, is 15 feet high. The wall consists of three sections; the central 4 feet thick, the others 5 feet; it probably had another terrace, 4 feet 6 inches thick, as it is 19 feet 6 inches thick in other parts. The gate faces S.S.E., its lintel, 7 feet 9 inches x 1 foot 4 inches x 3 feet, resting on side walls and corner posts; its outer face was blocked; and, as I saw it, the space was occupied by a colony of hedgehogs. A walled and sunken passage led eastward through the chevaux de frise, probably to compel assailants to advance with their shield arm away from the wall. The inner enclosures extend in a fairly regular band around the western edge, where the wall is 7 feet high. The chevaux de frise is in two sections; the inner, about 46 feet wide, thickly set with pillars about 3 feet high, with smaller spikes between, and still nearly impassable, save to the south. A second band extends for 50 feet more, but is less thickly set with stones; it has a border mound set with large blocks, one nearly 7 feet x 2 feet 7 inches x 1 foot. A large hoard of silver coins "of Edward II" were found at the foot of a pillar and, much more precious to the occupants, a streamlet wells out on the southern side. Several groups of blocks remain in the adjoining field...".

A substantial structure of this scale with the additional and unusual distinction of a chevaux de frise was presumably the property of an elite member of Burren society, whose wealth and rank was reflected not only in monumental stone work but also in the possession of fine metalwork, cattle and slaves. Whether tentatively assigned to the prehistoric Iron Age or to the early historic period, the proliferation of stone forts and other enclosures is remarkable. Robinson (1977) has recorded about 450. Some, particularly the larger and more complex sites, are a likely indication of a preoccupation with the visible expression of power and status, and possibly reflect a more aggressive society.

Small or large, they are a prominent monument type and it is interesting to note how contemporary burial evidence is scarce in the extreme. Indeed, the Burren offers a striking example of one of the most intriguing contrasts between the archaeological record of early prehistory and that of the later prehistoric and early historic periods. The earlier phase is remarkable for conspicuous burial monuments and a dearth of settlement evidence; the reverse situation obtains in the later period. Perhaps we are seeing social differences, for instance, being expressed in markedly different ways, but other interpretations are possible too. The explanation for this shift of emphasis is just one of the many challenges of the archaeology of the Burren.

Acknowledgement for illustrations

Illus. 4.1	Photo, Anne Korff
Illus. 4.2	Drawing, Anne Korff
Illus. 4.4	Drawing, Anne Korff
Illus. 4.5	Drawing, Anne Korff
Illus. 4.6	Photo, Ann Lynch and Con Brogan, Off. of Public Works
Illus. 4.7	Photo, Anne Korff
Illus. 4.8	Drawing, from De Valera and ONualláin
Illus. 4.9	After O.S. map and De Valera and ONualláin
Illus. 4.10	Drawing, Anne Korff
Illus. 4.11	Drawing, Anne Korff
Illus. 4.12	Photo, Anne Korff
Illus. 4.13	Drawing, after Hencken
Illus. 4.14	Photo, U.C.G., Dept. of Archaeology
Illus. 4.15	Drawing, Anne Korff
Illus. 4.16	Photo, National Museum of Ireland
Illus. 4.17	Drawing, after Burgess and Gerloff
Illus. 4.18	Drawing, Anne Korff
Illus. 4.21	Photo, National Museum of Ireland
Illus. 4.22	Photo, Paul Gosling
Illus. 4.23	Photo, U.C.G., Dept. of Archaeology
Illus. 4.24	Drawing, Anne Korff
Illus. 4.25	Photo, National Museum of Ireland
Illus. 4.26	Drawing, T.J. Westropp
Illus. 4.28	Photo, U.C.G., Dept. of Archaeology

4.28. Hut circles of unknown date on Turlough Hill.

5.1 Cathair Dhúin Irghuis , on Black Head (alternatively Ceann Bóirne) overlooking Galway Bay, is one of those timeless cashels which could be of prehistoric or even medieval date. Note the vertical joint in the drystone walling to the left of centre: such structural joints may have resulted from the use of different construction gangs, each working on a different section of the cashel wall.

The Burren in Early Historic Times

Paul Gosling

The Beginnings of History

Doluid dono aniar a mathair .i. Luachair Bairennach a hainm a Boirind Corcumruad di

Then from the west came their mother, Luachair-Boirennach was her name, and from Boirenn in Corcomruad was she

These words, from the story of Liamun in the Dindshenchas (Stokes 1894, 3212), are one of the earliest written expressions of the place we know as The Burren. And it is fitting that they should occur in this famous 11-12th century collection of stories, prose and verse about the names of noteworthy places in Ireland. For it is such a sense of place that gives this Burren, like many another corner of this island, part of its uniqueness and fascination. It is there, named and, by inference, defined, at the dawn of Ireland's history some 1000 or more years ago. Defining place is a political act and in manuscripts like the Dindshenchas we can sense its flux - Boirenn in Corcumruad. Today, these ancient names give themselves to two contiguous baronies in north Clare . Though technically a simple administrative sub-division of our counties, solidified in the the 16th and 17th centuries, many baronies are based on much older territorial and tribal boundaries. This phrase, Boirenn in Corcum-ruad, suggests an unequal relationship, a relationship of possessor and possessed; the stony place belonging to the people of Mruad. Here too is a pointer for our understanding of its past, for the Burren is named not from its inhabitants but from it geology. However, the fact that has come down to us with the separate status of a barony, suggests that it may once have been a distinct socio-political entity. But though geologically distinct, its social and political role in the historical era appears to have been peripheral: always a part of some greater entity, frequently a borderland, and consequently, a place condemned to the fringes of historical narrative.

In the 5th-6th centuries, at the time when the early clerics were just beginning to set down the first written words of Irish, the Burren appears to have been under the political sway of the Eóganacht Árann, an obscure branch of the powerful Eóganacht dynasty of Munster, based in the Aran Islands (Byrne 1973, 178). That such a close political relationship should have existed between two so closely related geological areas seems teasingly symbiotic. Whatever its origin, character or previous duration, this geo-political umbilical cord appears to have been severed soon after, probably as part of the general decline of the Eóganacht from the 7th century onwards .

Exactly what this would have meant for the Corcomruad, the earliest named people of the Burren, is unclear. The Corcomruad were just one of the dozens of minor tribes of Early Historic Ireland: small tribal groups, occupying a usually discrete area or tuath , and comprising a number of extended families with a common bloodline and/or origin legends. Governed by a king, or rí tuaíthe , they existed as semi-independent petty kingdoms, free in theory to enter into, and dissolve, alliances and dependencies with other kingdoms (Mac Niocall 1972). The Corcomruad themselves, for

instance, appear to have been overlords of the Crecraige (Byrne 1973, 67), a tribe perhaps based in the Burren itself. They were, in turn, a subject tribe, recognizing the overlordship of the kings of more powerful neighbouring tribes.

After the demise of the Eóganachta Árann, the Corcomruad may have come under the sway of the Uí Fiachrach Aidhne, a tribe in south Galway which enjoyed a brief hegemony over Connacht and north Munster in the 7th century (ibid., 243). Thereafter, they became a subject tribe of the great Eóganachta over-kingdom of Loch Léin, until its decline in the early 9th century. By that time, however, the Corcomruad may already have ceased to exist as an independent kingdom, as annalistic entries for the early 8th century indicate that it and the adjoining tribal group to the south, the Corcu Baiscind,were coming under pressure from kingdoms south of the Shannon estuary. In the year A.D. 705, for instance, we read of the death of one of the leading figures of the Uí Figente in battle against the the Corcomruad, and in 744, the annals record the annihilation of the Corcomruad, in battle, by the Déis Tuaiscirt of east Clare (O Corráin 1972, 7, 30). It was this tribe, later to become widely known as the Dál Cais of Thomond or Tuadmuma , who spectacularly filled the power vacuum left in the wake of the collapse of Loch Léin. By the 9th century, the Corcomruad were being driven into the Burren itself, and by A.D. 930, a branch of the Dál Cais , the Uí Thairdelbaig, had established itself temporarily over them (ibid., 114). It was probably during the long overlordship of the Dál Cais, that the Corcomruad finally surrendered the last vestiges of political independence, as they, along with many other petty kingdoms, were subsumed into the larger political units which characterized the emergence of the powerful

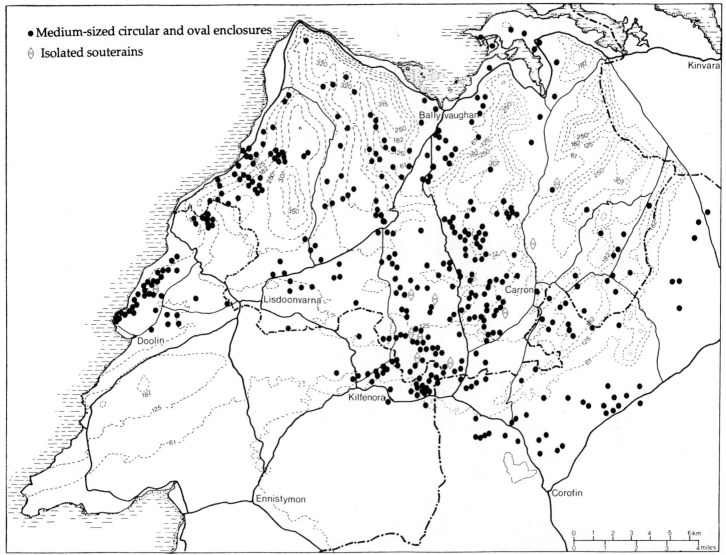

Legend:
● Medium-sized circular and oval enclosures
◊ Isolated souterains

Map labels: Kinvara, Ballyvaughan, Lisdoonvarna, Doolin, Carron, Kilfenora, Ennistymon, Corofin

Scale: 0 1 2 3 4 5 6 km / 0 1 2 3 4 miles

5.2   Early Historic Settlement in
The Burren: distribution map of
isolated souterains and medium-
sized circular and oval enclosures
(20-60 m in diameter), in the
Burren (after Robinson 1977).
Most of the latter are probably
ringforts, but in the absence, to
date, of a comprehensive
archaeological survey of the area,
one cannot be certain.

5.3 Near vertical view of Tullagh Fort, a fine single-banked, earthen ringfort (rath) at Commonage , c.2 km east south-east of Kilfenora.

5.4 Cathair Chonaill , c.1.5 km south of Poulnabrone, is one of the best preserved examples of a stone-built ringfort (cashel) in the Burren. The circular enclosure visible on right may have been a second cashel, or alternatively a related enclosure for penning cattle.

lordships of the 10th-12th centuries.

Hearths and Homesteads

Next to its round towers and high crosses, the ringfort is surely the most characteristically Irish of our ancient monuments. And within Ireland, it is in the Burren that one will find the most diverse, dense, and best preserved series of these enclosed settlements. However, eighty years after T. J. Westropp's pioneering work on the 'forts' of the Burren, estimates of their numbers are still vague. Westropp himself calculated the total for the barony at 306 (1902, 417), Tim Robinson marked 450 on his map (1977), but both these figures appear to be totals of the surviving remains only: even in

5.5 Aerial view of Cathair Mhór, near Aillwee, one of the ringforts in the Burren occupied until late medieval times. The outer wall of this large bivallate cashel has been partly cut through by the modern road from Leamaneh to Ballyvaughan (visible at bottom). The whole monument is now much obscured by recently regenerated hazel scrub (compare with Illus. 7.2), illustrating the fact that some of the present woodland in the Burren is of relatively modern origin.

the Burren, the improving hand has taken its toll of these vulnerable monuments.
Though often variously labelled as lios, rath, dún, cathair, caisel or "fairy fort", these family homesteads are now described generically as ringforts, irrespective of the materials used in their construction. Their principal characteristics are; their size and shape, 20m to 60m in maximum internal dimensions and usually circular or oval on plan; their enclosing elements consist of one or more substantial stone walls or earthen banks (the latter frequently accompanied by fosses, with the presence of one entrance, usually on the eastern side. Finally, their siting is also consistent, being characteristically on the summits or slopes of local hills,

hillocks, or in the case of the Burren, limestone bluffs and terraces. That said, however, it can still be difficult to distinguish, without scientific excavation, individual ringforts from certain types of ritual, funerary and other settlement enclosures of prehistoric vintage. The laying out of annular areas, for whatever purpose, is one of the simplest and oldest ways of defining space. From the archaeological excavations conducted in the Burren and elsewhere, it appears that the majority of these enclosures were built and occupied within what we know as the Early Historic Period (A.D. 400-1200) in Ireland. Thus, a simple plot of all the medium-sized annular enclosures in the Burren, as in Illus. 5.2, can be misleading, as many of the monuments included in it may be of divergent age and purpose, extending well before, and after, this 800 year time span.

That said, the Burren contains some of the most spectacular and perfectly preserved examples of the stone-built ringfort, otherwise known as cashels. The majority of these are relatively simple affairs, such as Cathair Scríbín, near Leamaneh Castle, Cathair Chonaill, near Poulnabrone, or the string of cashels ranged along the lower terraces of the Gleninagh valley, to the south-east of Ballyvaughan. In these instances, a single stout wall, faced internally and externally, defined the living area, now generally featureless and sometimes overgrown. Though they may at first appear to be more exotic, 'cliff-forts' such as Lios Mac Síoda , also in Gleninagh, are probably the result of innovative responses to the natural attributes of the chosen location.

Such cashels were probably the dwelling places of the *soer* or freeman grades described in the early Irish law tracts. Early Irish society was extremely inegalitarian, and status was of extreme importance for a person's capacity to own property and perform legal acts. The two main categories of freemen appear to have been the *ocaíre* and *boaíre* classes, roughly equated by modern historians with the 'small farmer' and 'strong farmer' of 20th century Ireland. In the surviving law tracts such as the Críth Gabhlach, painstakingly detailed accounts are given of the property entitlements of these classes, defining in the case of the *ocaíre*, for instance, the size of his house, value of his land, his stock, as well as his entitlement to share in a plough team, kiln, mill and a barn (Kelly 1988). While much of this information cannot be taken too literally, it does give us something against which to assess the social and economic role of the hundreds of simple ruined ringforts which grace the valleys and

plateaus of the Burren. Above and below the *soer* were the *nemed*, or privileged grades and the *doer*, or unfree. Whether through our misconceptions or not, it is with the more complex ringforts that we are tempted to equate as the dwelling places of these latter grades, the aristocracy and their servants and slaves. Cathair Chomáin, south of Carron, Cathair Mhór near Ailwee or Dún Torpa, at Gleninagh, are just three of a total of dozens of ringforts in the Burren with traces of more than one enclosing wall and/or bank (multivallate). Why exactly some ringforts should have additional walls or banks is far from clear, but it generally accepted that it was not related to defensive considerations. One passage in the Críth Gabhlach on the role of the *rí tuaíthe*, or tribal kings, is illuminating, as it uses the phrase 'rampart of vassalage' in describing additional ramparts around the dwelling of the king (Binchy 1941, 22). From this it may be suggested that some of the ramparts of multivallate ringforts may have resulted from a form of labour tribute, undertaken perhaps, as a tangible display of the loyalty and resources of the tribe, which in the process enhanced the stature of the king and the status of this residence (see Illus. 5.1).

Within the ringfort would have stood the various buildings of the household - the kitchen, main house and, perhaps, a subsidiary house - as well as structures, and defined areas, related to the livelihood of the family; a grain store, corn-grinding area, kilns and hen house. Other buildings may have been situated outside the fort, or perhaps in an adjoining enclosure. To date, Cathair Chomáin is the only ringfort in the Burren to have been scientifically excavated. However, this excavation, undertaken as part of the Third Harvard Archaeological Expedition in Ireland, in 1934, produced a wealth of information and artifacts

which help to illuminate the material culture and economy of one community which lived in the Burren sometime in the 8th -10th centuries A.D. (O'Neill Hencken 1938).

Spectacularly situated on the edge of a 30m high cliff overlooking a wooded ravine, Cathair Chomáin must have been an impressive place during its hey-day. Even in its present ruinous state, the innermost of its three stone ramparts is a formidable affair, up to 8.5m in thickness and still 4.3m in height at one point. The two outer semi-circular walls, though less impressive, were no doubt adequate for their probable dual role as indicators of the status of the site, as well as delimiting useful areas for livestock, outhouses and stores. The Harvard team, under the direction of O'Neill Hencken, concentrated their efforts within the area, circa 30m in diameter, enclosed by the inner rampart. Here, amidst the debris from two phases of occupation they uncovered the remains of 13 separate structures. These included six houses with hearths, two souterrains, and 16 other hearths, all now largely obscured by a protective layer of stones and sod. Half of the hearths were concentrated in and around a series of low walls in the southern part of the enclosure, apparently a working area and kitchen. This was underlined by the finds from this area which included the majority of the quern-stones found (Illus. 5.16), nearly half of the bone points, as well as spindle whorls (Illus. 5.15), pounding

and grinding stones, and worked fragments of bone and antler. The two principal dwellings of the ringfort were circular houses, c.6-7m in diameter, each with a central hearth. Apart from the notable concentrations here of personal ornaments (bracelets of lignite and bone combs), the entrance to one of the souterrains was located in the back wall of one of these houses. Such stone-built, subterranean refuges are common occurrences in the ringforts of the Burren (Illus. 5.7). In this instance, the souterrain consisted of a low, narrow passage which ran northwards from the house to an opening in the ringfort wall along the cliff-edge. At this

5.6 The entrance to Cathair an Ard Dorais - the fort of the high door - a fine, but ruinous cashel near Gleninsheen. Many ringforts had impressive lintelled doorways, secured by stout wooden doors, and possibly surmounted by a wall-walk. In earthen ringforts (raths) these were built of wood, and consequently do not survive.

5.7 The interior of a souterrain at Gortclare, near Turlough, showing the classic drystone-walled construction, corbelled inwards towards the top. The small doorway in the end-wall gives access to another chamber via a low creep-passage 2.4 m long, but only 0.75 m high and 0.65 m wide. Such deliberate obstructions are a feature of souterrains, and made them ideal temporary refuges for people and valuables.

5.8   Aerial view of Cathair Chomáin , the well-known trivallate cashel perched on the edge of a ravine, c.2km south of Carron. It is the only ringfort in the Burren yet to have been scientifically excavated, and is now a National Monument.

5.9   Reconstruction drawing of Cathair Chomáin , as it probably looked in the 9th century A.D. The structural details and activities shown are based on the results of the archaeological excavations carried out in 1934: A, Principal houses; B, working area and kitchen; C, a work gang is building the buttress against the outer face of the inner cashel wall to contain a bulge in the latter, while; D, other gangs are at work completing the outer enclosing wall; E, sheep-shearing in progress; F, a hunting party returns with a red deer.

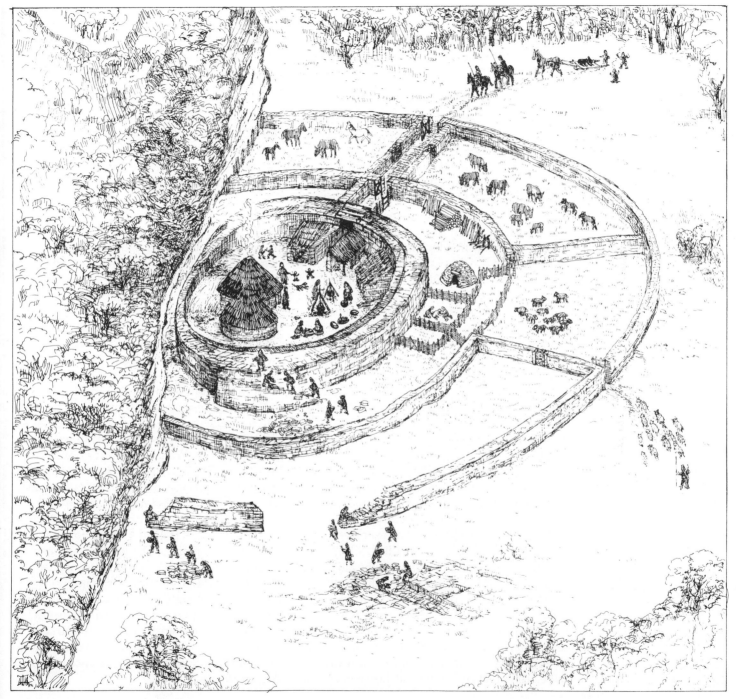

point, there is a narrow vertical crevice down the face of the precipice, which with the aid of a rope would have provided a quick and secret means of exit from the site.

Families and Farms

Ringforts like Cathair Chomáin were probably occupied by an extended family group: the Harvard team estimated its population as 'at most 40 or 50 inhabitants' (O'Neill Hencken 1938, 2). D. A. Binchy, the Celtic scholar, once laconically descried Irish society at circa 800 A.D. as 'tribal, rural, hierarchical and familiar', using the latter word in its older sense to indicate a society in which the family, rather than the individual, was the primary social unit. Though other family groups are also described in the early law tracts, the kin-group most commonly referred to is the *derbhfine*, or true group, whose members were all descendants, through the male line, of the same great-grandfather. Apart from possessing its own land, each kin-group also bore responsibility for the actions of, and injuries to, its members, as well as choosing its own family-head whose role it was to speak for the kin on public occasions (Kelly 1988).

The economy of these family groups was based largely on argriculture, and most ringforts were probably the centres of one hundred plus hectare farms. Often well-preserved, but undated, traces of old field walls survive around many of the ringforts (Illus. 5.13 and 14). In recent years, research with the aid of aerial photography has also identified extensive series of large, regularly laid out, co-axial field systems on the Burren plateaus which some archaeologists now suspect may be contemporary with a number of the ringforts (Fleming 1987). Though tillage must always have been practiced on the patches of deep soil

in the Burren, - witness the numbers of querns found at Cathair Chomáin - , the principal attraction of these uplands for farmers in the Early Historic period must have been the existence, by then, of large tracts of grassland. Thus, the oft quoted words of General Ludlow in the early 1650s, are memorable not only for the use of literary device to describe this landscape, but also for their perceptive insight into the essence of the Burren's appeal for farming communities stretching back into prehistoric-times:

'Of this barony it is said that it is a country where there is not water enough to drown a man, wood enough to hang one, nor earth enough to bury them. This last is so scarce that the inhabitants steal it from one another and yet their cattle are very fat. The grass grows in tufts of earth of two or three foot square which lies between the limestone rocks and is very sweet and nourishing'(O Cillín 1977).

The origin of open grassland in the Burren is problematic and the limited published research into the pollen record as preserved in the lake-sediments of the region does little to settle the question. W. A. Watt's work on two small lakes, Loch Gealáin and Rinn na Móna, on the south eastern fringes of the Burren (1984), does however, identify a big increase in the clearance of woodland after circa A.D. 300, which is a noted feature of Ireland's vegetational history at this period. Though this has been generally linked to the introduction of new farming practices, in particular to improvements to the plough, the latter can hardly have had a major impact in the Burren. Rather, it was probably a desire to expand the already existing areas of upland grazing that acted as the main stimulus for forest clearance in the Burren after A.D. 300.

On the evidence of early Irish law tracts, annals and folk-tales, and archaeological excavation, cattle, particularly dairy cattle, are generally accepted to have been by far the most important type of livestock in economy of Early Historic Ireland (O Corráin 1972). Likewise in the Burren, cattle have traditionally been the main livestock, and a number of writers have commented on the continuing local practice of grazing them in the valleys during the summer, before driving them up on to the commonages on the plateaus each October to take advantage of the good natural winter pasture (Gibson 1988, 58). This practice, which is a complete reversal of the usual pattern of booleying (transhumance), is likely to be of some antiquity. Out of a total of 4,187.25 kg of animal bones recovered during the excavations at Cathair Chomáin, for instance, those of cattle accounted for about 97% of the total, sheep and goat 1%, pig 1%, while the remaining 1% was made up of horse and red deer. When translated into food equivalents, the predominance of cattle becomes even greater. However, such calculations give only estimates of meat values, and do not necessarily reflect the importance of each type of livestock in the local economy.

One of the most numerous finds at Cathair Chomáin was the spindle-whorl, an essential part of the humble spindle on which the wool is drawn out into a thread before being spun on the wheel (Illus. 5.15). Though it was assigned no particular significance in the 1938 report on the excavations, recent research by Brian Hodkinson (1987) suggests that the importance of wool production at this site needs to be re-evaluated. His review of the archaeological evidence for weaving in Early Historic Ireland, reveals that the collection of 55 stone and bone spindle-whorls, and 20 possible pin beaters, from Cathair Chomáin, represents by

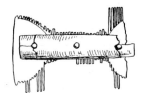

5.10 Fragments of bone combs from Cathair Chomáin. Scale: 1/3 actual size.

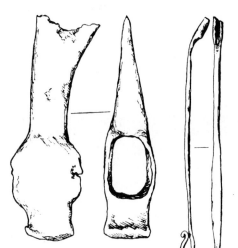

5.11 Iron axe-head and wood-working tool from Cathair Chomáin. Though the axe could have been used as a weapon, there is a notable absence of specialized weapons from this and other ringforts, emphasising their domestic character. Scale: 1/3 actual size.

5.12 Bill-hook from Cathair Chomáin. Scale: 1/3 actual size

far the largest group of artifacts connected with weaving in Ireland during this period. In this light, the traditional view of the ringfort dwellers of the Burren as cattle ranchers may need to be revised. While the whorls indicate the processing of wool, the pin-beaters, used for beating down the weft during weaving, suggests the presence of looms and the production of woven cloth. From the numbers of both objects found, it would appear that Cathair Chomáin can be interpreted as an important wool-processing station where shearing, wool production, and weaving was undertaken on a relatively large scale. Whether there were other such stations in the area, and of more regional significance, whether the importance of sheep in the econ-

5.13 A circular cashel and associated field system on upland terraces at Tullycommon, c. 1.2 km south-east of Carron. The rectangular walls of Cnocán Fort are also visible at extremem right.

omy of the Burren contributed to the increased pace of woodland clearance after A.D. 300, are teasing questions which demand further consideration.

The existence of a wool production centre in the Burren, alongside the obvious importance of cattle farming, raises the question of the distribution of surpluses in such a rural and tribal society. In the absence of towns and formal markets, the *óenach*, or assembly, is thought to have been the venue not only for the settling of legal matters and for games, but also for the exchange and barter of commodities (Kelly 1988, 4). Though we have no contemporary references to the existence of any *óenach* sites in the area, the site of the former racecourse and fair at Turloughmore, near Glencolmcille, is likely to be of some antiquity. Situated on the fringes of the Burren, beside ancient routeways into these uplands from the east, this is a likely location for an *óenach*. In this context, it is also easy to forget that the Burren is delimited on the west and north by

5.14 Cashel in cleared land at the head of the Gleninagh Valley, close to the present limits of cultivation. Traces of at least three periods of fields are visible:
1. meandering field walls possibly associated with the cashel itself;
2. ridge and furrow cultivation within and immediately outside the cashel, possibly of pre-famine date; 3. the regular pattern of strip fields at present in use.

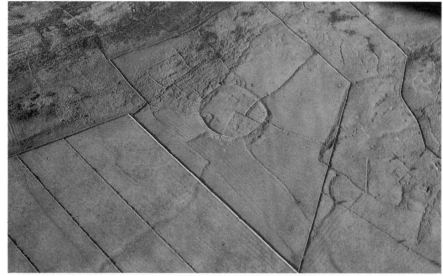

the sea, whose shores and routeways offer other routes into the region. The safe haven of Ballyvaughan Bay, in the north and the sandy shoreline at Fanore on the west, may also have been of particular importance in the economic life of the area. Mussel, scallop cockle and oyster shells were all found at Cathair Chomáin, for instance, which is 5 miles from the coast at its nearest point. The presence of the sub-rectangular house excavated by Etienne Rynne at Fanore (1968), when coupled with the occasional stray finds from the sand dunes in the area, hints that Fanore may have been of importance as a seasonal camp for harvesting the two great resources of the sea; food and salt.

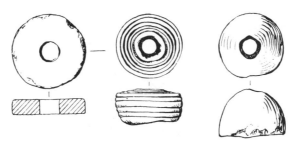

5.15 Three of the spindle whorls from Cathair Chomáin. Each whorl was mounted on a short thin tapering pin, or spindle, used in hand spinning for twisting and winding the thread out of the raw wool.

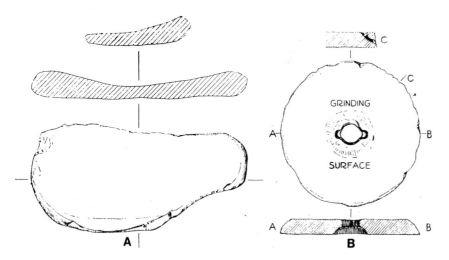

5.16 *A saddle quern (A) and a rotary, or disc, quern (B) from Cathair Chomáin. The archaeological excavations produced six saddle querns and a total of two whole, and fragments of 33, rotary querns. Used for grinding corn, their presence shows that tillage farming, for the production of grain, was undertaken. The presence of both types of quern at the site is puzzling, as the saddle quern is generally regarded as being of prehistoric date, replaced in the Early Iron Age (c.500 B.C. - A.D. 400) by the more advanced rotary quern. This has led some archaeologists to suggest that Cathair Chomáin is much older than its accepted dating of 8th-10th century A.D. (Rynne 1982, 6).*

Acknowledgements for illustrations

Illus. 5.1   Photo, A. Korff
Illus. 5.3   Photo, Dept. of Archaeology, U.C.G.
Illus. 5.4   Photo, Dept. of Archaeology, U.C.G.
Illus. 5.5   Photo, Dept. of Archaeology, U.C.G.
Illus. 5.6   Drawing, A. Korff
Illus. 5.7   Photo, P. Gosling
Illus. 5.8   Photo, Cambridge University Collection of Aerial Photographs
Illus. 5.9   Drawing, A. Korff
Illus. 5.10 After Hencken 1938, Fig. 26
Illus. 5.11 After Hencken 1938, Fig. 31
Illus. 5.12 Photo, National Museum of Ireland
Illus. 5.13 Photo, Dept. of Archaeology, U.C.G.
Illus. 5.14 Photo, Dept. of Archaeology, U.C.G.
Illus. 5.15 Drawings, after Hencken 1938, Fig. 27
Illus. 5.16 Drawings, after Hencken 1938, Fig. 36
Illus. 5.17 Photo, National Museum of Ireland

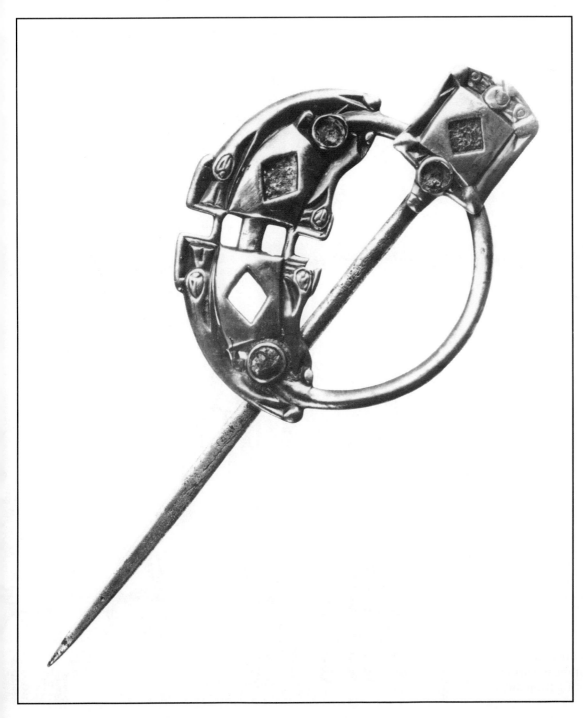

5.17 *The fine silver, pseudo-penannular brooch from Cathair Chomáin. It was found on the floor of one of the souterrains in the ringfort, where it may well have fallen from its wearer's cloak. The ring is only 60 mm in diameter, and the pin, which is of bronze with a square silver head, is 140 mm in length. Note the elongated animal decoration on the latter and on the terminals. It belongs to the same category of brooches as the Tara Brooch, in which the original functional role of the penannular ring and pin, as fasteners, was abandoned in favour of rich ornamentation. Such brooches were obviously prestige objects, the possession of which probably reflected the status of the wearer.*

T. J. WESTROPP

The Father of Burren Archaeology

The great philosopher Alfred North Whitehead once wrote that the history of philosophy could be seen as a series of footnotes to Plato and Aristotle. In a similar way, a convincing case could be made that virtually all modern archaeological research and field work in the Burren consists of a series of footnotes to the work of Thomas Johnson Westropp.

T.J. Westropp was born in 1860, the son of John Westropp of Attyflyn, Co. Limerick, and his second wife, Charlotte Lousia Whitehead. Educated at Trinity College, Dublin, he took his Master of Arts Degree in 1885. His work as an engineer and surveyor took him to many parts of the country and his early interest in the antiquities of Ireland led him to devote time, energy and considerable scholarship to researching and recording, in meticulous detail, all aspects of the abundant archaeological remains found throughout the country.

In 1886, Westropp became a member of the Royal Society of Antiquaries, and a Fellow in 1893. Eventually, in 1916, as a result of his many activities, he was elected President of the Society. By the time of his death in 1922, he had almost single-handedly laid the foundations that transformed antiquarian research into the archaeology of the Burren into a science.

During his life Westropp contributed literally hundreds of articles and papers to various journals, examining everything from mega-

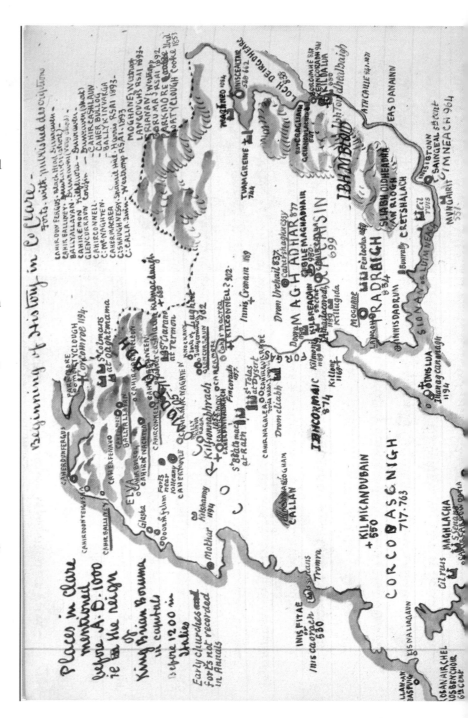

Manuscript by T.J. Westropp, from "Notes on Clare", 1890, 3A40, page 210. By kind permission of The Royal Irish Academy.

lithic tombs and ring forts to castles and medieval churches. Unencumbered by considerations of academic censure or criticism, he brought a fresh and enquiring eye to all he encountered.

Alone or in the company of similarly-minded enthusiasts like his good friend George Macnamara, he tramped the hills and valleys and open plateaux of the Burren, notebook and pen in hand, exploring, measuring and recording a wealth of detailed information that has proved indispensible for subsequent archaeologists.

His interests were all-embracing. For example, he did pioneer work in Clare folklore, winning the confidence of local people who shared with him their fast-vanishing traditions. He combined a scholarly and a speculative mind, tempered by a healthy scepticism, that made such papers as his fascinating examination of "Brasil and the Legendary Islands of the North Atlantic: Their History and Fable. A Contribution to the 'Atlantis Problem'", all the more valuable. Even his sense of humour adds a special dimension to his otherwise carefully documented articles and papers.

A trained artist, his notebooks, now in the library of The Royal Society of Antiquaries, contain hundreds of beautifully executed drawings and watercolours which are important not only as providing striking visual records of the many sites he visited, but as impressive artistic creations in their own right. With George Macnamara, another skilled photographer, he documented for posterity many hundreds of scenes that help the contemporary archaeologist understand more clearly the way both sites and the landscape itself has changed since his day.

Considering T.J. Westropp's enormous contribution to Irish archaeology, it is surprising that the precise nature of his work and life is not better known. The late Hubert Butler, in his challenging "Lament for Archaeology", describes the contribution made by men like Westropp, who lived at a time when the antithesis of professional and amateur had not yet been invented. Adopting the term "lay pretender" to describe such people, Butler argues that archaeology "owes an incalculable debt" to the open-minded, enthusiasm of those pioneers, like Westropp, who did the groundwork for subsequent generations of researchers and field-workers. In the Obituary Notice published in the Journal of The Royal Society of Antiquaries in 1923, the writer concluded that Westropp's "memory will live as an inspiration to those who knew him; and his name will remain written high on the Roll of Honour of Ireland, long after many men, who make a much greater noise in these times of ours, have dropped into the oblivion that awaits them".

T.J. Westropp at entrance of unidentified cave or souterrain, photographed by George U. MacNamara. Courtesy of Clare County Library

The Churches, Monasteries and Burial Grounds of the Burren

D.L. Swan

In the words of Daniel Binchy, Early Irish society was 'tribal, rural, hierarchical and familiar', and slowness to change, as well as a strong and conservative adherence to tradition is a fundamental characteristic of such societies. Nowhere is this more obvious than in the tenacity with which Irish society through many vicissitudes, through misfortunes and catastrophies, and for more than a millenium, has held fast to its traditional churches and burial place. In these circumstances, the church as a key focus of worship and communal ritual, provides a fixed point in a shifting landscape, against which settlement, growth, development and change may be measured.

The middle centuries of the first millenium of the Christian era were to see two profoundly significant changes in Irish society. Firstly came the change from a Celtic to a Gaelic society, while the following centuries witnessed the transformation of this society from paganism to Christianity. This latter development was to have momentous consequences, not alone for Ireland, but for the whole of western culture and learning, as well as for Christianity itself. Ireland, as is well known, was the first European country lying outside the Roman Empire to have been Christianised. Because it had never been conquered by Rome, it lacked the administrative structures based on the provincial capitals and the secular, bureaucratic framework, which underpinned the diocesan organisation of the western church.

In the absence of provincial capitals, or indeed, towns of any kind, as well as any semblance of centralised administration, the Irish church evolved its own structures and organisation, loosely modelled on the pattern which characterised secular society. Thus, for example, the church sites were laid out within a circular enclosure, mirroring the earthen or stone ringforts of the nobility and the landholders. Ecclesiastical ranks were graded in the same manner as that which applied to lay society, and gradually the body of laws was adapted to take account of the new developments.

Yet, all authorities agree with the tradition that these major changes took place in a relatively painless manner, and that continuity rather than a sudden and dramatic breaking with the past, marked out this period. An example of this can be seen in the survival of the tradition and ritual attached to the Holy Wells. Many, if not most of these must have been focal points for communal ritual in pagan Ireland, as in all probability was the case throughout much of pre-Christian Europe. Nonetheless, the level of survival here was remarkable. One scholarly study estimates the total number of these wells to be in excess of three thousand throughout the country as a whole. The firmly established association of the vast majority of these with early saints and with their churches and monasteries, shows how readily they were accommodated, and how easily absorbed into the Christian tradition. The same point can be made with regard to the many pillar stones, which dot the countryside. Numbers of these are found in association with early church sites, not infrequently, within the churchyards of the Christian era. Occasionally, a cross or other symbol of Christianity is found on these, signifying its adaptation to the new order as well as continuity from the older.

One striking result of recent research into Early Christian Ireland is the realisation of the huge numbers of sites involved. For example, the total numbers of churches and ecclesiastical establishments recorded in Doomsday Book for England in the late 11th Century is approximately 2000. From other sources a further 500 or so might be added to give an overall total of 2500. For the County Clare alone, there are about 170 potential early sites while for the country as a whole the average per county is approximately 120, giving a probable total not far short of 4000. Such figures reflect a density of population, an intensity of ecclesiastical settlement and level of wealth and resources at the disposal of the early medieval church in

Ireland, hitherto unsuspected and unrecognised. It does however help to explain the awesome achievements of the Early Christian society of early medieval Ireland, in magnificent metal-working, in illuminated manuscripts, and in stone-carving, as well as in its missionary activities continuing over several centuries, extending from northern Scotland to the Black Sea, and from the North Sea to southern Italy.

The Typical Ecclesiastical Site

It is not easy for us to picture what these early ecclesiastical sites might have looked like over twelve centuries ago, and it is frequently a disappointing experience for the interested traveller to arrive, not without difficulty, at one of these early churches. Here there may be an undistinguished and fragmentary ruin, with few if any architectural details surviving, within a crowded, overgrown and unattended churchyard. Features of interest, if there are such, will not easily be located, and detailed information is hard to come by. Nevertheless, there are certain characteristics and features which are common to all early ecclesiastical sites, by means of which they may be identified and recognised. These also help in the necessary task of dating such sites and in establishing even an outline chronology for the structures within.

As was already stated above, one of the most important and consistent features is the ecclesiastical enclosure itself, which in almost all cases, surrounded the site, providing both a practical defense and a ritual boundary. Within this boundary, only ecclesiastical law applied, thus affording a measure of sanctuary

6.2 Templeline Church, Site, No. 30

6.3   *Kilvoydan Church and Burial Ground, Site No. 66.*

The complete outline of this huge enclosure is visible surrounding both the churchyard in the background and the complex of farmhouse and farm-buildings with which it shares its interior.

6.4   *Kilkeedy Church and Burial Ground, Site No. 56*

(Also known as Cross Abbey) the full extent of this enclosure , partly incorporated into the more modern field walls, can be seen in the aerial photograph.

to fugitives from the civil powers. The enclosure consisted either of an earthen or of a stone and earthen bank with outer ditch, or of a substantial dry-stone wall with inner and outer coursed facings and a rubble core. Although reflecting in their general form the secular ring-forts and cashels of earth or stone, there were important differences. Most obvious was the relatively large size of the ecclesiastical site which could vary from less than 40m to over 500m in diameter, the average being between 70 and 120m. By way of contrast, the average diameter of the ring-forts throughout the country is reckoned to be 30m.

Strangely, these extensive, ubiquitous and sometimes hugely impressive field monuments have until recent times remained largely unrecognised, and detailed examinations of ancient ecclesiastical remains have instead concentrated on the structures and features within, on the ruined fragments of the churches, the crosses or carved slabs, or the later medieval stonework. The study of these enclosures is now however recognised as being fundamental to our understanding of the early Christian period, and their identification and recovery is a vital component of archaeological field work and survey.

The enclosure was generally circular or oval in outline and in most if not all cases was topped with a stout palisade fence, as an effective deterrence against intrusion. Thus, entry was gained through the formal gateway, references to which abound in the early documents. In the case of a major foundation, this took the form of a defended gatehouse, with permanent gate-keeper who had responsibility for the security of the establishment. Where evidence survives, it indicates that the entrance was consistently to the east of the enclosure, a feature also commonly found in contemporary ring-forts. However, it appears likely that in the case of the ecclesiastical sites the entrance was marked by a cross, sometimes referred to as the Entrance Cross, a few of which have survived either outside or directly inside the enclosure. Originally these crosses would have been of timber, and only where a stone replacement was erected could survival be expected.

The entrance cross would have been but one of a number of crosses positioned around the enclosure, both inside and outside. There are frequent references to west crosses, positioned facing towards the door of the church. South crosses were known, some of which have survived in the more important sites, and in certain cases there were known to have been crosses placed to the north. Thus it is possible that crosses were positioned at each of the cardinal points, that to the east marking the entrance; the west cross being the first object to catch the eyes of the members of the congregation on emerging from the church; the south cross marking the burial area; and the north cross completing the circle of protection.

In addition to the crosses, there were other standard features and structures which would have been found on all such sites. A church, or churches would have occupied a central position within the enclosure. It is important to note however, that the earliest churches would have been of timber, even in areas where timber was a scarce commodity. The Venerable Bede, writing in the early 8th cen-

tury in his monastery in Northumbria refers to the construction of a wooden church by St. Aiden of Lindisfarne 'in the manner of the Irish', and he comments on the 'dowel holes and dowels which secured it ... in a most extraordinary way'. No doubt, he was impressed by the joinery skills of the Irish just as he was astonished at the use of timber for such a structure, a matter which would however have evinced little surprise in Ireland at this time. An early reference to a stone church is found in the Life of Patrick by Tireachan, dating to the late 7th century, and for the 8th century there are only two such references. Even in the 9th and 10th centuries, it is clear that only some very few important sites had stone churches, and it was not until the 11th century that these became common throughout the country. Thus it is unlikely that any traces of the earliest churches have survived, and that even the earliest churches which we find today are but replacements of replacements. Nonetheless, it can be presumed that the stone built churches occupy the sites of their timber predecessors, maintaining a direct link with the earliest development of the site.

Despite the fact that the standard house type in Early Christian Ireland had, for many centuries, perhaps even since the Late Bronze Age, been circular in plan, there can be no question but that the earliest churches were laid out as rectangular structures. They adhered rigidly to an east-west alignment, and invariably the altar was to the east and the single doorway to the west. The single window of these simple, early buildings was always positioned in the east wall, over the altar, to catch the rays of the rising sun. Our oldest stone churches conform

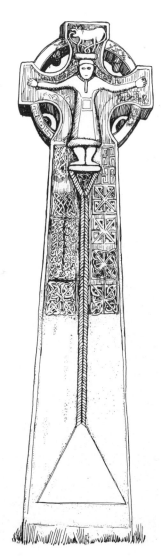

6.5   *West Cross, Kilfenora, west face, Site No. 50*

99

to this basic plan, and also provide simple structures with few elaborations or architectural embellishments. Yet, they follow an indigenous tradition, owing little if anything to influences from elsewhere. Among the features which can be recognised are some which can be claimed to have derived from their wooden ancestors, such as antae, where the side walls project beyond the lines of the end walls, providing support for the bargeboards which would have supported a shingled or thatched roof. Likewise, at the ends of the ridge-pole where the sloping bargeboards would have joined and crossed, stone finials are found, sometimes carrying simple decorative devices. The doorways were of simple trabeated form, which would have descended directly from their wooden prototypes, but which also echo those of the great stone forts of the Iron Age, with a single, massive lintel forming the door-head. This often forms a decorative feature, and occasionally, a carved

*6.6. Oughtmama west gable.
Site No. 15*

or inscribed cross will be found either on the outer face or soffit.

Most characteristic of all is the method of wall construction, which is sometimes described as cyclopean. Instead of coursed masonry, the walls are formed of huge, regular slabs of stone set on their edges, and forming outer and inner faces, with a mortared rubble core between. Even where the original walls have not survived intact, the re-use of these huge slabs makes the recognition of the technique, and thus of their early origin fairly simple.

The corners, and occasionally the jambs of the trabeate doors tend to be of quoined construction in side alternate fashion, a feature which adds considerably to the attractiveness of their outer appearance.

However, the most dominant aspect of their construction which marks the early stone churches of Ireland out from those found elsewhere in Europe in the early medieval period, is the ubiquitous use of battering. Generally, it will be noted that the door-jambs incline inwardly towards each other from base to lintel, and this inward slope is reflected in a similar slope of the sidewalls from foundations to wall tops.

The single east window tends to have a wide inward splay, and a round head, frequently carved from a single stone, or, in later times from a series of precisely shaped pieces of stone, carefully fitted together.

In some cases, the antae of the earlier series of churches were replaced by protruding corbels, attractively sculpted, and performing a similar function. These are found at the four corners, high up in the end walls, and can be considered another architectural embellishment.

The late 11th and early 12th centuries saw the introduction of the larger nave and chancel plan, and the phasing out of the simple, single cell churches. Churches also tended to become larger, and elaborate sculpted ornamentation around the doorways and the chancel arches, as well as an elaboration of the east windows characterised the finest manifestations of the Romanesque style. Windows in the north and south walls were now acceptable, and richly carved, decorated stonework, especially, representations of the heads of ecclesiastics, proliferated.

All this was to change with the introduction of the Anglo-Norman tradition in the 13th century. Thereafter, the doorways were inserted in the south or more rarely, the north wall, transepts were introduced: pointed, Gothic arches replaced the round headed Romanesque arches and dressed, carved limestone was preferred to the warm, red-toned sandstone of the earlier period.

These developments continued through the 15th, 16th and even the 17th centuries in some cases, despite the occasional iconoclasm of the Reformation, but by then, those churches which were not required for the use of the greatly diminished congregations of the newly established Church of Ireland had been abandoned and the process of decay had begun. Thereafter, the churches for the most part became mere burial grounds, and communal

religious ritual, if it survived, was focussed on burial and occasionally on pilgrimage and pattern.

The Holy Well, which was most frequently the focal point for patterns, and occasionally for pilgrimage, has already been referred to. It is necessary only to reiterate the importance of these in the context of the ecclesiastical sites, and in particular to emphasise that not infrequently they preserve the memory and tradition of the original dedication of the site, and

6.7 Toomullin church, east window, Site No. 37

6.8 Oughtmama (smallest church), east gable and window, Site No. 15

6.9   *Rathborney Church, south doorway, Site No. 7*

provide a useful pointer, where other evidence is lacking, to the early origins of the church sites.

Where so much destruction has taken place, some deliberate, but much as a result of neglect and the passage of time, those features of the early sites which survive, and which can be recognised by the interested visitor, tend to be durable, and not easily erased. Likewise, features of an overtly religious character frequently do not survive. Thus, elaborately carved crosses, or cross slabs are relatively scarce, especially those dating from the pre Norman period. They are however, of supreme importance, not merely as historical artefacts, but because they are often in themselves, major works of art, while also serving to

fill the gaps in the historical documentation, which is, unfortunately, all too sparse.

Thus, while stone baptismal fonts are extremely rare, the somewhat enigmatic bullaun stone is reasonably common on such sites. This consists of a large glacial erratic, an earthfast boulder, or rock outcrop, having one or more regular, circular depressions set into its upper surface, as though they were small basins. That these were already objects of reverence or devotion in the pre-twelfth century, may be deduced from the reference in the early life of St. Maccreiche, identified as one of those responsible for the introduction of Christianity into Clare. He, it was said, having fasted for the forty days of Lent, had a doe drop her milk into the bullaun stone at the door of his church on Easter morning, to provide him with nourishment after his long deprivation. Presumably, the non-religious character of these allowed for their survival, even though they are associated mainly with ecclesiastical sites.

Burial has always been an important feature of the church sites, even from the earliest times, and this has always tended to be concentrated in the area south of the church. A reference to the expressed wish of Cuthbert of Lindisfarne to be buried to the south of his church, close to the holy cross which he had erected there, indicates the antiquity of the tradition, further strengthened by the frequent references to the area north of the church as the "strangers' corner", a place often reserved for paupers, suicides, executed criminals and unbaptised infants. As has been pointed out, the post-Reformation period saw the burial ground as the focus for communal ritual, rather than the church, but whether it had always been the case that as a matter of course all the members of the community or neighbourhood would have similar rights of access, even in the earlier period, is still unresolved. Since however, these sites were originally occupational in nature, and thus served primarily as dwelling places for a substantial community, it is unlikely that extensive burial would have been allowed. Indeed, it is probable, that for much of the time between the 12th and 16th centuries, burial in the major sites especially, was a privilege which only the very wealthy could afford.

Other architectural features found in association with these sites are round towers or a record of same, and souterrains, both of which serve to emphasise that these sites were primarily communal dwelling places. The round tower was known as the cloig-teach, or bell-house, and its function, as its title indicates, was as a belfrey, although it might also be used as a place of storage or of refuge. The souterrain also served as a place of storage and of refuge, though rather than monastic treasures or precious objects, the souterrain probably held perishable foodstuffs.

Finally, a most important factor in the recogni-

6.10 Killilagh Church, Site No. 35

tion of these sites is the place name. Elements with an ecclesiastical connotation, such as Kil, Temple, Killeen, Monaster, Donagh, Aglish and Caldragh, are among those most commonly encountered, all of which indicate an early foundation. These terms derive from early Irish usage, in some cases such as Temple Aglish, Donagh and Monaster, being of Latin origin (Templum, Ecclesia, Dominus, Monasterium). In many cases the names also incorporate the name of a saint, almost invariably the supposed founder or one closely associated with him. These too provide invaluable evidence regarding the establishment of the site.

Ecclesiastical Sites of the Burren

A study of the Monastic sites and Churches of the Burren poses particular problems, not least of which is the difficulty in defining the area to be considered. The use of the parish and barony boundaries, while not entirely satisfactory, does at least provide a useful and logical framework within which to work, since both have early, if unelucidated origins, the latter possibly in early political units, and the former in ecclesiastical administrative divisions. The parish for this purpose is taken as being the civil parish, which coincides in some measure with the late medieval and early post-medieval ecclesiastical unit.

Thus, in these terms the Burren consists of the barony of Burren with its ten parishes as follows: Gleninagh, Killonaghan, Kilmoon, Rathborney, Abbey, Oughtmama, Kilcorney, Noughaval, Killeany, and Carran; the barony of Corcomroe with the following parishes: Killilagh, Kilmacreehy, Killaspuglonane, Kilmanaheen, Clooney, Kilfenora, Kiltoraght, and Kilshanny; the barony of Inchiquin with the following parishes: Kilkeedy, Killinaboy, Rath, and Ruan. Thus the whole of Burren and Corcomroe, and all but two parishes in Inchiquin have been included, the two omitted being the parishes of Dysart and Kilnamona, both of which lie well south of the Burren proper.

Studies show that the vast majority of such parishes have one, two or less frequently, three ecclesiastical sites within their boundaries. This is not the case in this region, however, where out of a total of twenty two parishes, only seven have one or two sites, while fifteen have three or more. Two parishes, Kilkeedy in Inchiquin Barony and Carran in the Barony of Burren, have each nine sites; Killinaboy in

6.11 Kilnaboy Round Tower, Site No. 65

104

Inchiquin has seven sites; Ruan, in Inchiquin, has six sites, and Rathborney in Burren has five sites. The distribution in Corcomroe is more even, with each of the parishes having one, three or four sites. It can thus be seen that in the distribution of ecclesiastical sites, the Burren is quite exceptional, both in their numbers and their density, and this is so to quite an extraordinary extent in the cases of the five parishes listed above.

In this context, no differentiation is made between churches and monastic sites, nor indeed, between either of these and the Childrens' Burial Grounds, some of which may have had a monastic origin, and a number of which contained a church or other ecclesiastical structure. During an earlier phase, some have also had adult burial. Each of these requires individual and detailed examination before it can be fully assessed.

A listing of the saints whose names are associated with the Burren churches reads like a roll-call of the early saints of Ireland. Here are found Colmcille, in the little church of Glencolmcille (No. 28), in the parish of Carran. The circular enclosure still survives, as well as the shaft of a cross, a sacred stone with the mark of the saint, and to the north is the Holy Well. It is of interest to note that the cross shaft is located outside and to the east, where one would have expected the entrance, had it survived.

Kilmoon (No. 6), in the parish of the same name, claims a somewhat tenuous association with the great navigator, St. Brendan, with its Holy Well to the north, and within, the re-

mains of a late medieval church. Tradition associates Maccreiche with the sites of **Drumcreehy** (No. 10) and **Kilmacreehy** (No. 38), and even though many of these early saints are at best, shadowy figures, the existence of some traces of cyclopean masonry in part of the north wall, gives this site an origin of respectable antiquity. Bishop Lonan gives his name to the site of **Killaspuglonane** (No. 41), where the recovery in recent years of a Romanesque carved stone head, which had been placed beside the Holy Well, allowed the recovery and recognition of this early site, where traces of its original, large enclosure may still be seen. No trace of the church survives, but considerable quantities of dressed limestone, built into the walls of the graveyard, testify to its existence and destruction. The small, circular enclosure which still surrounds the site of **Kilcameen** (No. 52), now only contains burial and a fragmentary ruin,

6.12 Drumcreehy Church (Bishopsquarter), Site No. 10

The remnants of the curving line of the enclosure can be seen extending towards the right from the line of the church-yard wall, on either side of the entrance. Its continuation is partly visible in the background, behind the church ruin and in the field below the church-yard in the foreground.

but it recalls St. Caimin of Inishcealtra, and provides an unusual Christian name for young boys and men, unique to this region.

Templecronan, in terms of its architecture as well as of its surviving features, is one of the premier sites of the Burren (No. 29). It is associated with St. Cronan, and provides for the visitor an almost unique survival of the main features of an early site. The church,

6.13 *Priest's Dwelling attached to Kilmoon Church, Site No. 6*

6.14 *Killonaghan Church, Site No. 3*

with its trabeate west doorway, now blocked up, is an excellent example of its type, and has both the protruding corbels, delicately shaped, and a number of carved stone heads, indicating its period of origin. The east window with its inclined jambs, mirrors the inward-sloping jambs of the west doorway, while the rounded head on the outer face of the window combined with the internal lintelled head, is a detail almost unique in Irish church architecture. Outside, part of the enclosure still survives, while to the west is the shaft of a cross. The Holy Well is to the south, and close to the east gable are two shrine tombs. These belong to a rare group of such features, almost always associated with very early sites, but in themselves, are not necessarily of very early date. They most probably represent an unusual survival of the cult of relics, having its origin in the reverence in which the founding saints were held, but frequently surviving, sometimes in debased form, into the post-medieval period.

Oughtmama (No. 15) is said to have been founded by the three Colmans, but the attribution is as uncertain as the personalities are obscure. It has been suggested that they may have had some connection with Colman Macduagh, but this can be no more than speculation. Be that as it may, we should forever be indebted to the founder or founders, for having left us one of the most perfect early sites to be found anywhere in the country. In its setting it rivals Glendalough, while its architectural interest is comparable to that of Clonmacnoise itself. It is a huge site, with traces of an enclosure measuring upwards of 200m east-west, while to the south are indications of a much larger enclosure on the outside. It has its mystery, too, for there are at least two accounts which indicate that there were here a number of early stone slabs, carved with crosses, or inscriptions, or both, which seem to have disappeared without a trace. It is difficult to imagine these having been stolen from such a remote and inaccessible place, but nothing is known of their present whereabouts.

What does survive, however, is sufficiently impressive. There are the extensive remains of three churches, with many early features, including trabeate doorways, cyclopean masonry, and projecting corbels. A decorated stone font survives, while a cross base is located on the northern periphery of the enclosure. A mill-race, and the site of a water-mill are pointed out, reminding us that this was an important aspect of the economy of many ecclesiastical sites, as well as providing a necessary service for the wider community, individual members of which would have been unlikely to have owned a mill or otherwise to have access to its services. It is not surprising, therefore, that increasingly, millstones are being recognised as part of the surviving furniture of these sites, and are more frequently being recovered. The well of St. Colman lies at a distance of 650m to the northeast, further up the limestone slopes from the valley floor and from this vantage point the whole of the site is visible in its incomparable setting.

It is gratifying to note that this well is still in use, as recently-placed votive offerings testify.

One of the most visually impressive sites in the

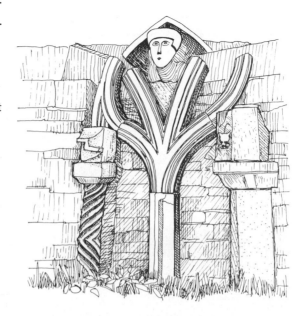

6.15 *Wall Tomb in Kilmacreehy Church, Site No. 38*

Burren is **Corcomroe Abbey** (No. 12) in the parish of Abbey. According to the late 17th century historian Ware's De Hibernia, et Antiquitatibus ejus, the Abbey, also known as Sancta Maria de Petra Fertilis (Saint Mary of the Fertile Rock), was founded in 1194 by Donal O'Brien, King of Limerick, as a daughter house of Inishlounaght in Tipperary. The aisled nave of the cross-shaped church, parts of which were blocked up in the 15th century, is divided from the choir by a stone screen topped by a simple tower. It has been suggested that the north aisle was never completed.

The quality of stonework on the capitals between the choir and the chancel is very high, with delicately carved representations of plants and human heads. The chancel itself retains its original roof, an altar tomb, sedilia, and a graceful lancet window. Features of special

6.16 *Head in Carron Church, Site No. 26*

The full extent of this large settlement is traceable in the curve of the field-fences in the foreground, complemented by the echoing curve of the rising valley slope in the background. There is a good indication of part of an inner enclosure surrounding the two church buildings in the centre.

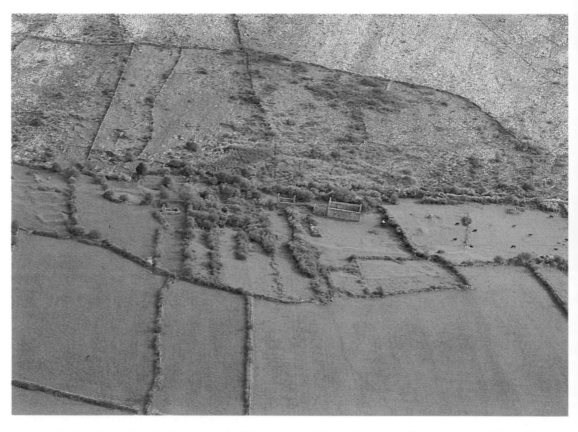

6.18 Oughtmama Churches, Holy Water font and baptismal font, Site No. 15

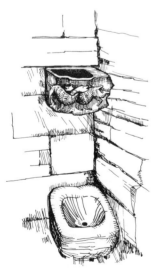

interest in the chancel include a carved effigy of a bishop on the north wall, and below one of the few effigies of an Irish chieftain found in the country, said to represent Conor O'Brien who was killed in a battle fought nearby in 1227. Traces of medieval polychrome painting can also be discerned on the walls and ceiling, as well as on the East window.

Part of the ruined cloister also still stands, as well as what may be an infirmary guest house, and a fragment of the fine pointed arch gate-house, described by Samuel Lewis in his Topographical Dictionary of Ireland (1827), that fell in 1840. In addition, considerable portions of the original enclosure wall are still visible in the immediate vicinity of the Abbey.

Other types of ecclesiastical sites are found in the region, including twenty of the type known as Childrens' Burial Grounds. **Formoyle**, a **Childrens' Burial Ground** in the parish of Killonaghan (No. 5), is an example of such a site, which appears to have degenerated from a church site to the status of a killeen, or burial place for unbaptised children. The occurrence here of a bullaun stone, together with indications of a destroyed structure place this site in the classification of early ecclesiastical sites.

Substantial evidence for enclosures exist at a large number of sites, including **Ballyallaban**

(No. 9), which also has a bullaun stone, at **Rathborney** (No. 7), **Kilcorney** (No. 19), **Glenamanagh** (No. 17), **Cushacorra** (No. 60), **Templeline** (No. 30), while aerial photography has revealed enclosures at **Templemore** (No. 58), **Kilvoydan** (No. 66) and **Kiltonaghty** (No. 53).

Kilfenora

There is however, one site which more than any other, might be said to typify the ecclesiastical sites of north-west Clare. Kilfenora is located on the south-west border of the Burren, and its present modest appearance scarcely hints at its former glory. Tradition brings us back to the latter half of the 6th century, when it is said, a church was founded here by St. Fachtnan, also associated with Ross Carbery in Cork. In the year 1055, it was of sufficient significance to receive the unwelcome attentions of one of the Dal gCais kings, when its stone church was destroyed. Having been passed over in the race to achieve diocesan status at the Synod of Rathbreasail in 1111, it was determined that this omission should be rectified in the next round. It is likely that as a result of this determination to demonstrate its eligibility for such distinction, we may today admire and appreciate one of the most impres-

Kilfenora High Cross, west face.

6.19 Corcomroe abbey, Site No. 12

The symmetrical planning and architectural lay-out of this splendid building can best be appreciated from the air.

sive concentrations of fine stonework to be found on any of our early sites. Thus, no less than seven carved stone crosses are associated with Kilfenora, six of which still survive in whole or in part, the seventh having been removed to Killaloe. It may be noted that three of these crosses are positioned to the north, the south and the west, around the present churchyard. To the north is the Holy Well, and traces of an enclosure may be found to the north-west and south-west, partly aligned along the townland boundary. These indicate a very large site, with a diameter of not less than 300m. Centrally located is the Cathedral, for which Kilfenora strove so mightily, now reduced to the status of a parish church, with its ruined chancel, still containing a strikingly eclectic collection of medieval carved stones.

Unfortunately, Kilfenora was unable to live up to its ambitions, and though it became an independent diocese at the Synod of Kells in 1152, its slender resources from just thirteen parishes, were unable to sustain its achievement. To-day, though administered by the Bishop of Galway, in the Catholic Union, Kilfenora can claim the distinction, uniquely in Ireland, of having for its Bishop, the Pope of Rome.

6.20 Corcomroe Abbey, decorated capitals, Site No. 12

6.21 Corcomroe Abbey, decorated capitals, Site No. 12

A Note on the Map

The accompanying map (page 114) indicates the location and distribution of the ecclesiastical sites of the Burren, and shows what can be claimed to be the densest concentration of such sites to be found anywhere in the country. Just as in the case of Kilfenora, so in the Burren as a whole, the moments of glory had passed, and advancing impoverishment, diminishing wealth and unfavourable circumstances led to the abandonment and despoliation of perhaps the greater number of these sites. Nevertheless, at places such as Oughtmama, Glencolmcille, or Kilfenora, it is possible in some measure to recapture something of this past glory, and to seen in the ruined churches of the Burren something of what was one of the most remarkable achievements of Early Christian Ireland.

It is certain that further work will reveal additional features at many of the sites dealt with here, as well as adding further numbers to the present impressively large total.

6.22 *Formoyle Childrens' Burial Ground, Site No. 5*

6.23 *Ballygastell Grave Yard, standing stone, Site No. 25*

6.24 *Kilfenora, Site No. 50*

The curve of the village street to the left and the straggle of field-fences at bottom right help to define the enclosure. The partly natural rocky platform extending from beneath the church-yard may represent an inner enclosure.

6.26 *Kiltonaghty Church and Burial Ground, Site No. 53*

Enclosure appears as circular feature partly enclosing the rectilinear graveyard, defined as a dark curve in the background.

6.25 *Gleninagh Church and Burial Ground, Site No. 1*
Line of enclosure can be seen to right of the church-yard, curving towards the laneway in the foreground and partly enclosing the ploughed field.

6.27 Manuscript by T.J.
Westropp, Kilfenora Cathedral,
from "Note on Clare", 1887,
3A39, page 337, R.I.A.

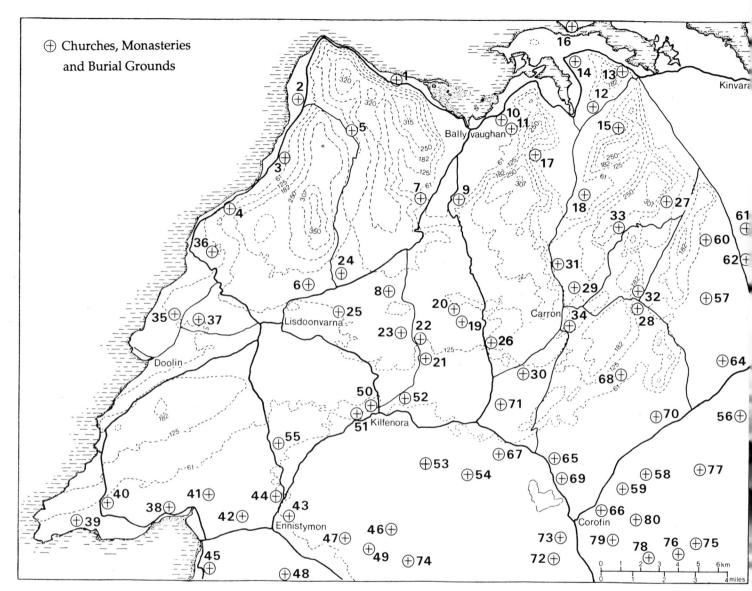

6.28 *Map showing the Churches,*
Monasteries and Burial Ground of
the Burren.

Inventory of Sites

Barony of Burren

Gleninagh Parish:
1. Gleninagh Church and Burial Ground
2. Murroogh Church site and Burial Ground

Killonaghan Parish:
3. Killonaghan Church and Burial Ground
4. Crumlin Church and Burial Ground
5. Formoyle Childrens' Burial Ground

Kilmoon Parish:
6. Kilmoon Church and Burial Ground

Rathborney Parish:
7. Rathborney Church and Burial Ground
8. Kilbrack Church and Burial Ground
9. Ballyalabban Church and Burial Ground

Drumcreehy Parish:
10. Drumcreehy Church and Burial Ground
11. Killoghill Church site and Burial Ground

Abbey Parish:
12. Corcomroe Abbey and Burial Ground
13. Rossalia Childrens' Burial Ground
14. Mortyclough Childrens' Burial Ground

Oughtmama Parish:
15. Oughtmama Churches and Burial Ground
16. Aughinish Church
17. Glenamanagh Childrens' Burial Ground
18. Killeenacurry Childrens' Burial Ground

Kilcorney Parish:
19. Kilcorney Church and Burial Ground
20. Kilcolmandara Church and Burial Ground

Noughaval Parish:
21. Noughaval Church and Burial Ground
22. Kilballymurphy Childrens' Burial Ground
23. Kilballymahony Childrens' Burial Ground

Killeaney Parish:
24. Killeany Church and Burial Ground
25. Ballygastell Grave Yard

Carran Parish:
26. Carron Church and Burial Ground
27. Keelhilla Church and Burial Ground
28. Glencolumbcille Church and Burial Ground
29. Templecronan Church and Burial Ground
30. Templeline Church and Burial Ground
31. Rannagh East Church and Burial Ground
32. Kilnaloone Childrens' Burial Ground
33. Kilnatulla Childrens' Burial Ground
34. Castletown Childrens' Burial Ground

Barony of Corcomroe

Killilagh Parish:
35. Killilagh Church and Burial Ground
36. Oughtdara Church and Burial Ground
37. Toomullin Church and Burial Ground

Kilmacreehy Parish:
38. Kilmacreehy Church and Burial Ground
39. Kilconnell Church site and Burial Ground
40. Dereen Childrens' Burial Ground

Kilaspuglonane Parish:
41. Kilaspuglonane Church and Burial Ground

Kilmanaheen Parish:
42. Kilmanaheen Church site and Burial Ground
43. Kilcornan Church and Burial Ground
44. Calluragh West Burial Ground
45. Calluragh South Burial Ground

Clooney Parish:
46. Clooney Church and Burial Ground
47. Killeinagh Church and Burial Ground
48. Mooghna Church and Burial Ground
49. Carnakilla Church and Burial Ground

Kilfenora Parish:
50. Kilfenora Church and Burial Ground
51. Kilcarragh Church and Burial Ground
52. Kilcameen Church site and Burial Ground
53. Kiltonaghty Church and Burial Ground

Kiltoraght Parish:
54. Kiltoraght Church and Burial Ground

Kilshanny Parish:
55. Kilshanny Church and Burial Ground

Barony of Inchiquin

Kilkeedy Parish:
56. Kilkeedy Church and Burial Ground
57. Ballyaglish Church and Burial Ground
58. Templemore Church and Burial Ground
59. Kells Burial Ground
60. Cushacorra Convent Ruins, Graveyard, Childrens' Burial Ground
61. Cloonselherney Childrens' Burial Ground
62. Rockvale Childrens' Burial Ground
63. Rathorp Childrens' Burial Ground (not on map)
64. Shantaghphubble Chapel in ruins

Killinaboy Parish:
65. Killinaboy Church and Burial Ground
66. Kilvoydan Church and Burial Ground
67. Parknahilly Graveyard
68. Poulnalour Church, Graveyard, Friary
69. Coad Church and Burial Ground
70. Lisheenaloughill Childrens' Burial Ground
71. Lemanagh North Childrens' Burial Ground

Rath Parish:
72. Rath Church and Burial Ground
73. Cahercorcaun Childrens' Burial Ground
74. Drinagh Childrens' Burial Ground

Ruan Parish:
75. Ruan Church and Burial Ground
76. Ballymacrogan West Church and Burial Ground
77. Kilranaghan Church and Burial Ground
78. Kilkee East Church and Burial Ground
79. Kylemore Childrens' Burial Ground
80. Rineen Burial Ground

6.29 *Church ruins, Oughtmama,
photographed for the Lawrence
Collection, 1914. Note the
absence of trees at that time.*

CHURCH RUINS, OUGHTMAMA, CO. CLARE. 4094. W.L.

Acknowledgement for illustrations

Illus. 6.1   Photo, T. Quinn
Illus. 6.2   Drawing, A. Korff
Illus. 6.3   Photo, D.L. Swan
Illus. 6.4   Photo, D.L. Swan
Illus. 6.5   Drawing, A. Korff
Illus. 6.6   Drawing, A. Korff
Illus. 6.7   Drawing, A. Korff
Illus. 6.8   Photo, A. Korff
Illus. 6.9   Drawing, A. Korff
Illus. 6.10 Brush drawing, T.J. Westropp, by
             courtesy of the Royal Irish Academy
Illus. 6.11 Drawing, T.J. Westropp, by courtesy
             of the Royal Irish Academy
Illus. 6.12 Photo, D.L. Swan
Illus. 6.13 Drawing, A. Korff
Illus. 6.14 Drawing, A. Korff
Illus. 6.15 Drawing, A. Korff
Illus. 6.16 Drawing, A. Korff
Illus. 6.17 Photo, D.L. Swan
Illus. 6.18 Drawing, A. Korff
Illus. 6.19 Photo, D.L. Swan
Illus. 6.20 Photo, A. Korff
Illus. 6.21 Photo, A. Korff
Illus. 6.22 Photo, A. Korff
Illus. 6.23 Photo, A. Korff
Illus. 6.24 Photo, D.L. Swan
Illus. 6.25 Photo, D.L. Swan
Illus. 6.26 Photo, D.L. Swan
Illus. 6.27 Manuscript, by courtesy of the
             Royal Irish Academy
Illus. 6.28 Drawing, based on O.S. Map
Illus. 6.29 Photo, courtesy of the National
             Library of Ireland

Carved Head on West Gable, Templecronan Church.

7.1   Ballynalacken Castle.

The Burren in Medieval Times

Paul Gosling

It is doubtful if the landing of the Anglo-Normans in Wexford in the summer of A.D. 1169 had much significance for the families and herdsmen of the Burren. Like the Vikings some 300 years before, the most immediate effect of their arrival in Ireland may well have been an increase in the range of goods available to barter. The church reform movement of the late 11th and 12th centuries, with its visible effects at Kilfenora after 1152, and the arrival of the Cistercians at Corcomroe c.1194-95 (Stalley 1987), were far more important events locally. Though the Anglo-Normans did make occasional raids into north Munster in the 1180s, it was not until the 1230s that their thirst for land had any tangible effect on the lives of people in the area. With the construction of stone castles in the first half of the 13th century, by the de Burgos at Galway and Kiltartan in south Galway, by the Walters at Nenagh, in Tipperary, and by de Musegros and de Clares at Clarecastle and Bunratty, county Clare was effectively ringed by the new colonists.

Within this area, however, the population groups which made up the O'Brien kingdom of Thomond appear to have continued to live and die by their traditional lifestyle based on the family, farming, and the expanded clan (Nicholls 1972). This kingdom included the Burren, where the O Lochlainns, O Conors and Mahons appear to have been the lineal descendants of the Corcomruad. Though by now reduced from independent *tuaíthe* to the status of dependant clans, they were by no means servile: Conor Roe, King of Thomond, was killed, and his forces routed, by the O Lochlainns 'at the wood of Siudain', in the heart of the Burren, in 1268, having gone to 'the upper cantred to tame it'. However, though there there are occasional references, like that just cited, to the death of leaders and the succession of clerics in the area, neither the Irish or English historical sources contain much detailed information on the everyday life of the Burren's inhabitants between 1200 and 1600.

Settlements and Society: Continuity and Adaption

There is, however, a significant body of archaeological evidence on the character of settlement in the Burren during this period, albeit as yet not fully recorded or studied. This includes not only innovative elements, like the fortified tower houses or the parish churches, each reflecting significant changes in social and religious organisation, but also a strong element of continuity in settlement from the Early Historic Period. The presence of gateways of medieval date at Cathair Mhór (Illus. 7.2) and

Cathair Mhic Neachtain (Illus. 7.3), for instance, provides solid evidence that both these cashels were occupied in the medieval period: the latter cashel was, in fact, the site of an important medieval law school. Both gateways consisted of passageways built of mortared stone, roofed with timber supported on corbels, above which were stone towers of two storeys, possibly more, in height. While both were clearly additions to preexisting cashels, their presence indicates that at least some ringforts in the Burren were still fully occupied, and undergoing refurbished, in the 15th-16th centuries. Whether or not ringforts were still being built anew after A.D. 1200 is a problematic question, but from what is known of the political and social organisation in the Burren at this period, the possibility certainly cannot be ruled out. A monument such as An Ráth, the fine, circular, earthen enclosure at the foot of Aillwee, though traditional in form, displays a number of features more characteristic of medieval than early historic settlement. Its situation, on level ground at the foot of a hillslope, its regular broad-banked layout, and its water-filled fosse, are all reminiscent of an Anglo-Norman moated site.

Further evidence of the continuity of traditional settlement forms in the Burren is also to be found in the presence of fortified tower houses within two other ringforts in the area: Cathair Cholgáin, to the north-east of Toomaghera, and Baile Uí Dhanair, to the north west of Leamaneh . As will be outlined below, such tower houses can date from the 14th to the 17th centuries, but Westropp has shown that the building of these 'peel towers' in County Clare does not appear to have begun until the early 15th. Their construction within cashels reflects not only a continuity of settle-

7.2   The photographer's Eye. Cathair Mhór, through the lens of T. J. Westropp, in the 1880s is revealed as devoid of the hazel scrub which now mantles it. Substantial portions of the late-medieval gate-house still survived at that time, though the single lintel over the gate, to the right of centre, looks much as it is today. Note the female photographer on the left with her (to our eye) cumbersome glass-plate camera.

ment, but also the adoption of the modern fashion for stone and mortar within a native settlement type, traditionally based on drystone walling, wattle, sod and thatch.

From the manuscript entitled Caithréim Thoirbhealaigh, thought to have been composed in the mid-14th century as a narrative record of the 40 year dispute over the succession to the O'Brien kingdom of Thomond (Westropp 1891), we get rare historical confirmation of this picture of settlement continuity.
Describing the aftermath of the Battle of Corcomroe, which took place in 1317, its author, Sean Mac Ruaidhrí Mac Craith, paints the following outline of contemporary settlement in north Munster:

'During autumn's and winter's revolution, after that battle of the Abbey they kept quiet: chiefs abiding in their holds, chieftains in their

7.3   The gateway and part of the wall of Cathair Mhic Neachtain, a substantial cashel c.3.5 km north of Noughaval. From manuscript evidence, and the design of the gateway, this cashel was certainly still being fully occupied in the late 16th century and was the site of an important late medieval law school.

strong places, tanists among their households; men-at-arms, each in his own quarters; hospitallers in their dwellings, ollaves in their raths, coarbs in their respective churches; every 'son of a good man' in his own residence, every layman in his liss, and every bishop in his august see'

Though couched in rhythmic prose, teeming with alliteration, and no doubt heavily influenced by the heroic narrative style, this passage is notable for the way in which each grade of society is mentioned, along with the type of residence appropriate to each. Moreover, the society described is still rooted in tribalism, and while allusion is made elsewhere in the Caithréim to markets and towns (Ennis, Limerick) as well as to the stone castles of the English, there is a noted absence here of any reference to either burgesses or knights.

Amongst the medieval Gaelic clans, the professional learned classes (physicians, jurists, harpists and poets) formed a distinctive element. These professions were generally based on hereditary families, and their continued existence was very much intertwined with the maintenance of many aspects of Gaelic culture. Such families were often closely associated with particular clans, and amongst the jurists, one of the most prominent were the Mac Clancys (Mac Flannchadha), one branch of whom were the legal experts of the O'Briens of Thomond (Kelly 1988, 254).

The Mac Clancys had a law school at Cnoc Finn, near Doolin, on the southern fringes of the Burren. This was one of three late medieval law schools in north-west Clare, the others being situated at Parkmore, near New Quay, and at Cathair Mhic Neachtain . Though little is known of the former school, the latter

appears to have been the principal school of the O'Davorens (Ua Duibhdabhoirenn), who were the lawyers of the O Lochlainns. Though they were a relatively minor legal family, they are known to have possessed an extensive collection of early legal texts, and are attributed with the compilation of one of the most important Irish legal manuscripts, now called Egerton 88. Apart from the texts themselves, the abundant marginal comments in their documents provide a vivid insight into life in a 16th century law school. One document in particular, dated to 1675, gives a fascinating description of the buildings of the school at Cathair Mhic Neachtain, mentioning 'the big house of the Caher within' and 'the kitchenhouse', as well as a number of other houses which appear to have stood outside the cashel wall. Although there is little evidence of legal innovation in the work of these medieval jurists, Fergus Kelly's recent research has shown that they were important for preserving and interpreting early legal texts, and they undoubtedly served an important function in the drafting of legal documents and in the settlement of disputes according to the Irish legal system, or Brehon law. In this regard, the survival of these schools in the Burren until the close of the 16th century, indicates that society in the region was still very much rooted in the old Gaelic culture right to the end of the medieval period.

The Medieval Landscape

The Caithréim is also important for the rare glimpses it affords of the Burren's landscape in the 13th century. Watt's pollen work in the Mullaghmore area(1984), shows a continued increase in the levels of grassland pollen at the expense of that for trees, between the 9th and the 16th centuries, indicating that further areas of woodland, particularly hazel, were being opened up for grazing. The persistent presence of cereal pollen in the diagrams, albeit in small amounts, also indicates that some tillage was being undertaken. Whether these developments were confined to the south-east fringes of the Burren, the palaeo-ecologists cannot yet say, and the processes by which the forest was removed - burning, overgrazing or deliberate clearance - are as yet little understood. However, the foundation of Corcomroe Abbey by the Cistercians, in the mid-1190s, certainly led to some land clearance in its vicinity. On what scale this took place is unclear, but the rule of this order did include a significant element of manual labour, and the Cistercians are generally regarded as having been at the forefront of agricultural techniques in the middle ages (Barry 1987). Unfortunately, exact details of the abbey's landholdings are now lost: the '11qrs. of land' listed as belonging to it in the late-16 early-17th century gives no clues as to the quality or use of these holdings. However, a passage in the Caithréim describing the route of Dermot Mac Turlough Mor's army through the Burren in 1317, records at one point that having gone 'through Coill an Air ominously and persistently they passed out into the Abbey of Corcomrua's clear land'. This hints at the existence of a managed farmland of some extent by that date. Dermot's approach was from the south through Carron, and the 'clear land' referred to was probably in the Turlough valley. The area known as Gleann na Manach, on the west side of the valley to the south of Moneen Mountain, is listed as part of its possessions after its dissolution.

What type of farming was practised by the Cistercians at Corcomroe, or what influence it may have had on farming practices in the Burren, are tantalising questions that can only be broached here before being set aside for future researchers to answer. Other references in the Caithréim, to 'Lenane's diary lands', situated somewhere to the north of Kilnaboy, along with such general references to the Burren as a country 'flowing with milk', indicate the continued importance of dairying in the region. And with the evidence for wool processing in the Burren in the 8th-10th centuries on our minds (see Chapter 5), it is interesting to note the presence of sheep amongst the inventory of spoil taken on a raid into Mahon O'Briens lands around Inchiquin and the southern borders of the Burren, in 1318.

Despite the clearances, however, significant tracts of woodland still remained in the late 13th and early 14th centuries when the events portrayed in the Caithréim took place. The 'wood of Suidain', already alluded to, appears to have been situated at Muckinish, to the north east of Bell Harbour, and the march of Dermot Mac Turlough Mor's army in 1317, brought them through Coill an Áir , the Wood of Slaughter, at Deelin and Poulaphuca, between Carron and Turlough. Even in 1655, when the Down Survey was being made, sizeable tracts of woodland were still intact, particularly in the eastern part of the Burren, at Creevagh, Oughtmama and Drumcreehy (Westropp 1909, 273). Information on the western part of the region is harder to come by, but Westropp's study of the placenames in the area, suggests that the deep valley of Gleninagh was also once heavily wooded, though whether this still survived until medieval times is unclear. Thus Ludlow's oft quoted words on the Burren (see page 00), while they do convey the essence of the region's character, cannot be taken too literally. Though it was in medieval times, as it still is, a 'land of white stones', a 'hilly grey expanse of jagged points and slippery steeps' with 'high pinnacled coasts', by 1600 it must still have presented the traveller with a patchwork of forest and cleared land in the valleys, and large open, upland terraces and plateaus where the gryked and runnelled limestone pavements were probably still dotted with diminishing hazel thickets.

Trade and Routeways

Such a landscape must have been inimical even to the stoical drover, as it undoubtedly was to the medieval knight, merchant and burgess. As with other upland areas in medieval Ireland, the 'narrow ways' and 'fastness begirt tracks' of the Burren mentioned in the Caithréim, would not have been attractive to the Anglo-Norman settlers even if they had overcome the O Lochlainns and O Conors. Even today, the region is characterized by the total absence of agglomerated settlement. In fact, only a handful of the villages and towns of north Clare and south Galway predate the 17th century (Illus. 7.15). Given the Anglo-Normans espousal of a market economy, the contrast between Medieval Thomond and Leinster, where dozens of market sites and boroughs were established in the late 12th and 13th centuries, could not be greater. Yet though medieval shipping must have used Ballyvaughan Bay as a safe haven and mooring for off-loading merchandise, this activity appears to have left no lasting mark there until the construction of a quay in the early 1800s sparked the development of the present village.

However, on the eastern and southern fringes of the Burren, at Turloughmore, Kilfenora and Noughaval, there is some evidence that medieval markets may have existed prior to A.D. 1600. None of these places appear to have historical documentation to confirm the presence of a regular market, but it hard to believe that Kilfenora, as the site of a medieval bishopric, would not have attempted to commercially exploit its position as a diocesan centre. The presence of the fair green, with its very fine paying stand, on the north edge of the village, certainly attests the presence of regular markets here in the 18th century. Only 4km to the north east lies Noughaval (Nuachongbháil), where there is a fine medieval market cross, or more accurately stone (Illus. 7.5) close to the ruined, 13th century church. From its associations with St. Mogua, the origin of this place as an ecclesiastical site certainly extends back into the first millenium A.D.. However, the conjunction of the name Nuachongbháil, meaning 'new holding, settlement, [or] (monastic) establishment' (Meyer 1906), with a parish church and market stone, suggests this was once more than just the focal point of a medieval rural parish. In the 19th century there were 10 houses and 64 inhabitants here, and it is possible that the place was some form of nucleated settlement in medieval times. If so, then its situation, on an old routeway close to the boundary between the baronies of Burren and Corcomroe (Illus. 7.4), may also be significant. Though further research may disprove it, it is tempting to suggest that Noughaval may be an example of an Irish-sponsored market centre: a native response to the Anglo-Norman 'borough', which set up the legal framework, including a market, from which most of Ireland's medieval towns developed.

As noted above, Noughaval appears to have been situated on one of the main routeways through the Burren, from Kilfenora, in the south, to the broad valleys at Turlough and Ballyvaughan in the north. Though they were

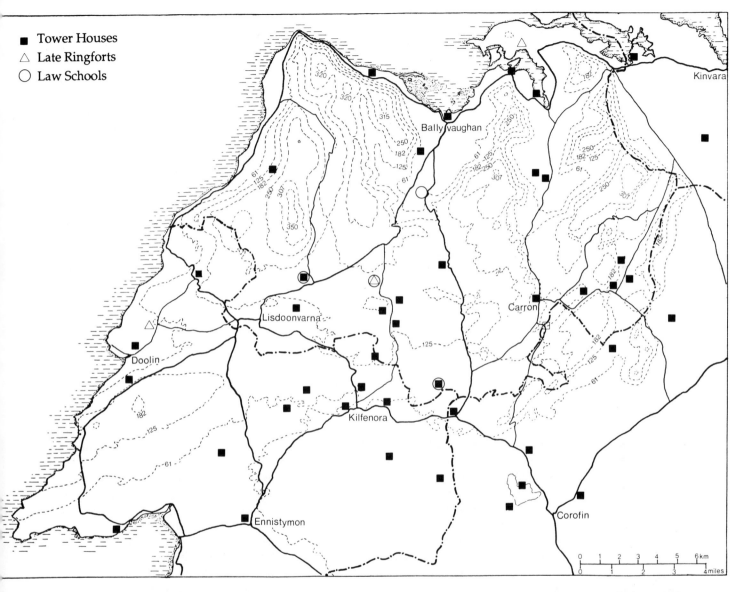

Tower Houses
△ **Late Ringforts**
○ **Law Schools**

Kinvara

Ballyvaughan

Carron

Lisdoonvarna

Doolin

Kilfenora

Ennistymon

Corofin

0 1 2 3 4 5 6km

0 1 2 3 4miles

7.4   Medieval Settlement in the Burren: tower houses, and late ringforts (after Gosling), and law schools (after Robinson).

125

unlikely to have been more than poorly defined tracks, such routes would have been important in medieval, if not prehistoric times, as narrow arteries for communication and transport. In fact, Noughaval may well have been situated at an old route junction: one route running north-eastwards, via Caherconnell and Poulaphouca, to the Turlough valley; the other northwards, via Corkscrew Hill where the line of the old road down this steep descent is still traceable, to the Ballyvaughan valley. The antiquity of the former route is attested by the detailed descriptions, in the Annals of the Four Masters, of Hugh Roe O'Donnell's long range cattle raid into Connacht and North Munster in August 1599 (O'Donovan 1851). Though no such sources exist for the northern route, the presence of three O Lochlainn castles within 1km of each other at Ballymahony, Ballymurphy, and Lissylisheen, just to the north of Noughaval, suggests that they were strategically located here to command this northern route (Illus. 7.4).

The principal approach to the Burren from the south in medieval times appears to have been along Bothar na Mac Rí, which the present road from Corofin to Kilnaboy follows. From Kilnaboy, there were routes westwards to Kilfenora, and northwards to Turlough. The latter route, through Crevagh, Carron and Deelin into the Turlough valley and on to the coast at Bell Harbour, is described in detail in the Caithréim, when Dermot Mac Turlough Mor's army followed it, in 1317, on their way to victory at the Battle of Corcomroe.

It is no coincidence that the routeways described so far all run roughly north-south, as the geology of the Burren has a marked bias along this axis. However, a number of ancient east-west routes are also known to have existed. The most famous of these is undoubtedly Carcair na gCléireach, now the Corker Pass, which crosses the saddle to the north-east of Corcomroe before making the steep descent onto the plains of south Galway. Even as a modern routeway, it provides a convenient short-cut for the traveller entering or leaving the Burren, avoiding the much longer coastal route, via Burrin, around the northern foot of Abbey Hill. As a routeway, the Corker Pass certainly dates back to the end of the 16th century when Hugh O Donnell and his followers crossed it with a massive spoil of cattle from Thomond, on their way back north. Its proximity to Corcomroe Abbey must have been convenient for the monks there, and one wonders whether its original name - the slope of the Clerics - arose from their constant use of it, or because the enterprising Cistercians actually opened it up as a routeway themselves.

The only other possibly ancient pass into the Burren from the east appears to have been via Glencolmcille, to the north-west of Mullaghmore. Apart from the presence of the old fair site at Turloughmore, immediately to the east of it, the existence of numerous wayside penitential stations at the summit of the pass, suggest that this was once a popular routeway. When coupled with the presence of four castle sites in Glencolmcille itself, along with two others at Carron and Castletown, immediately inside the pass, it also suggests that it was also of strategic importance (Illus. 7.4). Finally, Westropp has also suggested that the steep trackway which crosses the ridge from the

7.5   The medieval market stone at Noughaval. Octagonal in shape, it is a squat pillar built of close-fitting, mortared limestone blocks, standing on a stepped base. According to Westropp, lines drawn on the stone served as measures of length for people attending the market.

Gleninagh valley into the Caher valley, via 'Ca-heranardurrish', may also be an ancient route-way connecting Fanore and the Ballyvaughan valley.

Tower Houses:

The castles referred to above belong to a type known as fortified tower houses which were built in great numbers in Ireland in late medieval times (Leask 1951). Westropp recorded over 70 castles in the Baronies of Corcomroe, Inchiquin and Burren, 20 of which were within the latter barony. Of these, only ten survive to any height, though all of them were probably tower houses. Their presence in the Burren indicates that the local clans kept apace with the contemporary architectural fashion and living styles of late-medieval times. While tower houses are generally dated between the

7.6   Newtown Castle.

7.7   Donegore Castle, near Doolin, is one of only three cylindrical medieval tower houses in north west Clare: the others are at Newtown, near Ballyvaughan, and Faunarooska, above Fanore.
    a) pictured a century later, in 1978, just after its restoration as a private residence.
    b) drawn by T. J. Westropp in 1878.

127

14th and mid-17th centuries, Westropp argued that those in Clare appear to date mainly from the 15th. However, the absence of accurate dating evidence for the Burren tower houses is notable. Due the excellent preservation of a number of them, principally Leamaneh, Newtown and Donegore, they do provide us with a vivid first hand impression of the living conditions of the upper levels of late Gaelic society.

As the name implies, fortified tower houses were essentially dwellings, built with an eye to defence. The main component of their design was the vertical arrangement of the living quarters which gives them their characteristi-cally tall, slender profile (Illus. 7.9 and 7.10). Similar towers are known from Scotland and northern England, but it appears more likely that these groups were independent responses built, like the Irish examples, by wealthy families seeking security and status in the unsettled late-medieval societies in which they lived.

Built of limestone and mortar, their design and layout is best understood at sites such as Muckinish (Illus. 7.8), and Glencolmcille, where partial collapse has fortuitously exposed vertical cross-sections. The ground floor usually comprises a doorway, entrance hall with a "murder hole" above, spiral stairs, and a dimly lit store room, usually roofed by a stone vault. Traces of the wickerwork matting, on which the vault was built, are often visible on the ceiling (see Illus. 7.12). The upper floors, often three or four in number, contained the principal reception and living quarters of the household. These often consist of a main room with small bed-chambers, store-rooms and latrines opening off them.

Apart from those on the top floor, the windows are generally narrow slits, set in wide internal embrasures designed to maximise the light. Originally the only fireplace would have been in a brazier on the top floor, the smoke exiting through a louvre in the roof. However, formal stone fireplaces were later added to many castles (Illus. 7.11). Around the steeply pitched roof (thatched or slated) was a parapet walk, invariably with a machicoulis , or defended projection, directly above the ground floor doorway.

Around the base of each tower was a court-yard, or bawn, usually surrounded by a stout rectangular wall. Apart from providing additional protection for the castle, the bawn

7.8   The pattern of collapse at Caisléan Muicinis Nua, near Bell Harbour, reveals the structural detail and layout of a typical 15th-16th century fortified tower house: the vaulted second and fourth storeys, the positions of the wooden floors (now gone), and the wide internal embrasures to the narrow windows.

also contained the principal buildings of the household, as outlined below for Leamaneh. Good examples of these bawns survive at Shane-Muckinish (Illus. 7.13), and Lissylisheen, near Noughaval. At Cathair Cholgáin, and Baile Uí Dhanair, already mentioned, where the castles were built within cashels, these earlier enclosures presumably performed the same function. However, at the latter places especially, the tower house can be viewed simply as a modern replacement for the principal house of the settlement.

Two castles, at Gleninagh, near Black Head, and Cathair Cholgáin , near Toomaghera, also have churches nearby. This juxtaposition of temporal and spiritual power is a classic feature of rural settlement elsewhere in medieval Ireland, and these two examples serve to remind us of the close relationship between the church and local clans.

Apart from their distribution on routeways, already noted, there also appears to be some correlation between the Burren tower houses and the barony boundary. Of the 21 castles shown on Robinson's map within the Barony of Burren, for instance, 11 are situated within 1km of its boundary. While the reasons behind such distributional biases are always difficult to unravel, they may be related here to the protection, by the O Lochlainns, of their ancestral lands with their valuable upland grazing. Certainly, the distribution pattern around Kilfenora and Noughaval, with four O Lochlainn, and three O'Brien castles ranged on either side of the barony boundary, has all the appearance of a local borderland.

Finally, the existence of vertical jointing in some of the Burren tower houses also deserves mention. From its presence in the masonry of

7.9   Gleninagh Castle.

7.10 Ballynalacken Castle in 1878. This drawing, by T. J. Westropp, shows one of the two gates into the castle bawn, or courtyard. Note the three corbels above the gate, the remnants of a small machicoulis, or defended projection, protecting the entrance. The bawn at Ballynalacken occupied the whole of a large flat plateau defined by a near vertical cliff. The castle itself, visible in the background, was built in two phases.

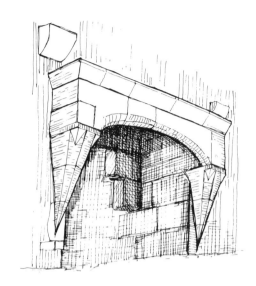

7.11 *Fireplace in Ballynagown Castle, at Smithstown, near Kilshanny. Though a relatively common feature of tower houses, fireplaces and chimneys are often additional features, inserted into the fabric some time after the original construction to give some warmth to the dark interiors. Wood and turf would have been the standard fuel.*

7.12 *Spiral stairs and doorway in Leamaneh Castle, by T. J. Westropp. Note the traces of wickerwork on the ceiling, the 'hanging eye' (at top right) from which the door was hung, and the bolt slot (at centre left) for securing the door.*

the towers at Ballynalacken and Leamaneh, it is evident that they were built in two phases. In both cases, the initial phase consisted of a tall slim block containing the doorway, spiral stairs, and small chambers. Furthermore, on each storey there were blocked doorways, indicating the clear intention that a second phase was to follow. While possibly suitable for defence, the diminutive proportions of these towers must have limited their use to store rooms and sleeping quarters. The lack of reception and living rooms was rectified by the second phase at Ballynalacken which consists of commodious rooms disposed in three storeys over a vaulted ground floor: a similar intermediate phase may also have existed at Leamaneh. Though the social implications of this little studied feature (Leask 1951, 00) have yet to be understood, it has at Leamaneh provided us with a rare example of the full transition from fortified tower to castellated mansion house.

Leamaneh, in fact, provides us with a useful summary of the settlement history of the Burren from A.D. c.400 to 1600. For when coupled with the crumbled walls of Cathair Scribin, the early historic ringfort on the hilltop behind it, this late medieval tower and 17th century mansion encapsulate over one thousand years of history: from the fort of a tribal family group on the Corcomruad, through the fortified tower of the O'Brien clan of Thomond, to the mansion of a gentleman farmer of the County Clare.

7.13 *Picturesque view of Caisleán Sean-Muicinis (the old-castle of Pig Island), at the turn of the century, from the Lawrence Collection. The castle is strategically situated at the landward end of the island, commanding the narrow neck of land which connects it with the mainland. Though one half of the castle fell in the mid-1880s, and the crenellations on the bawn wall are modern, this picture gives a good impression of the original appearance of this 16th century O Lochlainn tower house. The scene is little changed today.*

Acknowledgements of illustrations

Illus. 7.1 Photograph, A. Korff
Illus. 7.2 Photograph, National Museum of Ireland
Illus. 7.3 Photograph, National Museum of Ireland
Illus. 7.5 Drawing, A. Korff
Illus. 7.6 Drawing, A. Korff
Illus. 7.7a Photograph, A. Korff
Illus. 7.7b Drawing, Royal Irish Academy
Illus. 7.8 Photograph, P. Gosling
Illus. 7.9 Drawing, A. Korff
Illus. 7.10 Drawing, Royal Irish Academy
Illus. 7.11 Drawing, A. Korff
Illus. 7.12 Drawing, Royal Irish Academy
Illus. 7.13 Photograph, National Library of Ireland
Illus. 7.14 Photograph, A. Korff

7.14 Leamaneh Castle.

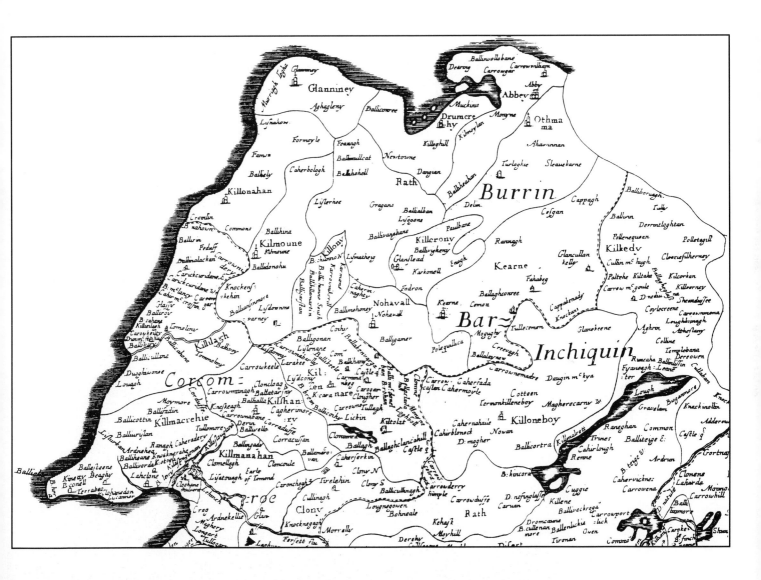

7.15 *The earliest detailed map of north-west Clare is that by William Petty from his* Delineatio Hiberniae *, published in 1683.*
Apart from the barony (broken lines) and parish boundaries (solid lines), it also shows many of the castles and churches. Note the
absence of the names Ballyvaughan and Lisdoonvarna. The scale is approximately 1:0000.

133

1   *Drawing of Leamaneh Castle as it might have looked in A.D. 1500, shortly after its construction. The small dimensions of the tower (1) suggest that it was probably used only as sleeping quarters and as secure storerooms. Most of the meals and business of the household are likely to have been conducted in an adjacent hall (2). The walled bawn (3) probably also contained the quarters for servants (4), and stables (5). There are also likely to have been a number of houses and outbuildings outside it (6), including a well (7). In the background we can still see the crumbling walls of Cathair Scríbín (8), possibly still partly occupied.*

Leamaneh
An O'Brien Castle and Manor House

Jeff O'Connell/Paul Gosling

One of the most spectacular sites in the Burren is the ruined castle and manor house of Leamaneh, situated at the junction of the Ballyvaughan, Corofin, and Kilfenora roads. Taking its name from either leim an eich, "the horse's leap", or leim an fheidh, "the deer's leap", it was the residence of that branch of the O'Brien family from which the Barons Inchiquin of Dromoland Castle trace their descent.

According to Strafford's 17th century survey of Clare, there was a fort at Leamaneh called

2. *Leamaneh Castle, 1991*

Cathair Inine Rua, or the Fort of the Red-haired Girl, although the only ruined fort in the immediate vicinity hearing a name today is Cathair Scribin.

It is likely that the original tower house at Leamaneh was constructed about 1480, possibly by Turlogh Donn, one of the last independent kings of the old kingdom of Thomond. In 1548, Turlogh Donn's son Murrough the Tanaiste (an Irish word meaning "the expected one" or designated heir) surrendered his ancestral title to Henry VIII who in return created him First Earl of Thomond and Baron Inchiquin. In his Will, Murrough left his Leamaneh property, as well as land at Dromo-

land (near present day Newmarket-on-Fergus), to his son Donough. However, Donough O'Brien joined the Earl of Desmond's ill-fated rebellion in 1580-81. After it was suppressed he was hanged at Limerick and his lands declared forfeit to the Crown.

The Leamaneh property was saved for Donough's son, Conor, when Queen Elizabeth granted it to Sir Torlach O'Brien of Duach (near present-day Ennistymon) who acted in the role of guardian until Conor came of age. Conor married Sir Torlach's daughter, Slaney, about 1594 and they are known to have lived at Leamaneh Castle. It is recorded that Boetius Clancy, High Sheriff and M.P. for Clare, who

4.   *"Maire Rua"*

ordered the execution of Spanish survivors of an Armada ship that ran aground near Doolin, presented a large table made from the wood of one of the ships to Conor and his wife. This table can now be seen in Bunratty Castle.

Conor O'Brien died in 1603 and his son and heir Donough MacConor O'Brien married Honora Wingfield, daughter of Robert Wingfield of Robertstown, County Limerick. Of their six children, it is Conor, born in 1617, whose name, together with that of his remarkable wife, Maire, is most intimately associated with Leamaneh.

Maire Rua (so-called on account of her red hair) was the eldest daughter of Sir Torlach and Mary MacMahon of Clonderlaw Castle, near Killimer, Co. Clare. In 1634 she married Daniel Neylon of Dysert O'Dea and had three children before her husband's untimely death in 1639. To satisfy the legal requirements, her cousin, a Protestant, was appointed by the Court of Wards as guardian of her eldest son, William. Another decision by the Court granted her the lease of her son's extensive

3.   *Circa 150 years later at Leamaneh, the transition had been made from fortified castle to castellated mansion. While there may have been an earlier extension to the tower, the wide-windowed mansion we now see (9) was constructed against its west wall in the early 1600s. Formal gardens, including fish ponds (10), were also laid out, and embellished in the course of the of 17th century by the ornamental gateway (11), turrets (12), and a summer house (13).*

lands and permission for her to receive the issue and profits. Thus she commanded a substantial income that gave her considerable independence and made her a very rich young widow.

Just seven months after her husband's death in 1639, Maire Rua married the twenty-two year old Conor O'Brien and Leamaneh Castle became their home. The eldest of their five children was Donough, born in 1642.

The splendid mansion, now such an impressive ruin, may have been mostly Maire Rua's creation, financed by the money she was able to draw upon from her son's estate. Her husband, meanwhile, soon became heavily involved in military affairs connected with the Irish dimension of the English Civil War that broke out in 1642.

In contrast to the fortified tower which it adjoins, it is a wide-windowed and multi-gabled house, very modern for its day. Such mansions were just coming into vogue in the first half of the 17th century. Though its exact date is unknown, it is more than likely contemporary with the fine ornamented gateway, now at Dromoland Castle, which originally stood on the line of the courtyard wall in front of the mansion (Illus. 5). An inscribed slab above the gateway arch records that it "was built in the yeare of our Lord 1648 by Conor O'Brien and Mary Ni Mahon alias Brien wife to the said Conor".

Maire and Conor had only a few short years in which to enjoy their fine house. In January 1649 King Charles I was executed in London. In Ireland the Royalists - an uneasy social and religious mix of the native Irish, the Anglo-Irish and English opponents of Parliament - were no match for the well-equipped and highly disciplined army of Oliver Cromwell that landed in 1649.

Cromwell was recalled to England before the campaign could be carried into Clare, but in the summer of 1651 his son-in-law Henry Ireton led the attack from the Limerick side, while Edward Ludlow moved into the Burren from the North. Conor O'Brien, leading a troop of horse, attempted to stop Ludlow's advance into West Clare at a place called Inchecroghnan, in the vicinity of Ennis (unfortunately it is not possible to identify precisely where it is).

According to the anonymous diarist who accompanied the Parliamentary army, on July 25th Ludlow "heard of the enemyes drawing together at a pass neare Enis, he fell into their quarters, killed many, tooke some prisoners and pursued the rest 3 or 4 miles. Among others was there slaine Connor O'Brien of Lymenaugh in the county of Clare...the most considerable person in the county...his cutting off gave a stop to the proceeding of the enemy and did breake that regiment of horse commanded by him".

According to an old family tradition, the body of Conor O'Brien was brought back to Leamaneh. The body was laid to rest in the O'Brien family tomb in Ennis Abbey. In late Autumn Ludlow, together with Ireton, moved the Parliamentary army into Clare. Reaching Leamaneh, where two nights were spent, Ludlow described it as being "indifferent strong, built with stone, and having a good wall about it". The decision was taken to garrison the house. Clearly, Maire and her children were no longer there.

Maire O'Brien, now a widow and in a very

5. *These drawings of Leamaneh Castle, made by T.J. Westropp in August 1884, record the fine 17th century ornamental gateway shortly before its removal to Dromoland Castle, near Bunratty. As the lower drawing shows, the gateway stood in front of the castle, on the line of the inner bawn wall. It bears the arms of the O'Brien's and Mc Mahon's, and the date 1643.*

precarious position regarding her property, moved swiftly to safeguard her eldest son's inheritance. The method she chose was, in the circumstances, quite understandable. She contracted marriage with Cornet John Cooper, a junior commissioned officer in the Parliamentary Army. Little or nothing is known about Cornet Cooper. It is likely that the marriage took place in 1653, and one immediate consequence was the decision to raise eleven year old Donough as a Protestant in order to avoid the taint of being associated with the discredited Catholic cause.

Contrary to the popular folklore surrounding Maire Rua, the marriage was a success. A son was born, and John Cooper increased the estate he managed on behalf of his wife and her children. The date of his death is not known, but Maire outlived him, dying in 1686. Where she lies buried is unclear, but it is likely to be either Coad Church, near Kilnaboy, where two of her daughters are buried, or in the O'Brien family tomb in Ennis Abbey.

Leamaneh suffered badly during the Commonwealth period. After the Restoration, attempts were made to undo some of the damage resulting from its military occupation. After again taking up residence, Sir Donough O'Brien had erected the handsome gate porch in which his arms as a baronet are incorporated. But the fine parkland of trees had been cut down, and the deer park destroyed. Sometime around 1685-86, Sir Donough moved to Dromoland Castle. He was the last O'Brien to live at Leamaneh.

Apparently Leamaneh was occupied, on and off, until the end of the 18th century. After that, this once-fine castle and mansion gradually became a ruin. Drawings made of it by T.J.

LEMENEAGH CASTLE 1884

Lemineigh Castle from the Lisdoonvarna Road.

Gate at Lemaneigh with arms of Sir? Donat O'Brien Bart.

Lemineigh Castle

139

Westropp towards the end of the 19th century show it derelict. A fine fireplace is now in The Old Ground Hotel in Ennis, and in 1902 the gateway was removed to Dromoland Castle.

Acknowledgements for illustrations

1. Drawing, Anne Korff
2. Photography, Anne Korff
3. Drawing, Anne Korff
4. Drawing, Anne Korff
5. Drawing, by courtesy of the Royal Irish Academy
6. Drawing, by courtesy of the Royal Irish Academy

6.   *Drawing by T.J. Westropp, from "Notes on Clare".*

8.1   Birchfield House near Liscannor, built sometime around the beginning of the nineteenth century and now a ruin, was the home of Cornelius O'Brien who sat as Member of Parliament for Clare from the 1830's until his death in 1857. A colourful character, he was a conscientious landlord who was publicly praised for his work in Famine relief. So much of a mark did he made in the district that one observer noted that "he built everything around here except the Cliffs of Moher".

Post-Medieval and Modern Times in the Burren

J.W. O'Connell

The seventeenth Century was one of the most momentous and turbulent in all of Ireland's history. In 1601, the greatest challenge ever presented to continued English control of the country - the seven year war led by Hugh O'Neill, the Earl of Tyrone - was ended at Kinsale by the decisive victory of Lord Mountjoy over the Gaelic military coalition. At the beginning of the eighteenth Century, in 1704 and again in 1709, acts of Parliament were passed which aimed at extinguishing not only the Catholic faith of the majority, but ensuring that the equation of land-ownership with social and political power was transferred from the old Gaelic Catholic population to the new Protestant ":ascendency". Through the operation of the so-called "Penal" legislation, the proportion of land held by Catholics fell, during the eighteenth century, to about 5 per cent.

Two disastrous wars dictated the pattern of events in the seventeenth century. The first, beginning in Ulster in 1641, ended with the subjugation of the country by Parliamentarian forces, and was followed by a massive scheme of transplantation designed to destroy the power base of the old Gaelic aristocracy. Only those Catholic land-owners who could demonstrate they were not involved in the rebellion were exempted from the large-scale confiscation of estates, and even this group was to be compensated with land in the western counties, notably the area of Clare west of the Shannon.

Cromwellian Ireland was harsh. The fate of many of the ordinary people was transplantation to English colonies such as Barbados, while soldiers who had served the Irish cause fled abroad, many distinguishing themselves in the Irish Brigade of the army of France.

It was during this decade also that the relentless attempts to eradicate the Catholic church laid the foundations for that legacy of bitterness the Irish folk memory has preserved over the last few centuries.

The Restoration in 1660 revived hopes that the worst excesses of the Cromwellian period might be reversed. But the new king, Charles II, was persuaded that any leniency towards Catholics would antagonise his Protestant subjects. The only substantial change of policy was the easing of religious persecution.

The accession of the Catholic James II in 1685 once more kindled hopes that some form of the old order might be re-established. But his defeat at the Battle of the Boyne, and in 1691, Sarsfield's defeat at Aughrim, ended all possibility of this. Although the original terms of the Treaty of Limerick were moderate, for example, granting Catholics the same religious liberties as enjoyed under Charles II, the Protestant-dominated Irish Parliament succeeded in imposing a narrower and more punitive settlement.

By the end of the seventeenth century a dominant minority - English in origin and Protestant in religion - was in the process of achieving complete political, economic and social superiority over the Catholic majority. Although a certain number of Catholic landowners remained, the severe Penal legislation ensured that economically they were virtually destroyed as the eighteenth century progressed. Rights of inheritance between Catholics were done away with, and other parliamentary acts forbade their participation in professions and public life. The only method by which Catholics could hold on to their property and take part in the public and political sphere was by conforming to the established Church, a prudent path taken by many of the old Irish landed class.

From Penal Times to Catholic Emancipation

The history of the diocese of Kilfenora, which has the distinction of being the smallest in Ireland, provides us with an insight into the situation of the Catholic Church in the Burren during the century and a half that followed the passage of the Penal Laws.

For a period of about sixty years - from the death of Hugo MacGlanchy, who was consecrated sometime after 1572, until Andreas Lynch was consecrated by the Papal Nuncio, Runuccini, in 1647 - Kilfenora had no bishops but was administered by vicars apostolic. This papal decision to appoint priests to act in the place of bishops, was a direct result of the spread of the Reformation and became common throughout the Irish Church during the first half of the seventeenth century when the normal organisation had broken down. And after the death of Lynch in 1673 Kilfenora was again administered by vicars until 1722.

Although the spread of the Reformation in the Burren was slow, it is reasonable to assume that one of the first losses suffered by the Catholic Church was their places of worship. In 1615, the Royal Commissioners were informed that one of the ten canon's portions belonging to Kilfenora - a sum of fourteen shillings - was used to repair the cathedral, an indication that it was already in a neglected state.

Documentary evidence for this poor diocese is meagre, but occasional references from material in the Galway diocesan archives throw a little light on the situation prior to the first Penal legislation. For example, in 1632 the Catholic Archbishop of Cashel reported after a visit to Kilfenora that the priests had no regular income or fixed residences but "go from house to house". And we learn that in 1681 the council in Dublin ordered the Sheriff of Clare to arrest Denis O'Dea, a priest of Kilfenora, who had ordered a fast in the parish of Killilagh contrary to the law.

In 1697 an Act was passed in the Irish Parliament ordering all bishops and clergy bound by vows and living in community - monks and friars - to leave the country by May 1st, 1698, and laid down harsh penalties for any such persons attempting to enter or re-enter the country. The Act left the secular

8.2   *East Window of Kilfenora Cathedral.*

clergy - priests living in the world - alone, but it was felt that, with no bishops to ordain new priests, the Church would die a natural death.

In 1704, an Act for the Registration of all secular clergy was passed, ordering all priests to register with the civil authorities, to indicate the parish or parishes where they ministered,

143

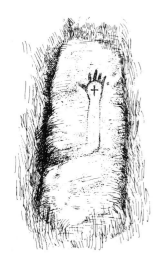

and to provide sureties of £50 each for their good behaviour. The registration list for the Kilfenora clergy provides us with the names of ten priests ministering throughout the diocese. For example, William O'Daly was parish priest of Kilfenora, Kiltoraght and Noughaval. 52 years old and living at Ballykinvarga, he had been ordained in 1671 by Archbishop James Lynch of Tuam. His sureties were paid by James Davoran of Lisdoonvarna (he was also responsible for the O'Davoran Chapel standing to the north-east of the medieval church at Noughaval) and Charles McDonogh of Ballykeel.

An indication that the clergy were suspected of either aiding or turning a blind eye to social discontent in the area is provided by another reference from 1712 when William Butler, High Sheriff of Clare issued orders for imprisoning the Kilfenora clergy because of the recent houghing of cattle. This practice - the

ham-stringing of cattle - was a protest against the conversion of arable land into pasture, which resulted in many small farmers losing their tiny holdings.

From the 1730's, strict enforcement of the Penal Laws was progressively relaxed. Masses were held in simple barn-like structures - some may have actually been converted barns - and, although the numbers of priests were still small, a dispensation had been granted by Rome to allow the ordination of young men under the strict canonical age so that they could assist as curates. A Report by the Protestant Archbishop of Tuam in 1731 states that there were eight priests officiating, and several others, not registered and possibly members of the illegal religious orders, concealed, who were active, saying Mass and preaching. Thirteen Mass-houses were known, as well as other places - probably private houses - where Mass was celebrated. There were no friaries or nunneries, but there were ten schools where grammar and other subjects were taught.

The ruins of some of these Mass-houses or chapels can still be seen in the Burren. For example, in the townland of Fermoyle East there is a simple structure resembling a house, with a small room having its own entrance so that the priest could arrive and depart without being seen and reportedon by informers. Not far from this structure, which may have been used during the period of strict enforcement, is another, less hidden chapel which was in use up until the 1870's. Glenaragh Church, a much more substantial building, not far from the 14th century Rathborney Church, was in use

8.3   Stone with Engraved Hand near Ballykeel. According to local tradition, it was carved during Penal Times and when the Sun shone on the thumb, it indicated where the Mass vessels were hidden.

8.4   O'Davoran Chapel and Outdoor Altar at Noughaval Church.

until the middle of the nineteenth century.

James O'Daly had been consecrated bishop of Kilfenora in 1726, but after his death in 1749, Pope Benedict XIV decided to unite the tiny, poverty-stricken, diocese with Kilmacduagh, in County Galway, under Dr. Peter Kilkelly. From an interesting letter sent by Dr. Kilkelly to Rome in 1771, outlining the state of the diocese, we learn that eight priests were ministering to a Catholic population of over 10,000 people. The Cathedral was in the hands of the Church of Ireland, whose members numbered scarcely 200.

It is evident from Dr. Kilkelly's letter that the ordinary functions of parish life were returning to normal. Baptisms were registered and marriages were celebrated. Catechism was taught every Sunday and Holy Day to the young people of the diocese and regular meetings of parish clergy were held monthly except during the Winter.

We are also given a glimpse of the people of the diocese. "Since all of the people live in country districts and almost all earn their food and clothing by the sweat of their brows, they have none of the vices one associates with a life of ease and luxury. There are some few who are weak-willed, whom their parish priests strive earnestly to strengthen".

By the beginning of the nineteenth century, the Catholic Church was no longer seen as a threat and more and more provisions of the Penal Laws were relaxed. Although full legal emancipation did not occur until 1829, by that time the dark days of persecution were little more than a fading memory. Through a combination of zeal and prudence, the Catholic Church had not only successfully negotiated its way through the eighteenth century legal disabilities, but had shown itself to be essentially loyal to the existing order. The story of the nineteenth century Church runs parallel with the steady decline of the Church of Ireland until its disestablishment in 1869.

Landlord and Tenant

The Burren cannot have presented a very attractive prospect for the new Protestant landowning class that came to dominate affairs throughout the eighteenth century. And in fact, despite the consequences of the Williamite Settlement, various branches of the O'Brien family continued to hold extensive properties in the area. It is also worth mentioning that a number of landlords - the Martyns of Gregans,

8.5 Glenaragha Parish Church, now in ruins, was a simple t-plan chapel built for the Catholic community by the Marquess of Buckingham in 1795. It continued in use until the present church of Ballyvaughan was built towards the middle of the nineteenth century.

8.6   Ballykeel House near Kilfenora, built early in the nineteenth century and no longer occupied, was the home of the Blake-Forster family.

8.7   Decorated Keystone from entrance to garden at Finavarra House, home of the Skerrett family from the end of the eighteenth century. The house is now in ruins.

old upland pastures.

The staple food was the potato, a crop that flourished in the thin acidic soil of the Burren. It is difficult now to imagine the monotony of a diet based largely on potatoes. Yet the traveller Arthur Young wrote that the people "live the year through on potatoes, and for half the year have nothing but water with them". Remains of many small gardens containing spade-formed potato ridges, or "lazy beds", can be found all over the Burren. Exclusive reliance on this one food crop was to prove disastrous during the mid-1850's when the sinisterly-named Phyophthora infestans fungus blighted the crop.

Eighteenth and nineteenth century farm houses of the type seen, either still occupied or in ruin, in the Burren, were simple, single-storey structures, with one large room and several smaller rooms off to the sides. At one end of these byre-dwellings might be housed animals as well. A late seventeenth century

the Blake-Forsters of Ballykeel, and the Skerretts of Finavara - were Catholics who had managed to hold on to their lands.

As for the ordinary people, it is likely that farming and grazing practices in use for centuries continued during much of the eighteenth century. Farms were small, and the population large, making land both a precious and a steadily diminishing resource. Roads in the Burren were very bad in most places, and until towns like Lisdoonvarna and Bally-vaughan began to grow, the common pattern was clusters of small cabins scattered through-out the region. One of these now deserted villages can still be picked out at Fermoyle East. The expansion of population in the Burren also led to many otherwise "landless" people occupying whatever land, however poor, was available - hillsides, boglands, and

description by John Stevens gives some idea of what the poorer of these dwellings were like:

"...there is generally one flock bed, seldom more, feathers being more costly; this serves the man and his wife, the rest all lie on straw, some with one sheet and blanket to cover them others with only their clothes and blanket to cover them. The cabins have seldom any floor but the earth...some have windows, others none. They say it is of late years that chimneys are used, yet the house is never free of smoke. That they have no locks to their doors is not because there are not thieves but because there is nothing to steal".

The search for fuel was a pressing concern. Turf constituted the main source, but as the

8.8   House ruins at Fermoyle East.

8.9   During the Great Famine, public relief projects were sponsored by the Government, among them road-building and the construction of stone walls.

Killeen
by Brian Mooney

Was it because never
having experienced conflict
they shared the loneliness
of the warriors in their long
barrows men honoured them?
Singled them out as that distant
part of themselves which,

once indifferent to shadow,
now scarce knew how to
recognise light. Their lives
a suffusion, they grew
ingorant of the dark iodine
of death, of love's
fretful art. And the whole, slow
haemorrhaging of time, like lichen,
staining the grey midden
of the heart.

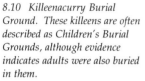

8.10 Killeenacurry Burial Ground. These killeens are often described as Children's Burial Grounds, although evidence indicates adults were also buried in them.

148

population grew, so did the use of available bogs. In that case, anything might be used, from straw and dung to trees cut down at the edges of landlord's demesnes.

Several serious outbreaks of agrarian violence, the first from 1815 to 1817, prompted by the economic distress caused by the end of the Napoleonic War in 1815, the second in 1830-31, as a response to poor harvests, swept over West Clare. Landlords saw no alternative but to raise rents, while secret societies like the Terry Alts responded by taking the law into their own hands. Fields belonging to landlords were dug up, hay-ricks burnt, and cattle hamstrung. One particular incident deserves mention. On January 21st, 1831, Mr. William Blood, a Resident Magistrate who lived at Applevale House, Corofin, was murdered by his servant. The government response was swift. Eight men were arrested and hanged at gallows erected at Corofin, Rath and Kilfenora.

It was not until the 1880's, after the establishment of the Irish National Land League, and the successive Land Acts passed under the administration of Gladstone that tenants finally achieved security and the right to purchase at reasonable terms the land they had farmed, in some cases, for generations.

The Growth of Towns

Towns are a relatively late arrival on the Irish scene. Apart from those areas in the south and east that felt the impact of the Vikings and later the Normans, only a very few villages and what could be called towns, using a little descriptive leniency, existed in the Burren before the seventeenth century.

What villages and towns there were grew out of markets and fairs, such as those for which there is some evidence at Turloughmore, Noughaval and Kilfenora. In 1618, for example, John Sterne obtained a grant to himself and his successors to hold at Kilfenora

8.11 A nineteenth century print showing a typical clustered village on the way to extinction. Poverty, famine and eviction led to depopulation throughout the Burren during the century, and traces of many villages can be seen at various places in the region.

149

8.12 The Spa at Lisdoonvarna
was the chief reason for the growth
and popularity of the town in the
nineteenth century and it
continues to attract people in large
numbers today. Writing towards
the end of the nineteenth century,
Professor Mapother, a former
President of the Royal College of
Surgeons in Ireland, described the
Gowlaun Sulphur Spring as
"most efficacious in cases of scaly
skin diseases, in acne and eczema,
in chronic rheumatism, rheumatic
and atonic gout, scrofulous
swellings, also in some diseases of
bones and joints...The proper dose
of the Gowlaun water is from two
to eight tumblers, or half pints,
daily, and the more divided this
quantity the better, a stroll for
some minutes intervening".

a Thursday market and two fairs a year at the rent of 20 shillings.

Ballyvaughan, with its position on the seacoast, was undoubtedly an ideal site for the growth of a town, but there is little evidence of its growth until the early years of the nineteenth century. Samuel Lewis reported it contained 23 houses and a population of 151 persons in 1831, "since which time several new houses have been built, and it is progressively improving". A new quay was constructed by the Fishery Board in 1829, and such was the subsequent growth of the fishing industry that by 1837 another quay was called for. A market for corns and pigs was held weekly on Thursday, and fairs, "lately established", Lewis tells us, were held on June 24th and September 23rd. A court was held every six weeks and

district sessions were also held on a regular basis. By 1841 there were 35 houses and a population of 255 people. With its own work-house, coastguard station and police barracks, it had become a place of some considerable importance.

Probably the most substantial town in the Burren is Lisdoonvarna. It is almost entirely the creation of the nineteenth century and gained its prominence through the shrewd development and exploitation of the medicinal properties of the sulphur waters first remarked upon by Dr. Sylvester O'Halloran in 1751.

"Taking the waters" became a very fashionable pursuit in late eighteenth and early nineteenth century Britain. The beautiful city of Bath, which became the haunt of those who considered themselves the pace-setters of society, was itself established around a spa like Lisdoon-varna. So, although Lisdoonvarna did not even find a place on the original Ordnance Survey map of 1840, by mid-century it had grown considerably. In 1847 a post office was established. By 1859 a small Protestant Church was built, a sure sign that those who could afford the luxury of travelling to the spa had arrived. A simple Catholic church was built in the 1860's, and before long Catholics were coming in great numbers. In fact, the spa wells became a favourite haunt of bishops and clergy of all denominations. In 1872 there were already 67 houses, and a number of fine hotels for the increasing number of visitors were built. Although the nearest station, opened in 1887, of the West Clare Railway was seven miles away at Ennistymon, people thought nothing of the trip by long car and trap to the

now famous and widely-advertised Lisdoonvarna Spa Wells.

Ironically, as towns like Lisdoonvarna and
Ballyvaughan expanded, others like Kilfenora
and Noughaval and Fisherstreet, near Doolin,
went into a long decline, only partially arrested, in the case of the former and latter of
these, during the last decade.

8.13 *Ballyvaughan Court House,*
c. 1900.

Acknowledgements for illustrations

Illus. 8.1   Drawing, A. Korff
Illus. 8.2   Drawing, A. Korff
Illus. 8.3   Drawing, A. Korff
Illus. 8.4   Drawing, A. Korff
Illus. 8.5   Photograph, A. Korff
Illus. 8.6   Drawing, A. Korff
Illus. 8.7   Photograph, A. Korff
Illus. 8.8   Photograph, A. Korff
Illus. 8.9   Photograph, T. Quinn
Illus. 8.10   Photograph, A. Korff
Illus. 8.12   Drawing, A. Korff
Illus. 8.13   Photograph, courtesy of the
              National Library of Ireland
Illus. 8.14   Photograph, G. V. Mac namara,
              Clare County Library, Ennis
Poem   by kind permission of Brian
              Mooney

8.14   Chimney Sweep, Michael Fitzpatrick, or "Mick-Fitz", of Corofin, from a photograph taken c. 1900. A now almost vanished occupation, chimney sweeps were once, like thatchers, in great demand, especially in the small towns and villages that grew up during the late eighteenth and nineteenth centuries.

Charles Ffrench Blake-Forster

Ballykeel House, about half a mile from Kilfenora, was the family home of a remarkable young man who combined in his brief life - he was only 23 years old when he died - the activities of a public servant and an historian. Charles Ffrench Blake-Forster, born in 1850 at Forster House, Forster Street, Galway, was the son of Captain Francis Blake-Forster and Mary Josephine Comerford, daughter of a successful merchant. He was educated privately by a tutor, and in England. His father owned property in the parish of Kinvara, and here, in an old mansion that had belonged to a branch of the Ffrench family, the young man had his principal residence.

Blake-Forster, despite his youth, played a prominent role in the life of Galway, as town Councillor and as a Poor Law Guardian. In 1874, the year of his death, he was appointed High Sheriff, and presided over the first elections held for Members of Parliament under the newly introduced Ballot Act. His health, however, was always fragile, and according to his obituary notice, "the great labour he had undergone in his untiring literary pursuits had affected his constitution, and the fatigue and mental anxiety consequent upon the illness and death of a beloved sister proved too much for him to bear". He died on 9th September, 1874 and was buried in Bushy Park Cemetery, outside Galway. His popularity, however, was such that after his death, as a mark of respect, he was elected to the East Ward seat on the town council he had been nominated for shortly before his final illness.

His principal historical work is "The Irish Chieftains, or A Struggle for the Crown, with numerous notes and a copious appendix", published in 1872. Best described as an historical novel, it is set in the South Galway-North Clare region and describes the troubled period in Irish history from 1689 to 1745. The notes and appendices contain a wealth of documentary information related to the families of the district, many of whom were among his ancestors. Proud of his Irish ancestry, the publication of the book caused a sensation. According to his nephew, Blake-Forster "was expelled from the County Clubs of Ennis and Galway, and the principal clubs in Dublin, on account of his opinions, Jacobite and Nationalist...and because the binding bore an uncrowned harp".

Charles Ffrench Blake-Forster, painted by Joseph O'Malley (courtesy of the Mellett Family, Bellykeel)

His passion for antiquarian research was all-consuming and he devoted much of his energy to researching the history of Clare. Among his writings are "A Topographical Description of the County of Clare, its Castles, Abbeys and Round Towers", "The Genealogies of the Principal Families in the Counties of Galway and Clare", "A Collection of the Oldest and most Popular Legends of the Peasantry of Clare and Galway", and numerous compilations of historical material such as "The Annals of Corcomroe" and "The Annals of Kilfenora". Many of these were published in contemporary newspapers like The Galway Express and The Galway Vindicator and Connaught Advertiser.

One of his most interesting works is a charming novel which appeared in two parts in the Vindicator in February 1870 entitled "Lemenagh Castle. A Legend of the Wild Horse". Similar in style to "The Irish Chieftains", it is essentially a romance that brings together the author's historical research into the imposing figure of Maria Ruadh O'Brien.

9.1   Ennistymon Falls

Lore and Cures and Blessed Wells

Lelia Doolan

Our childhood gateway to the Burren was at Ennistymon. We spilled out of the memorable West Clare train, dragging cases, parcels, boxes and bicycles to be met by father's brother, our Uncle John, with the sidecar and Jimmy or a neighbour with the common car onto which all the baggage and maybe all three of the boys were heaped while our mother and the three girls squeezed up onto the sidecar to sway the four miles home in style. More often we came in dribs and drabs, some on the train and on the Limerick to Lisdoonvarna bus with many another returning Yank or emigrant; toiling up the three long hills from Kilshanny to land at Doolan's Cross in the middle of June with our aunt Anne waiting at the gate to welcome us in and grandpa lurking inside by the window.

From then until the beginning of September when scenes of desolation attended our return to Dublin, we were the adopted children of the place. We took part in the daily round of men's and women's work on a middle-sized farm, the nights of *cuairt*, the games and stories; and all the ways of thinking and turns of speech still liberally sprinkled with Irish words and sentence structure were grafted onto our own towney talk. Even the landscape was a vivid, living presence. Fields, bushes, boundary walls all had their own identity and name; Slieve Elva traced the horizon north of Lisdoonvarna; Mount Callan, an unmistake-able landmark in the Southern distance, was a forecaster of weather and a companion at all times.

Focal Gaeḋilge a cualas sa ḃaḋ.—

Geoṫán	Dasrín
Gráineóg	Scuacán
Ciseóg	Boḃarán
Banḃ	Buaḋreán
Crúiḃín	Spailpín
Scollán	Cáincín
Ciseac	Gaḃlóg
Spairc	Caorán
Spairceóg	Cadlicín
Cioróg	Maisrín
Ciorsc	Caorán
Crocacán	Praiseac ḃuiḋe
Bacac	Práiscín
Báimín	Bairéad
Ballán	Doirnín
Boṫán	Taoscán
Smicín	Súgán
Poll marḃ	Cruiscín
Suarac	Bacán
Bearc	Smuz
Cresrán	Sgearrán
Ciseóg	Eitín
Amadán	Faoileám
Crám	Pusacán
Luidín	Pearc

9.2   Irish Words that I heard at Home., - from a copybook in the Schools Collection

So I was not too surprised years later to discover from Máire Mac Neill's great book, The Festival of Lughnasa, that Mount Callan was a sacred place, one of the ancient heights on which festive assemblies were held to celebrate *Domhnach Chrom Dubh* or Cromdubh's Sunday, now called 'Garland Sunday'. She also lists St. Brigid's Well, north of Lahinch, as "one of the three most strongly lasting survivals of Lughnasa"—the other two being the Croagh Patrick pilgrimage and Puck Fair (which, she comments crisply, "has gained fame and renewed life in being made known by journalists to the bohemians of Dublin and London"!). Garland Sunday was usually the last Sunday of July, the end of Summer, and was celebrated by outings to Lahinch. Thus

the old religion and the new paced along in fairly agreeable tandem.

The life lived in the parish of Kilshanny did not differ to any great extent from the life observed, fifteen odd years earlier, by the American anthropologists, Arensberg and Kimball, who came to Luach and Rinnamona in 1932. Their study of family and community life was first published in 1940 and enlarged, from material collected on their initial two-year stay, to include six new chapters on the relationship of countryman with townsman, in a new edition in 1968.

Their concentration was on the realities of small-farm life: the structure of family and kin, the division of labour between sexes, the role of old people and the regulations and inter-dependencies of social and economic life. It is a great pity that, so far, there has been no re-study of the material. No doubt the effects of new media, of tourism, Vatican II, the EC and emigration would paint a different picture. Chris Curtin and Tony Varley's 1982 study of some bachelor farmers in the Burren region, while pointing up changes in farming activity, housework and social activities (the pub replacing the old rambling house, for instance), finds evidence of adaptation rather than social or personal breakdown.

The colourful and opinionated views of earlier visitors like Westropp, O'Curry and O'Donovan and their awe-inspiring, diligent attention to every detail, flesh out in fuller form emotions, dilemmas, beliefs, anxieties and superstitions that went along with the humdrum labours of everyday. "Burren", wrote O'Donovan, "is the wildest and ruggedest district I have seen...its history and topography are better preserved than those of any County I have yet visited". He and O'Curry began taking down the stories and tales of local seanchai and listing the healing qualities of wells and stones:

"Toberaduff (Well of the Black) Holy Well in Cahirfadda. Black sediment found at its bottom and from which it is named, used by the peasantry for colouring wool as well as for applying to swellings of the eyes and limbs".

They only remained in the area for ten short October days in 1839 and it was ninety years later that Séamus O Duilearga (Professor J.H. Delargy) who was later to be Honorary Director of the Folklore Commission at its establishment in 1935 took up the work. In Kerry he had conceived of the idea of recording what remained of the oral tradition and he came to a part of the Burren where the older generation still had Irish although the young were no longer fluent. In a short memoir, written forty years later, he brings to life the artistry and faithfulness of the storytellers, the scenes of hushed attention around the Ediphone recording machine and the sheer physical endurance required to carry on the work of collecting. His sense of desperation at the possible loss of the store of *sagen* and tales with the death of the old men who were their repository comes through touchingly. But there is also a sense of everyone lending a hand, as in one incident where on a night of

9.3   *St. Brigid's Well, still a place of pilgrimage, especially on February 1, and on Garland Sunday at the end of July. An atmosphere of strangeness and tranquillity surrounds the place.*

Sr COLEMANS WELL. Co. CLARE. 4092. W.L.

9.4   St. Colman's Well at Oughtmama in olden times and today (opposite page). The well was visited on November 5 and was said to cure eye ailments.

storm-force gales, he is sent on over the sand-dunes near Fanore to the house of Tomas O Húir with the promise, from one Sergeant Meara, that he would get a donkey and cart to haul the immense Ediphone machine and all its impedimenta to the house in time for recording. Amid thunder-claps and darts of lightning, the steadfast Sergeant pulls up to the door in good time, soaked but triumphant. The donkey could not be caught so he had pulled the cart all the way himself!

Between 1929 and 1935, during holidays from teaching at the University in Dublin, Séamus O Duilearga collected almost 500 tales as well as *seanchas* and extensive vocabulary from the

archivists of the district. The irony is that the tradition of story-telling died as the collection grew. (Perhaps the recent efforts of a group in Ballyvaughan to revive the art will have success). Some of the stories were published by O Duilearga in Béaloideas, as well as pieces of charms, verses and customs.

But most moving for me was the description of a remarkable man from the neighbourhood:

One of the visitors who came on *ragairne* almost every night was a neighbour, a middle-aged man named Sean Mac Mathuna. He was a good listener and in the beginning rarely contributed to the

night's entertainment, but as we got to
know one another better, I realised that in
him I had found a man who could help in
the work of saving something of the
tradition of Thomond. He was diffident
and shy, but his burning love for Irish, and
his poignant regret, so often expressed to
me, at the rapid decay of the language in
Clare, overcame his shyness and at length
he agreed to do what he could in the
neighbourhood. Before he died, 20 years
later, he had sent to the Commission over
11,000 pages of all kinds of folklore, 4,000
pages of this fine collection being diaries in
which besides much else he recorded his
experiences as a collector from Ballyvaughan to Milltown and from Aill Bheal
na Tulach to Ennistymon—a huge area for a

9.5   St. Colman's Well today

*9.6   Seán Mac Mathúna - or Mac Mathghamhna as he himself
spelled it. At the end of one of his notebooks he wrote:*

*"Farewell now little book and good luck to you on your
road into the great world and into the hands of other people.
Hard have I earned what is in you, gathering for you in a
hundred places so that I could speckle these traditions on to your
white pages...And may what I have written be to the advantage
of the old language of our country".*

working man to cover on Sundays and church holidays mainly, for the spade was more familiar to him than the pen. For twenty years, Séan Mac Mathuna walked the roads and boithrins of Corcomroe and the Burren, often wet, sometimes hungry...seeking out the old Irish speakers in search of the despised and neglected traditions which but for him would have gone into the clay".

Seán O Suilleabháin, Archivist to the Folklore Commission, later took part in designing a most adventurous scheme in which the schoolchildren of the country were asked to become folklore collectors among the older folk in their neighbourhood and write up their findings in school jotters which were then transcribed into special copybooks and returned to the Commission's offices in Dublin. The scheme lasted from June 1937 to December 1938 and resulted in half a million pages of material. In the whole of Clare, 176 schools took part, about twenty of these being in the Burren. This collection, on microfilm, is at the County Library in Ennis, under the benevolent care of Miss Mary Moroney.

It is a staggering treasure and up to now the general public has largely been unaware of its existence. However, there are plans to mount a full exhibition in University College Dublin in September, 1991, and hopefully this will later travel outside the capital. Since the pupils taking part were in the 11-14 age-range, there should still be youngsters in their mid to late sixties who may remember taking part. Although, even in the thirties, some people were sensitive about their ages, as a letter from the Convent School in Ennistymon shows:

9.7 Letter from Sr. Filumena which accompanied the copybooks sent to the Commission.

A Duine Uasail,

Is oth liom a rádh nach raibh na daoine a thug an t-eolas seo dos na daltaí sásta a n-aois do thabhairt doibh
    is mise
       le meas
         An tSr. Filumena

(I regret that the people who gave information to the scholars did not want to give their ages to them).

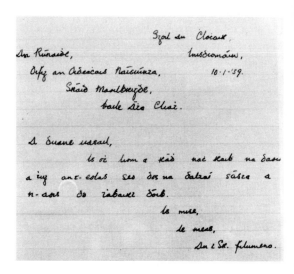

Among the songs and tales, prayers and fragments of history and myth, there are many interesting herbal and fantastical remedies for common or unusual ailments. Here's one list from Tadgh de Nógla, a pupil from Doolin:

Aicidí agus Tinneas

Bonn Leach	= sore on the heel of the foot
Ballsgóid	= gumboil
Craunra	= wart
Ath	= swelling
Plucamas	= mumps
Fiabras Dearg	= Scarlatina
Bruitíneac	= measles
Galar Incinne	= meningitis
Meathanach	= consumption
Scoilteacha nó deatacha	= rheumatism
Tineas droma	= lumbago
Aillis	= cancer
Gor	= ulcer
Tragaid	= pleuricy
Tinneas na sgainóg	= pneumonia
Slaghdán	= cold in the lungs
Miaban	= reel in the head
Lagacar	= weakness

This list was collected from Padraig O Cilltreáin (76 years), Fisherstreet, Doolin. I have not tampered with the spellings except where the sense is unintelligible.

In his book, Making the Cure, Dr. Patrick Logan lists many plant remedies and charms, several of which are to be found in the Burren school copybooks proving, perhaps, that their efficacy was a byword for generations where no conventional medical practitioner could be found. Animals were also treated with herbs and in Kilnaboy, two branches of the Curtis family practised cures - one for animals, the other for humans. The latter branch of the family - Brian, Robin and Maria Curtis - fell foul of the clergy and were excommunicated. Of the other branch of the family, Patrick Curtis, grandfather of Michael and P.J. Curtis and their father, Patrick Joseph (Pat Joe), were blacksmiths and trusted vets. They escaped clerical displeasure, perhaps due to the Catholic belief of the time that animals have no souls. The schoolchildren wrote about the Curtis gift of healing in their researches:

The Doctor of Kilnaboy
There is a man living near Kilnaboy and he has the power to cure liver complaints and also to cure cows that have swallowed raw potatoes. People have been known to come back from America to consult him. His entire predecessors possessed the same gift but this man (a blacksmith) was the only one who practised as a wise man.

With his human patients the blacksmith's method was simple. He made the sufferer lie on the anvil and pretended to strike him with a sledge hammer. While doing this he says a prayer: 'An t-ucht a bheith socair, Is do schairt a bheith reidh. In ainm an Athar agus an Mhic, Agus an Spioraid Naomh. (Let your chest be calm and your midriff be ready. In the name of the Father and the Son and the Holy Spirit).

9.8   Animal cures also occur in the Schools' notebooks. Here is an illustration for a cure for gripe or worms in cattle - the worm's knot, also called the vanishing knot: "The belief is that these knots, when made over the calf's tail, cures the calf of the worms".

161

This is done on three occasions, on two Mondays and a Thursday but in some cases once is sufficient. Local legends say that this gift was bestowed on him by St. Patrick whose horse cast a shoe near at hand. That man was also a blacksmith and he insisted on shoeing the horse freely and as a result of this all of the man's descendants have the gift of curing certain complaints. The man's name is Curtis.

There are other versions of this tale, differing only in detail. In some cases the man on horseback is a priest in penal times, on the run, and the smith puts the shoes backwards on the horse so that he may not be caught. The important figure is, in all cases, the smith.

Smiths were figures of mythic size in a folk tradition - as will be evident later in the story of the Smith's Wonderful Cow.

Michael Curtis still has his father's lance which he used to make incisions, especially in the

9.10   One of the collection of lances used by Pat Curtis and his son Pat Joe Curtis of Kilnaboy particularly in the treatment of farcy in horses.

case of farcy in horses. The disease is normally regarded as incurable when the hind legs swell and the veins distend. The vein is lanced and about a quart of blood is let and then the animal is given a dose of linseed oil and turpentine mixed. P.J. Curtis described having seen this procedure as a child - a similar treatment is described in Dr. Logan's book. Many farmers in the district and beyond still remember with gratitude Pat Joe Curtis's gift.

The human cures in the Schools' Collection may be divided into fabulous and herbal. There are several recurring ailments, of which warts are a prominent entry. Dr. Maccon McNamara of Corofin, while not pooh-poohing natural cures, says that 50% of warts disappear spontaneously within two years, while Dr. Logan says that almost all physical illnesses - over 80% of them - will get better no matter what treatment is given.

Here are a mixture of cures from Kilshanny School:

St. Anthony's Fire: To get the seventh son and to blow his breadth three times on the sore.
Yellow jaundice: To drink for three days but black tea.
Ringworm: To write your name with a pen and ink around it.
Warts: To get somebody to count the warts and whoever would count them it is they would take them.
or
Get an eel and cut the head of him, rub the blood to the warts and bury the eel. While the eel is rotting, the warts are curing.
or
Count the warts, get as many small pebbles and put them in a piece of cloth and leave it at the crossroads. Whoever found it and counted the pebbles it is they would get the warts - and they would go out of the person that would have them.
Sty: To look with the eye the sty is in through a pure gold ring (and, it is sometimes added, onto a green field).
Burns: To get a person who licked a lizard nine times to lick the burn and it would afterwards be cured.
Colds: To put garlic in your shoes and to eat it; to boil milk and onions and drink it.

Leigiseanna

Cures for Whooping Cough
(1) Ferret's leavings
(2) Garlic put into the stockings of the affected person
(3) Cure given by a man on a white horse :- "Fear an Capaill Bán"
no 3 is very simple. If you see a man passing on a white horse simply ask him to name anything to give to the person affected, and when this is given the cough disappears.

Warts :-
apply water found on rock when not looked for
apply the juice of the root of the Dandelion

Burns
A person who licks a lizard three times in the name of the Blessed Trinity and then licks the burn in the same way is sure to relieve the burned person.

Disease of the Liver :-
The sick person put on the smith's anvil and and the sledge raised by the smith over the person

Cures from a Ruan School Notebook - just outside the Burren.

The children of Kilnaboy National School of today procured the following statement from a local man, showing that old traditions are still alive:
Ring-Worm:
"I am the seventh son in our family without any girl and as such I have a cure for ring-worm. I did not know about this for a long time, but I was told to put a worm into my hand and keep him there for 4 or 5 minutes which I did and he shriveled up and died and ever since I have cured many people from all over Clare and even a little girl from England. The patient has to come to me 3 times starting on a Monday he will have to come 2 Mondays and a Thursday. Up to now I have a 100% success T.G. and I do not charge one penny for my services".
Signed: Joe O'Brien

Seán Mac Mathúna, the collector from Luach, was also asked to supply cures for ear, nose and throat conditions for a Dublin specialist, as practised in Seán's district. No stranger to colds from his journeys in all weathers, he provides a range of answers to the thirteen conditions listed, from the hot mustard bath to the milk and onion treatment; rubbing dry salt on the soles of the feet, mixing pepper with a hot drink - and so on. He is especially eloquent on a condition of relaxed uvula *(sine Seáin)*, treated by placing salt on the tip of a spoonhandle and lifting up 'the prone little tongue' at the back of the throat. And 'when the salting operation is over the "dr." lifts the patient by the hair of the crown of his head, off the ground'. To cap all this, he writes a note of apology for the 'meagre amount of information' he has been able to collect!

Not all the children's cures are of a magical turn. Máire Ní Chonmara of Kilfenora notes that red clover flowers are used for coughs and that tea made from cowslip flowers is an excellent drink for insomnia. An infusion of hop flowers for stomach and nerves, and marigold flowers for fevers completes the flower list. Of roots, she makes the following list:

Dandelion root	for kidney and liver
Golden Seal root	for liver and digestive tone
Rhubarb root	for diarrhoea
Lily of the Valley	dropsy and heart disease
Blue Flag root	liver complaints
White Bryony root	coughs and colds

There are too many examples to mention here but many are not unique to the Burren. Cillian Roden tells me that F.J. Foot's paper on the botany of the Burren does list one plant that is unique to the area - *Spirea filipendula* or Dropwort - found in Glencolumcille. Of it he says: 'It is well known to many of the peasantry, the Irish name being *Fillyfindillaun* (I could not ascertain the correct orthography of the word but this is its pronunciation), and is much used, when boiled in new milk, as a remedy for diseases of the kidneys'. Try as I may I have not been able to fathom what *fillyfindillaun* might actually be, in Irish. My cousin, Cyril O Ceirin, pausing momentarily in his struggles to bring a plant called *meacan aille* to heel, (it was used as a paste-poultice for *borr-phiast* - carbuncle, boil or scrofolus) suggests that it may be *fialla fiadháin*, a wild plant, or possibly the local pronunciation of *filipendula*, Latin being a passion of the hedge school-masters.

In making enquiries about present-day knowledge or use of old cures (the children of Kilnaboy school, through the prompting of their master, Tony Killeen, were good enough to start enquiries and came up with the old sty cure, and some familiar wart ones as well as moss or cobwebs to stop bleeding, and comfrey - also widely used in earlier times - for a disinfectant) I then had the good fortune of

9.11 A note from the collector. He then attached a dozen odd pages of detailed material!

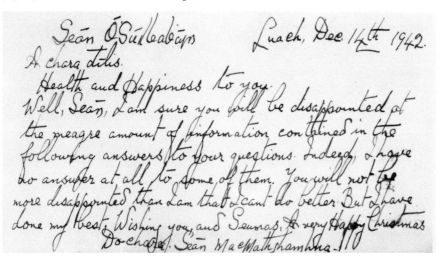

15

Cúram na gCos.

Fadó ní raib aon bróga á caiteam ag na daoine. Nuair a bíod siad ag dul go dtí an tAifreann do tógfad siad a mbróga in a lámta go sroisfead siad an séipéal. Annsan do cuirfead siad orta iad. Agus nuair a tagad siad amac bainfead siad arís díobta iad.

Is ceart do duine an t-uisge in a nigeann sé a cosa do caiteam amac má deireann daoine nac mbéad an t-ád ins an tig seo dá gcoimeádfaí siad istig é.

Caiteann na daoine go léir bróga anois. Ní caiteann na páistí

bróga ins an samrad. Bíonn siad i bfad níos fearr agus níos caodruime gan iad. Uaireanta geibeann na páistí "bunlocs" ó beit ag léimead ar na cloca. Sagas bíonán críd tagann leigeas air.

Do bí i bfad níos mó gréasuide fadó ná mar atá anois. Níl ac aon gréasuide ins an bparóiste seo. Comnuigeann sé i Lios dún bEarna. Ní caiteann na daoine aon bróga bonn admaid anois ac do caitfead siad cúpla bliadain ó soin iad. Tá siad ana mait cun siubail ar na cairigreaca.

meeting Mrs Teresa McCormack who turns out to be a descendant of Mr. F.J. Foot, and has obviously inherited a knowledge of botany and cures. She told me of a cure for gallstones that involves rendering down butchers broom in boiling water and stiffening it with a good dose of whiskey, and gave me many more recipes besides.

Almost as intriguing as the herbs and cures was information about good and bad days to do things on: 'it is lucky to leave cows out on a Friday. It is unlucky to get married on a Saturday', so wrote Micheál O Cuillináin of Rinnamona, while Aine Nic Mhathuna of Ballycashen wrote 'If a person cut his nails on Monday he will have no luck. Tuesday is an unlucky day for removing horses or cattle. If a person started any work on a Saturday and if he did not finish on that day he would not finish for a long time. Wednesdays and Fridays are lucky days for tilling. Friday is a lucky day for removing furniture. Wednesday is a lucky day to sow potatoes.' Noone should pay out money on a Monday 'because they would be giving it away for the year'. There are many other marvels of balancing the here and now with eternity: the care of the feet, casting a spell, local legends, songs, prayers, superstitions, holy days.

Each school that took part wrote about the townland's saint and pattern day and blessed wells. St. Martin, St. Senan, St. Austin, St. MacCraven, and Colman and Caimin and Mogua and Iníne Bhaoith and Brigid.

9.12 and 9.13

The Care of the Feet

Years ago people wore no shoes. When they went to Mass, they would carry their shoes in their hands until they reached the Church. Then they would put them on and when they came out they would take them off again. It is right that a person should throw out the water used to wash their feet in because people say that if the water is kept inside they would have no luck.

All the people wear shoes nowadays. Children do not wear shoes in the Summer. They are a lot better off and lighter without them.

Now and again, the children get callouses from jumping on the stones. The cure is to put a kind of needle through it.

There were a lot more cobblers years ago than there are now. There is only one cobbler in this parish. He lives in Lisdoonvarna. People do not wear any shoes with wooden soles now but they used to wear them years ago. They were very good for walking on the rocks.

From a copybook in Scoil Aill Bhéil an Tulaigh in the parish of Ballyvaughan

There are about forty holy wells scattered throughout the Burren. Not many are regularly visited any more. But their locations and the cures they promise - for warts and feet, for delicate children, for toothache; stone chair for a backache cure, stone arch for headache and many, the great majority, for eyes - all attest to a faithful hope against elements and fate. Some have a very special mood about them; being nearby offers tranquillity which must always be part of any healing. And the water itself is a balm. In almost every instance, too, there is a family living nearby who have knowledge of the well and its powers, as if they were guardians of the place.

I have my favourites but the most extra-ordinary of all, to my mind, is the place linked to the mythical tale of the marvellous cow and the beds and tracks and bare patches she has left all over the fabulous stone heights of the Burren.
The cow was called Glas Ghaibhneach:

"To make a long story short", writes Maire Mac Neill: "the Smith, Lón Mac Liomhtha, had three arms and one leg on which, however, he could travel swiftly. He was the first smith to make edged weapons in Ireland. He had stolen the marvellous cow in Spain and brought her to Slieve na Glaise

9.14 Visiting the Iníne Baoith Well (wart cure) with Paddy Healy below Baur North

166

because it was both a natural fortress and fertile. Here his seven sons, one for each day in turn, herded the cow whose gift it was that she could fill any vessel into which she was milked. All went well until a cunning woman milked her into a sieve".

But this wickedness turned into a munificence for the cow's milk flowing through the sieve formed into seven streams and these became the Seven Streams of Taosca at Slievenaglasha, once a place of pilgrimage. The cure there is for diabetes on one Monday and two   Thursdays or two Mondays and one Thursday. Like many places in the Burren, it seems to be empty and bleak. But it is full of spirits. As Thomas Westropp discovered, a hundred years ago, when he and Dr. George Unthank Mac Namara pursued their enquiries, the story was still alive in the area. An old man told him: "the cow used to feed near the herd's house and over Cahill's mountain, where she could get plenty of water out of Reeskagh. And she went away and how do I know where? And there were no tidings".

"But", as Máire MacNeill wrote: "there are tidings for us. The Burren keeps secret treasure and the apparently forgotten can be recovered".

Acknowledgements
Special thanks for generous information and directions to:
Mary Moroney, Clare County Library; Ríonach Uí Ogáin, Department of Folklore, UCD; Teresa McCormack, Kilfenora; Rita Cutlar, Galway; Maccon and Finola McNamara, Corofin; Br. Seán McNamara, C.F.C.; Patrick Cullinan, Poundtown; Donal and Michael Murphy, Knockauns; Patrick McCormack, Glenquin; Tony Killeen, Kilnaboy; Professor M.E. Mitchell, UCG; Michael Curtis, Kilnaboy; P.J. Curtis, Kilnaboy; Paddy and Mary Healy, Baur; Tony O'Brien, Glensleade; Maura Lynch, Carron; Antoinette O'Brien and Gerry Kennedy, Heritage Centre, Corofin; John Keane, High Commons; Tomás O'Dea, Coisceím; John Keating, Commons South, Donncha O hEallaithe, Indreabhán - and to my aunts: Brigid Considine (96) and Anne Doolan, also my godmother, who is 92 on the day of publication. All errors are mine.

9.18 Well of the Holy Cross at Gleninagh (Tobar na Croiche Naofa).

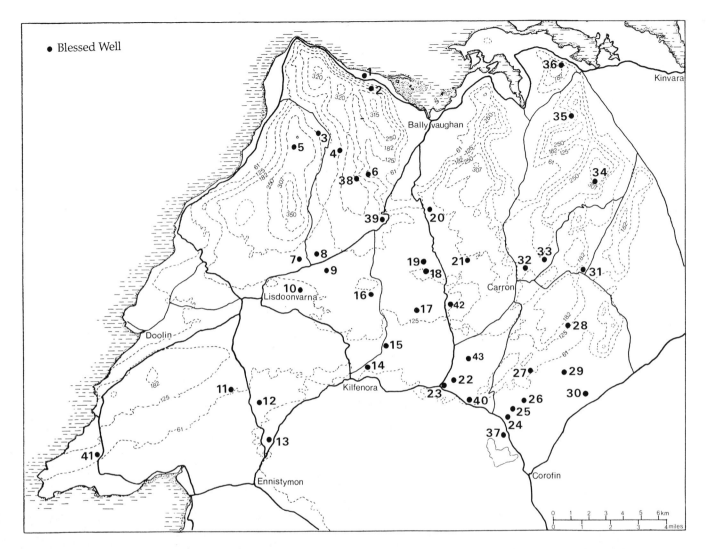

9.15 Blessed Wells in the Burren

1. Tobar na Croiche Naofa. Gleninagh.
2. Tobar Chornáin (Pinnacle Well). Gleninagh.
3. Tobar Bhran. Formoyle - Cahir River valley.
4. Tobar Lonáin. Derrynavahagh.
5. Tobar an tAlthar Calbach, also a well of St. Colanm (toothache and sore eyes). Faunarooska.
6. St. John's Well. Poulacapple.
7. Tobar Mhuadháin. Kilmoon.
8. Abhainn Tobar Leith. Cill O Éinne.
9. Tobar Cholmáin & arched stone. (headache cure)
10. St. Brendan's Well. Lisdoonvarna. (said to be for fertility in women)
11. St. Senan's Well. Kilshanny. (eyes)
12. St. Austin's Well. Kilshanny.
13. St. McCraven's Well. Celluragh. (eyes)
14. Tobar Chaimin. Kilfenora. (eyes)

15. Tobar Mogua. Noughaval.
16. Tobar an Spa. (headaches)
17. Tobar na nAingeal. Kilcorney. (eyes)
18. Tobar Iníne Bhaoith. Glensleade. (warts)
19. Tobar Cholmáin Bhaire. Glensleade. (eyes)
20. Gleninsheen. Two wells or bullauns (rock pools) for toothache.
21. Tobar Dearg. Eantymore. (dyeing & rheumatism)
22. Tobar Dubh, near Cahirfadda. Leamaneh. (dyeing and sore limbs & swellings)
23. Tobar Mhartáin. Opposite Leamaneh Castle. Saint's day, November 11 was traditionally a day "free from all wheel-work".
24. Tobar Mhaighdeáin. Kilnaboy. One of the many wells of Iníne Bhaoith. ("a daughter of the Royal line of Cormac Cas, of the Dalcassians" - White's History of Clare).
25. Tobar Iníne Bhaoith. Kilnaboy. (eyes & delicate children)
26. Tobar Iníne Bhaoith. Commons South. (See also 40, backache cure)
27. Seacht Srotha na Taosca. Seven Streams of Taosca. (diabetes)
28. Tobar na Glaise. Knockauns.
29. Bullaun Phádraic. Glan. (eyes)
30. Tobar Iníne Bhaoith. Ballard. (eyes)
31. Tobar Columchille. Glencolumcille. (eyes and feet)
32. Tobar Chronaín. Carron.
33. Tobar Fhachnan. Cosceím.
34. Tobar Cholmáin MacDuach. Slievecarran. (eyes, also cure for backache)
35. Tobar Cholmáin. Oughtmama. (eyes)
36. Tobar Phádraic. Abbey Hill.
37. St. Fleming's Well. Corofin. (eyes). Also blessed tree.
38. Glasgeivnagh Hill and Poulacapple. Marks and bed of Glas Geibhneach cow.
39. Marks of St. Brigid's knees. Corkscrew.
40. Suiochán Iníne Bhaoith. Roughan near Kilnaboy. (backache cure)
41. St. Brigid's Well. Liscannor.
42. St. Macreehey's Well. Poulacarran. (eyes)
43. Poll Insheen. Moygownan. (eyes)

9.16 Poll Insheen Wells. One of the two wells at Gleninsheen near Patrick Nolan's house (toothache cure).

169

257

Prayer to Saint Brigid.

[illegible] Ní Doċaiḋ a ċuireas flonnras ré ar comraic ċúirn féin ór léiṫí féin an oíḋċe anoċt Bríġid Ní Doċaḋ díon Inġean Aoḋa Ó Ṫúrafinn Fiaċra Mic Caisg Mic Cormaic Mic Ċairḃ Mic Ċaoin - gaċ oíḋċe dá gcuimhniġimíd ar flonnc Bríġde gan dearmad ní gontar sinn ní báiḋtear sinn, ní fágtar sinn ar dearmad. Ní dóġann teine na grian solais sinn, ní múċann uisce ná sáile sinn is linn féin buaḋ gaċ báire ó anoċt go bliaḋain ó anoċt agus anoċt féin. (Trí uaire oíḋċe Bríġde - [illegible]
An Paidir, Fáilte an Aingil, Cré na nAspal)

Told by:
Patrick Doolan.
Kilshanny.
Age 83

Written by:
Ellie Lysaght.
Kilshanny.

Prayer to St. Brigid in a Kilshanny School Notebook, collected by Ellie Lysaght from my grandfather, Pat Doolan, then 83 years of age. My Aunt, Brigid Considine, was a teacher at the school and still recites the prayer.

The first phrase is unclear but it then continues:

.........since tonight is her night, Brighid Ni Dochad, protected daughter of Aodh O Thurafinn Fiachra Mhic Caisg Mhic Cormaic Mhic Chairv Mhic Chaoin - every night that we remember without fail the family tree of Brighde we are not wounded, we are not drowned, we are not deserted. The fire of the sunlight does not burn us, the fresh water nor salt water does not extinguish us and ours is the victory in every contest from tonight until a year from tonight and tonight included. (Say this prayer three times on St. Brigid's night, the Angelus and the Apostles' Creed).

9.17 St. Austin's Well near Kilshanny, one of the loveliest settings for a well. The day for visiting is August 28th.

Photographs from the Schools' Collection and of Seán MacMathuna (9.2, 6, 7, 8, 9, 11, 12, 13, 19), courtesy of the Head of the Department of Irish Folklore, University College, Dublin.

Acknowledgements for illustrations

9.1   Drawing, A. Korff
9.3   Photograph, A. Korff
9.4   Lawrence Collection by Courtesy of the National Library of Ireland.
9.5   Photograph, A. Korff
9.10   Photograph, A. Korff
9.14   Photograph, A. Korff
9.15   Based on O.S. Map
9.16   Photograph, A. Korff
9.17   Drawing, A. Korff
9.18   Photograph, A. Korff
9.20   Photograph, A. Korff

9.20   Well of St. Colman MacDuach at Eagle's Rock, Slievecarran

1. *Shepherds shelter at Cragballyconoal. Photograph, A. Korff.*

The Shepherd's Folklore

Caoilte Breatnach

"South Galway and North Clare are the only hills in Ireland where sheep thrive best. First of all the hilly land is dry and grows short green sweet grass best suitable for cross bred sheep, - that is Cheviot mothers mated to a large Galway ram. The progeny are ideal, they love to travel and ascend the high hills like their grandmothers in Connemara. They are wild and cunning and go from one hill to another often tormenting and vexing their owners".

Michael Fallon of Gilroe, Tubber, Co. Clare whose above statement both summarises the suitability of the Burren landscape to sheep-farming and expresses the richness of the lore associated with this way of life, was one of the last of the old breed of shepherds at the time when he was recounting his way of life for the Irish Folklore commission in the late 1950's.

Species

In Michael Fallon's time, the species of sheep most popular in his area were the Galway ewe, Galway Cheviot (horny type), Border Leicester and Oxford Downs. The Galway ewe was

"the biggest ewe in the world carrying the heaviest weight and producing the heaviest fleece of wool, but very susceptible to disease. The Connemara horny cheviot is a small or I may say the smallest sheep in Ireland, yielding a very small grey fleece of excellent quality wool, and they are capable of producing twins or, as we say here, couples. The mutton of the Cheviot wether is the nicest and most delicate of all particular sheep".

Fairs

The Connemara sheep were bought from herdsmen who drove all their sheep together from the hills of Connemara to the fair, each man's flock being separated on arrival by dogs and men shouting commands in Irish. Of the many fairs held throughout his region in those days, Michael Fallon remarked that the greatest lamb fair was held at one time in Tubber. Buyers attended from Kerry, Limerick and Tipperary and most of them would know what kind of land the sheep were raised on, having dealt with their owners over the years. The fairs also kept the sheepfarmers in touch with each other, news was exchanged, anecdotes passed on and so forth. It was a common sight afterwards to see hundreds of lambs and sheep being walked the long journey home by drovers who would shear some of the sheep to lighten their burden, handing in their fleeces to houses along the way.

The biggest hogget fair was held in Kinvara and in Ballyvaughan the 'smallest mountain sheep' were on offer. In the Burren foothills, the Turloughmore sheep fair took place and was followed by the horse races a day later. Deal making was a complicated ritual, sometimes carried through with the help of an intermediary, who was also considered to bring luck to the buyer. Roger Nix was one of these. Porter, pigs crubeens (feet) and loaves of bread aptly called grinders were sold from tents where luck-money also changed hands, a custom which persists to this day, whereby the seller returns some money to the buyer for luck.

Shepherding

Patrick O'Connor of Bunahow, Crusheen, Co. Clare, a dog trainer who also herded 300 sheep in the Burren, remarked that a good dog was better than ten men for flocking sheep. In his day he trained all kinds of dogs, but the greyhound could not be trained, he said. Thomas O'Halloran of Crushoa, Kinvara, Co. Galway, herded sheep since he was ten years old. He knew 'the bleat of fear, the bleat when they are going roguing, the bleat prior to dropping, the bleat after and several other bleats known only to the shepherd'. The shepherds would arise at 6 a.m. and visit all expectant ewes, he said, and would give a 'peep' to the ewes with the lambs in the haggard.

"Then he eats his breakfast and after that attends to all the sheep, putting each individual lamb or lambs with their mother, and feeds them, then allows them off to pasture. During the day he gets a summons from some member of the household - one ewe impatient up there. The shepherd goes at once to the spot, he sees the ewe lying and rising now and then, scratching the ground with her right foremost foot, he says to himself 'too early' and 'leave very well alone'. He returns back and starts doing some other important work. But all the time he has his mind on the ewe".

Colman Coití O'Loughlin of Kinvara lived and shepherded in the Burren mountains at Carron.

"There was a lot of herding in Carron. I had no wage - 'freedom' was my wage. Two milk cows and a horse I had at first, I had permission to keep them on the land, and twelve sheep. - I had a few acres with the house. I had them for free, that was the kind of wage I had".

Quacks

Shepherds needed to recognise and respond to ailments fairly quickly and indeed some of them were expert sheep doctors or 'quacks'. It was said that there was no day that a sheep would not be sick, cured, or dead. The male fern, garlic and other plants had their uses. A form of temporary blindness was treated by applying nicotine 'juice' from the shepherds pipe to the affected spot. Copper wire was stitched like a shoe lace onto the sheeps body, so that the blue stone generating in the blood stream would kill the invading germ of Broxy. Thomas Comyns of Tubber would apply a plaster of tar and pitch to the spot above the ear where he had bored a hole with an auger on the head of the sheep suffering from 'head staggers'. Plasters of boiled potatoes, some lime and cow dung prepared in an old pot containing sour milk were also used. This was before the arrival of the veterinary profession, though the quacks assistance was still called for from time to time thereafter. As one farmer put it "when all fruit fails, welcome haws".

Martin Forde of Bunahow, Tubber, claimed that, apart from the carrion crow, the worst menace was the she-fox who carries home her prey to feed her young. In the mountainous regions of the Burren, stoats sometimes attacked sheep in their sleep, leaving the tell tale small punctured hole in the back of the dead sheep's ear. The 'marten cat' or pinemartin, at times would kill and carry away a lamb and the other nocturnal, the Badger, was blamed for decapitating the odd lamb, leaving the torso behind. However Forde said:

"In my time we were never opposed to badgers while minding sheep in Cregg demesne. I often saw 40 or 50 of them in the same field as the ewes and lambs. They would not touch the young lambs, they seem to be busy rooting for the bulbs of artichoke, worms, etc.".

During the lambing period, sheepfarmers would place a paraffin lamp in the field with the ewes. Sometimes a young dog was placed in a box near the sheep, in the hope that its constant barking throughout the night would deter any attacker.

Shepherds huts

Most shepherds learnt their trades from their fathers, some of whom had worked for land-owners such as Lord Gough and Frank Shaw Taylor, who owned thousands of acres and were well equipped with agents, labourers, herdsmen, stewards, fairsmen, drovers, milk-maids, servants and so on. Stewards rode from farm to farm on horseback and oversaw the regular transfer of sheep from one patch of ground to another in order to avoid disease. During the lambing season shepherds, some of whom were young teenagers, spent the night alone in makeshift tents, catching an hour or two of sleep while minding the flock. Shelter was also provided by timber frames over which a large haycock was built at harvest time. This 'hut' measured about 14' long x 6' wide x 4' high and housed sheep and shepherd during severe winter nights. Permanent structures containing no door nor windows were built at a corner of a big field on the bigger estates. They were thatched with wheaten straw, the angled inside walls were lined with oaten straw which was fastened with hazel rods. A straw mattress was also provided.

The shepherd's crook

The sheepcrook was once a common imple-ment, according to Michael Fallon. It was a 'tool' similar to that used by St. Patrick and was about 5 ft. long.

"When the shepherd wants to catch any individual sheep at maggot time, etc., he sticks the crook on her rear foot and pulls her to him. Then he can attend to her easily".
Michael Hanrahan, who was shepherding on a large estate, related the following story:

"One night in the month of February, I was sheltering in my hut. I had a big fire outside, the dog sleeping near the fire, then a strong breeze blew. The dog dashed into the hut, frothing and frightened, the hair stood straight up on his back, he saw something evil. I saw nothing. I made the sign of the cross with the sheep crook, then I lay on the crook - we believed by doing this, nothing evil could happen us".

Shearing and packing

When shearing time arrived in early May, the hand shears were used, a good man being able to shear 30 sheep in a day. Michael Fallon:

"Long ago before the Compulsory Education Act, it was a delight for young boys to be kept home from school, minding and keeping the sheep in their place, while father lets in a shorn one, and takes out another for the shears".
Each hour the shearers were handed a pint of porter as was the custom. Tar or pitch was used in branding afterwards and many lambs became instantly weaned because the smell of the tar and the absence of fleece on their mothers threw them into confusion.

Many farmers believed that wool would lose its weight when stored and consequently arranged for its immediate sale. One man did however remember seeing as a young boy a large pack of wool being suspended 6" above ground and hung between two trees, where it was stored unaffected by the elements for 12 months. The wool from the Galway ewe was believed to be the best and when this account was recorded it was still the custom to keep a black sheep, preferably a ewe, running with the flock in order to have a supply of black wool at home. If a member of the household had a headache, the father would apply a piece of the wool with a bandage to the sore spot. And with that anecdote I conclude this summary of the shepherds folklore.

Acknowledgements
We are grateful to Prof. Bo Almquist, Head of the Irish Folklore Dept., U.C.D., for permission to publish the relevant information contained in the Folklore Commission's archives. The source material for this article is contained in M.S. 1689 (p. 107-325) of the manuscript collection, Irish Folklore Dept., U.C.D., Dublin, and is being published by kind permission of the Head of the Irish Folklore Dept. We would also like to acknowledge the work of Joe Flanagan of Tubber who collected the material in the late 1950's.

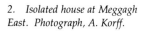

2. Isolated house at Meggagh East. Photograph, A. Korff.

10.1 *One of the many public-house traditional music sessions in the northern Burren*

The Bardic Connection
Traditional Music and Song in the Burren
Charlie Piggott

The footprints of an elder race are here,
And memories of an old heroic time;
And shadows of an old mysterious faith
So that the place seem haunted
And "strange sounds float in the wind".
(*Anon.*)

A Venerable Tradition

Why bardic? The story of traditional music and song of old Ireland is intricately and deeply connected with the ancient bardic orders and with the ageless holy chants and hymns. Indeed, it can be said that our fame in

177

10.2 *Horn-player on a grave-slab near the 12th century church at Noughaval. The site has many other interesting features including a stone market-cross pedestal, a special vault of the O'Davorens of the law school and a small ruined monastic settlement.*

10.3 *St. Colman's Bed on the southern cliff face of Slieve Carron in the Burren.*

music may, to a great extent, be credited to the bardic system. A folklorist studying singing styles on a global scale considers "Ireland to be part of the old Southern Mediterranean - Middle Eastern family of style called bardic....highly ornamented, free rhythmed solo or solo and string accompanied singing that supports sophisticated and elaborate verse forms"[1]. Our dance music can also be classified within this definition.

When we read bardic poetry we may imagine it being recited in much the same manner as poets deliver today. However, many of the bardic poets either sang or performed, using a kind of chanting recitation. The scholar Dr. Osborn Bergin further tells us that "a knowledge of one of the modern spoken dialects will give no idea of the rich and subtle music of the bardic poetry"[2].

One of the few direct cultural links we have with the past in the West of Ireland is traditional music and song. Like the Basques and Greeks within Europe, the Irish have a strong living tradition of music-making which has been performed unbroken since neolithic times and in the Burren area of North Clare the playing of this music is still alive and flourishing.

The "musical" boundary of the Burren includes the area enclosed by a line North of Doolin, through Lisdoonvarna and Kilfenora up to Kinvara.

Today these towns and villages (Ballyvaughan, Bell Harbour, Fanore and New Quay should be added) ring with traditional music in the form of public house "sessions", concerts and the occasional ceili. Although some of these places only skirt the Burren, in not too distant times, the music was played throughout the region at house dances and "cuirts", and in earlier centuries a strong tradition of bardic schools and the performance of ecclesiastical music existed.

During the 19th century music-making was very popular in the countryside and we are indebted to those hearty Irishmen and women of their time for creating and maintaining in circulation the thousands of jigs, reels, horn-pipes and airs that we have today. A certain family of Mahers, who lived near Bell Harbour in the heart of the Burren, had twenty-one children, all of whom played music! Neither did financial restraints block the way of this great love of music, as fiddles and flutes were home-made from materials as incongruous as old grease tins and discarded bicycle pumps respectively, which the children took to school in their satchels to practise and play at any opportune moment. Even families who had no musicians amongst their members passed on tunes from one generation to the next orally, a melody being learned from elders humming (called 'mouth music' or 'puss music') or whistling it. As in other regions, North Clare has a strong tradition of humming for dances in the absence of musicians or instruments.

Early Musical Instruments

In ancient times the dominant musical instrument in Ireland was the harp (according to the Brehon Laws the harpist was the only entertainer with independent legal status). But the horn, timpan (a dulcimer-like instrument), and bagpipes were in common use, as were two kinds of bells, either an open bell with a tongue, as used in churches, or a closed, pear shaped bell with a loose ball. The music of St. Enda's bell in the Aran Islands reputedly rang so loudly that it could be heard at Coleman's hermitage under Sliabh Carron in the Burren.

10.4 Johnny Doran (right) with Pat Cash and son. Johnny, together with his brother, Felix, travelled extensively in the Burren during the 1930's. Photo was taken in Green Lane, Terenure, Dublin in the '40's by John McCaffrey.

Right of Sanctuary

Outlaws in a place of stone
they left the road
and skirted hazel coverts,
climbed on rock and fed their eyes
on fern and Mountain Aven
softening the fissures.

The day was stolen from the world
and given to them. They tasted it
beside Sruthán na Naomh, listened
for the chant in Colmán's roofless
oratory, halting breath to hear
his breathing in the cave.

This must be how he knew it:
balm of secret meadow under Eagle's Rock
wind harping in hazels
and the mesh of men and laws
outlawed to the lowlands, rumoured
in the scripture of the stream.

By Michael Coady

Recently, replicas of unearthed examples of the timpan and horns have been fashioned and are once again in circulation within the tradition. Although no horns have so far been found in the Burren, four examples excavated in South Clare are of Bronze Age origin (1200-500 B.C.)[3]

A tradition of harp and pipe playing in the Burren region is well documented. An uilleann-pipe and flute making workshop run by Eugene Lambe is now in operation at Fanore. The legendary piper, Garret Barry played and travelled extensively in the area, as did his successor Willie Clancy of Milltown Malbay and, during the 1930's the Dorans (Johnny and his brother Felix), who were travelling pipers of incredible talent and were regular visitors to the villages of North Clare for races and fair days.

Movement of musicians throughout the countryside has always provided a basis for the exchange and survival of many tunes and airs. The popular East Galway musicians, Joe Cooley and Joe Leary, played and worked as tradesmen for many years around the Burren, leaving their stamp on many a bar-counter of the major hotels there. And John Kelly, the West Clare fiddler, once said he heard from the old people that many of the tunes played in Clare in these past centuries were introduced by migrant workers and itinerant craftsmen crossing the Shannon by ferry from the Sliabh Luachra region of East Kerry.

Later Musical Instruments

Today, traditional music is performed preferably on fiddle, flute, whistle, concertina and accordian, along with other instruments of more recent introduction.

The concertina, in particular, is popular in County Clare and the Burren region has its compliment of fine concertina players, among them Micilín Conlon, Paki Russell and Noel Hill of the Lisdoonvarna area, the Fahys and Droneys of Bell Harbour and the Corrucuns of Ballyvaughan. The reasons for the popularity

the introduction of the instrument into the county. The concertina music we hear in the Burren is very much unadorned, relying on rhythmic impulse for its effect, and this makes it particularly suited for set-dancing.

Fiddle, flute and accordian playing is also widespread in North Clare, where one can hear such great exponents as Tommy Peoples and Tony Linnane (fiddles), Bobby Gardner and Sharon Shannon (accordians) and the Clanceys and Hynes brothers from near Lisdoonvarna. Anthony Donaghue, a Fanore fiddler, having once constructed his own fiddle, played it and made the comment "Isn't

10.5 Well known South Burren concertina player, Noel Hill, from Corofin, Co. Clare.

10.6 A most colourful musical character who lives on the southern slopes of the Burren, Micilín Conlon is equally competent as accordian and concertina player.

of this instrument in the county are obscure but it would appear that they are grounded in the social system of the 19th century when concertinas appeared in great numbers. The contributory factors which may be cited are:

1. The fact that Limerick was a stopping point for trans-Atlantic trade in the 19th century.
2. The emergence of the hardware store as part of Irish trade, causing the expansion of retail of luxury goods.
3. The sending home of parcelled goods by emigrants, which often included a concertina.

Soldiers and sailors returning from the Napoleonic Wars in Europe also contributed to

10.7 *South Burren fiddler, Willie 'Beg' Shannon from Doolin.*

10.8 *The Bell Harbour Ceilí Band. From left: Joe Maher (fiddle); Cris Droney (accordian); Jack Daly (drums); Jim Droney (concertina) and Miko Linnane (pipe). Photograph was taken c. 1946.*

it grand the sound you get from horse hairs scraping on cat's gut"! The local style of fiddling has been described as "one of mood and sensitivity, through the use of the slightly plaintive long note and the light-hearted roll"[4].

Céilí Bands and Set-Dancing

Céilí bands, as we know them today, came into existence as a result of massive emigration into Britain in the post-famine years of the 19th century. At the southern gateway to the Burren one of Ireland's finest, "The Kilfenora", was established early in this century. Through this band an unbroken and unrivalled tradition has been carried on by such families as the Mulqueens, McCormicks, Linnanes, Lynches, Wards and Tierneys, consistently epitomising all that is best in the traditional music of the area - great fiery music, with a unique lift and rhythm. Other bands, including the Bell Harbour Céilí Band, flourished in the fifties and sixties in towns like Doolin and Lisdoonvarna and the Ballyvaughan Quartet (Martin Rabbit, concertina; Jim O'Kane, fiddle; Patrick Vaughan and Sean Neilan, concert flutes) were musically active in carrying on the tradition in the northern Burren, travelling from one house-dance to another by bicycle.

Set-dancing was a very popular activity at these house sessions and, although in form derived from the European quadrille (set-dance), it is still a vital part of the West and North West Clare tradition. Two favourite dances are "The Clare Set" and "The Caledonian Set" and the full-blooded 'battering' footwork with overall mastery of rhythm which can be witnessed at these dance gatherings must portray traditional dancing at its finest.

Bardic Connections

An interesting old bardic connection with the Burren region concerns a meeting, reputedly to have taken place at the residence of the 7th Century King Guaire near Kinvara, between the poet Marvan and the professors of the great Bardic Academy (led by the Chief Bard, Seanchan, son of Torpest) - a meeting at which Marvan revealed to the professors the origin of the poet's harp (the wind playing on the dried tendons of a stranded whale's skeleton) and how metre originated - the alternate beat of two hammers five times over on the smith's anvil (ti-tum, ti-tum, ti-tum, ti-tum, ti-tum). An example of this 'hammer-anvil' metre is found in the early poetic works of Chaucer in his "Canterbury Tales".

Livy has handed down a tale to us
About a knight surnamed Virginius....

10.9 *The Kilfenora Ceilí Band. This line up of 1957 shows, back row: Pat Madigan (double bass); Paddy Mullins (concert flute); Gerald O'Loughlin (drums); Jim McCormick (concert flute); Jerry Lynch (accordian). Front: P.J. Lynch (fiddle); Tom Eustace (fiddle); Gus Tierney (fiddle); Kitty Linnane (piano).*

Seldom any came but from remote parts to be at a distance from Relations and other acquaintances that might interrupt his study. It was necessary the place should be in the solitary of a garden, or within a sept or enclosure far out of the reach of any noise, which an intercourse of people would otherwise occasion.   (Cartoon drawn by Martin Turner.)

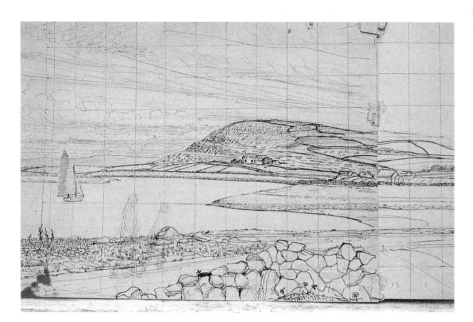

10.11 *View overlooking Bell Harbour near the O Dálaigh bardic school site. Drawing by Robert Gregory*

Wandering), the former being traditionally performed in the Burren to this day.

Eibhlín a Rúin

and the great love poet Robert Graves states that "Irish poetry is to English poetry, as the Pharasaic Synagogue is to the Christian Church: an antecedant which historians are tempted to forget or belittle"[5]. He further informs us that "the strongest element in English poetic technique (though certainly acquired at second or third hand) is the Irish tradition of craftsmanship"[6].

A bardic school in the Burren of which we have knowledge is the 15th Century O Dálaigh school at Finavarra. The foundation stones of the school can still be seen near the shore at Bell Harbour and the twin poets Cearbhall Mór and Donagh O Dálaigh are famed for their connection with this site[7]. Two folksongs associated with Cearbhall which survive in the Irish tradition are "Éibhlin, a Rúin" (Eileen, my love) and "Seachran Chearbhaill" (Cearbhall's

Local country people say that the song is the outpouring of the poet's passionate love for Eileen Kavanagh, the daughter of a Leinster chieftain who was to marry a kinsman of her father's choice. O Dálaigh arrived at the wedding disguised as a harper who was an uninvited guest and was not recognised, not even by Éibhlin herself, until, taking up his harp he broke into this devout love song: "Will you come or will you stay, Eileen my love". That evening the lovers escaped and were united. The composer, Handel, while staying in Dublin in 1743, on hearing the song commented that he would rather have been its author than of "all the music he had ever composed"[8].

184

Eibhlín, a Rúin

'Sheolfainn féin na gamhna leat,' Eibhlín, a rúin,
Sheolfainn féin na gamhna leat,' Eibhlín, a rúin,
Sheolfainn féin na gamhna leat, siar go Tír Amhlaidh leat,
Le súil go mbeinn i gleamhnas leat,' Eibhlín, a rúin.

'Sheolfainn féin bó leat-sa,' Eibhlín, a rúin,
Sheolfainn féin dhá bhó leat-sa,' Eibhlín, a rúin,
Do shiúlóchainn an saoghal mór leat, acht cleamhnas d'fháil óm shearc,
'S ní scarfainn go deo, deo leat,' Eibhlín, a rúin.

'An dtiocfaidh tú nó'n bhfanfaidh tú,' Eibhlín, a rúin,
'An dtiocfaidh tú nó'n bhfanfaidh tú,' Eibhlín, a rúin,
'Tiocfaidh mé 's ní fhanfaidh mé, tiocfaidh mé 's ní fhanfaidh mé,
Tiocfaidh mé 's ní fhanfaidh mé, 's éalóchaidh mé lem stór.'

'Céad míle fáilte romhat,' Eibhlín, a rúin,
Céad míle fáilte romhat,' Eibhlín, a rúin,
Céad míle fáilte romhat, fáilte is fiche romhat,
Naio gcéad míle fáilte romhat,' Eibhlín, a rúin.'

'I myself would drive the calves with you, Eileen, my love,
I myself would drive the calves with you, Eileen, my love,
I myself would drive the calves with you, back to Tirawley (Co. Mayo) with you,
In the hope that I would go into marriage with you, Eileen, my love.

'I myself would drive a cow with you, Eileen, my love,
I myself would drive two cows with you, Eileen, my love,
I would travel the great world with you, only to obtain marriage from my beloved,
And I would never separate from you, Eileen, my love.

'Will you come or will you stay, Eileen, my love,
Will you come or will you stay, Eileen, my love,'
'I will come and I will not stay, I will come and I will not stay,
I will come and I will not stay, and I will elope with my love.'

'One hundred thousand welcomes to you, Eileen my love,
One hundred thousand welcomes to you, Eileen my love,
One hundred thousand welcomes to you, one-and-twenty welcomes to you,
Nine hundred thousand welcomes to you, Eileen my love.'

Whereas "Éibhlin, a Rúin" contains poetic narrative, the other song we have from the O Dálaigh school, "Cearbhall's Wandering", consists of alternate verse and prose passages. One story we have is that Cearbhall was captured having eloped with Eileen Kavanagh and was taken before a judge. To show his talents he composed a story with each hand performing the prose and verse at the same time, again pouring out his love for her. This song forms part of the repertoire of the famed sean-nós singer, the late Seosamh O hÉanai. Here are the opening pieces of verse and prose from the song translated from the Irish:

*I spent a while looking at the queenly woman,
And she was a white-toothed and yello-haired maiden;
It would not seem a long while to me to look at her yellow hair
Or to beguile her until morning, although it is foolish to say it.*

And how more foolish is it for me to say that than for Fionn son of Cumhall, grandson of Tréanmhor, descendent of Baoiscne, to come on the mound, on the earth in pleasure, and to the Red Branch, listening to the cry of a beagle and to the howl of puppies, to the deeds of violent men and to the foolishness of little men, or, to Aogan son of Aogan, the first warrior who ever came to Ireland, making the three leaps of Brice Blaighe rather than be drowned and destroyed for the love of a woman from the Eastern world!

10.13 Eibhlín a Rúin by the bardic poet, Cearbhall O Dálaigh. The Irish welcome 'céad míle fáilte' has been taken from the concluding stanza of the song. The answer to the question whether Eibhlín eventually married Cearbhall or the chieftain prince has been lost in folklore. Mrs Daly of Bell Harbour however relates that the knowledge will be revealed to those who visit the Cistercian Abbey at Corcomroe at 12.00 pm on Christmas Eve (the supposed night of the wedding) when the feast day falls on a Saturday!

Another beautiful bardic poem by the Clare poet Aodh Bui MacCruitin (c. 1750) praises the ship of O'Loughlin of Burren, one of the great ruling families of the area. The poem contains some remarkable metaphors, speaking of the sea being aflame as the boat's keel inflicts its sharp wound on its surface - "An bhóchna ar lasadh mar ghearrag a cile creacht":

Beannaigh an barc bláthshruite béalchumtha,
Beannaigh an áirc, arrachtach éisiomdha,
Beannaigh an sál shnaimhteas, a Dhe dhúilimh,
Is gach calaithe, an tráth threactfas, i bhféichiúine....
(O bless the beautifully crafted shapely bowed ship
Bless this fine strong unique ark
Bless its stern as it floats, O God Creator
And every harbour into which it punctually sails)

10.14 Miko Russell (left) whistle playing at a session while under critical scrutiny by North Clare singer, Pat Keane (right).

Folksong in the Burren

Not far from the O Dálaigh bardic school site, on the Aughinish penninsula, one can listen to the singing of Pat Keane. A traditional North Clare singer with a unique repertoire, Pat learned most of his songs from older singers in the region, included among them "The Jacket of Blue" and "The Kerryman's Rambles to Tipperary". In constant touch with the un-shakeable spirit of Old Ireland, this mighty veteran at the ripe age of eight-seven still sips the elixier of life most nights of the week, springs to the floor when the occasion for a half-set lends itself and does not wait to be asked a second time when invited to "spake a verse of a song". "I wasn't born on a calm night" Pat will tell you, an expression he uses to demonstrate his wild rebel spirit and reckons that anyone who cannot sing, dance or play an instrument must have been born on a calm night. I have often asked him to sing a verse in a crowded bar to hear him exclaim that he would want "the jaws of a jack-ass" to rise above the noise!

At the other extremity of the Burren lives Miko Russell, another fine traditional singer and instrumentalist. Together with brothers Paki, who played concertina, and Gussie, playing flute, they comprise members of a family renowned for renditions of the 'Old Music'. His youth was spent absorbing the music of concertina players like Patrick Flannigan and Jack Donaghue, being deeply influenced by his mother who also played concertina.

In the true nature of the musical tradition, instrumentalists rarely resort to written sheet music but inherit the tunes "by ear", Miko being no exception to this rule. The folk music collector, Breandán Breathnach comments that his contribution to existing collections exceeds the century and on his style notes that "his skill in weaving the phrases together and an endearing variety of rhythmical ornamentation combine to make Miko a player of whom one never tires of hearing"[9]. A great favourite of his is the uplifting reel, The Limestone Rock.

Many of Miko's songs ("The Poor Little Fisherboy" and "The Well of Spring Water" etc.) were collected from old-timers in the Ballyvaughan region. A song I came across while visiting that area sings the praises of the valley at Fermoyle which cradles the only overground river (Abhainn na Cathrach) in the Burren.

The Vale of Fermoyle
There's a deep rugged valley away down in North Clare
To which the easiest access is by far from the air
Where the foxes and badgers do amble in style
On the high towering crags o'er the Vale of Fermoyle

If you could be there on a dark winter's night
To see those high towering crags by the lightning made bright
Or to pass by the roadside and hear the turmoil
Of the deep winding waters flowing down thro' Fermoyle

10.16 The Vale of Fermoyle. Written by Jack Carley in praise of the Fermoyle Valley. This song was collected from Mrs. J. Linnane, Caherbullog (1981) by the piper, Eugene Lambe.

"The Limestone Rock"

There stands the ruins of three churches renowned
Where our forefathers worshipped when faith was
kept down
When Cromwells fierce roundheads did plunder our
Isle
The good priests said mass on the Vale of Fermoyle

Of charms and beauty they are there galore
From Coiltemaoilean to the sea bitten shore
Where the Atlantic rolls in from the famed Aran
Isles
To meet the bright waters flowing down thro'
Fermoyle

It's residents are happy 'tis plain to be seen
They love their old homesteads they'd die for the
green
They neither play golf there or go in Exile
But live quite contented in the Vale of   Fer-
moyle

I was there once myself and a home I could make
But Fate so decreed that the road I should take
I could live my life long there and die with a smile
All I ask is a grave in the Vale of Fermoyle

So now that I'm gone and forgetfulness seek
I'll ream thro' this world existence to eek
Though hard be my lot and rough be the toil
O I'll never forget you Sweet Vale of Fermoyle

10.17 Folksong in the Burren. Summery of titles presented by Tom Munnelly to the Clare Archeological and Historical Society conference on "The Burren and it's People", Ennis, May 7th, 1988.

A lecture delivered by the collector, Tom Munnelly, to the Clare Archaeological and Historical Society (1988) gave some interesting findings of folksong in the Burren[10]. The "Mairnealaigh Loinge" taken from Katie

Droney seems to have been a popular song in the area and Miko Russell can be heard performing it today.

Another poet-songwriter, Francis A. Fahy (1854-1935) of Kinvara composed such well known songs as "Galway Bay", "The Auld Plaid Shawl" and "The Queen of Connemara", and the present day singer-songwriter, Sean Tyrrell, who has lived in the Burren for a number of years, is actively engaged in setting to music much of the obscure and forgotten earlier Irish poetry including the work of the Co. Meath poet, John Boyle O'Reilly (1844-1890).

Song Title	Singer and year of recording
Is Moch, Moch ar Maidin Mairnéalaigh	Miko Russell, Doolin (1987)
Loinge Bruach na Carrige Báine	Katie Droney, Fanore (1972)
	Paddy Killoughrey (Torpey) (1960)
Fair Margaret and Sweet William	Martin Howley, Fanore (1975)
The Ride in the Creel	Joe Connely, Kilshanny (1972)
The Golden Glove	Katie Droney, Fanore (1972)
The Cattle Drive	Mikey 'Straighty' Flanagan, Inagh (1976)

Names of Tunes

Names of tunes are a very interesting subject in traditional music, many of them being grounded in the poetic language of the countryside: "The Pigeon on the Gate", "The Hare in the Corn" and "The Mouse Trap", the latter tunes, according to concertina player, Cris Droney, being great favourites of the Maher family of Bell Harbour. We also find that a grand diversity of names and versions exist within tunes.

Very often an interesting anecdote or fine story is associated with the name of a tune, e.g. "The Tipsy Miller". This old slip jig (sometimes called "The Dusty Miller") was called for by the Corcomroe poet Cearbhall, but which the piper did not know. "Well, if it be your will, let me play it on your pipes" and Cearbhall played it and danced it with O(E,´)ibhlin, his lady love, at the same time. This tune is now a great favourite among Uilleann pipers.

The names of many tunes have associations with local places in the Burren, e.g. "Maire Rua" (called after Maire Rua O'Brien, the famed lady of Leamaneh Castle), "The Road to Lisdoonvarna", "Port Ceann Boirne" (e.g. Black Head, this jig being often called "The Cliffs of Moher") and "The Bell Harbour Reel". An old Kilfenora set of tunes include "The Kilrush Races", "The Dublin Reel" and "The Burren Reel".

Conclusion

A sense of environment is of paramount importance for the survival of traditional singing and musicianship and the majestic Burren hills provide a haven for these contemplative activities. P.J. Curtis, a Kilnaboy broadcaster and musician once wrote that "generations of North Clare musicians have listened with their inner ears, interpreting the 'strange floating sounds' (of the Burren) with open hearts - our lives are richer because of them"[11].

May they long continue to do so.

"The Road to Lisdoonvarna"

10.18 Musician and instrument-maker, Gary O'Brien, at the only fiddle-making workshop in the Burren, near New Quay, Co. Clare.

10.19 Eugene Lambe at his workshop in Fanore. His piping was greatly influenced by the playing of Tommie Reck and Seamus Ennis while his pipe making follows in the tradition of Matt Kiernan and Dan O'Dowd. One of his favourite tunes, "The Trip to Fanore" was composed by south Clareman, Paddy Donaghue while on a visit to Fanore.

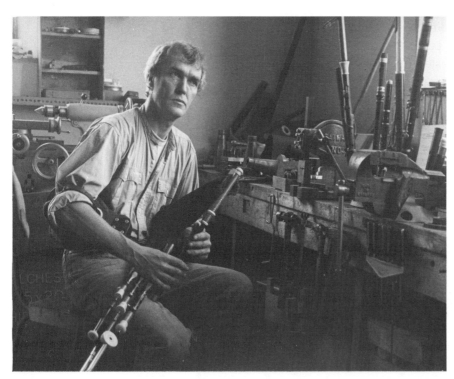

Acknowledgements for illustrations

10.1.   Photograph, Thomas Quinn
10.2.   Drawing, Charlie Piggott
10.3.   Photograph, Anne Korff
10.4   Photograph, Courtesy of Na Píobairí Uilleann
10.5   Photograph, Courtesy of Na Píobairí Uilleann
10.6   Photograph, Ilsa Thielen
10.7   Photograph, Ilsa Thielen
10.8   Photograph, Courtesy of Cris Droney
10.9   Photograph, Courtesy of Kitty Linnane
10.18 Photograph, Frank Miller
10.14 Photograph, Ilsa Thielen
10.19 Photograph, Ilsa Thielen
          Poem by kind permission of Michael Coady

The Artist's Eye

Anne Korff

To the eye of the 18th century landscape painter, the Burren had little to offer. Artistic fashion demanded the Italianate scenery of Killarney, Kilkenny or Upper Lough Erne. Not until the mid-19th century do we find visual record of the region.

In 1837, the Great Topographical Survey of Ireland was commissioned. This project was to provide not just a topographical record but an archive of the antiquities and National Monuments of the country. The Ordnance office, which undertook the Survey, employed George Petrie as draughtsman. He was joined by William Wakeman and George de Noyer in making the visual record. Fortunately these people were also fine artists and members of a coterie which included such people as Lady Gregory and W.F. Burton, the only artist mentioned who was actually from the Burren region, having been born in Corofin in 1816. Some fine drawings and watercolours of the region survive from this fusion.

In recent years the Burren has been the subject of such artists as Robert Gregory, Derek Hill, Barrie Cook and many others and today the surrounding region has become the adoptive home of many painters, sculptors, craftspeople and others who find in the region the ambiance for creativity which had lain fallow for so long.

George Petrie (1789-1866)
"Pilgrims at St., Brigid's Well, Liscannor".
Watercolour

George Petrie was the son of a Dublin Portrait painter. He had academic success at an early age and was the colleague and friend of some of the finest landscape painters of his time. He travelled extensively through Ireland and Wales, providing engravings for books and journals. He was a keen antiquarian and in 1833 took over the antiquities section of the Topographical Survey of Ireland.
He was the first watercolourist to be awarded full membership of the Royal Academy.

Frederic W. Burton (1816 - 1900)
"Galway Bay, Co. Galway".
Watercolour

Frederic William Burton was born to a landowning family at Corofin, Co. Clare. Like his
friend, George Petrie, his principal medium was
watercolour. He shared Petrie's interest in Irish
Antiquities and love of the Irish Landscape.

Nathaniel Hone (1831 - 1917).
"The Cliffs of Moher, Co. Clare".
Watercolour

Nathaniel Hone was a member of the family
which included Nathaniel Hone (1718 - 1784)
and the celebrated stained glass artist, Evie
Hone. He read engineering at T.C.D. and practised engineering briefly before going to study
painting in Paris in 1853. He travelled widely
on the Continent and returned to Ireland in
1872. In 1894 he was appointed Professor of
Painting at the R.H.A.

View from Turlough Hill Fort near Oughtmania Co Clare May 8 1906
Published RSAI XXXV.

Thomas J. Westropp (1860 - 1922)
"View from Turlough Hill Fort".
Watercolour, 16 cm x 21 cm.

Although better known for his pioneering work as an antiquarian/archaeologist, Thomas J. Westropp was an amateur artist of considerable skill and sensitivity. His watercolours, together with hundreds of drawings and sketches, are found alongside his antiquarian researches and notes in the notebooks he carried with him while he travelled through the Burren. In several cases it is possible to trace the origins of what later became finished works in the initial sketches he made while he was visiting various sites. Westropp probably never saw himself as an artist. But, like many other people of his class and time, he no doubt received basic instruction in certain artistic techniques. While much of his artistic work had a practical motivation, it is obvious that he possessed a keen eye for depicting the dramatic landscape of the Burren, as is evident in the watercolour here reproduced. It is probably also a reflection of his precision as a careful observer that his artistic work is remarkably free of any tendency to "romanticise" what he saw.

1

Robert Gregory (1881 - 1918)
1. "Bellharbour", Oil on canvas, 65 cm x 90 cm.
2. No title, Watercolour
3. No title, Watercolour
4. No title, Oil on canvas

Although better remembered as the subject of W.B. Yeat's poem "An Irish Airman Forsees His Death", Robert, the only son of Lady Augusta Gregory was an accomplished por-

traitist, landscape painter, set designer and photo-grapher. He studied at the Slade School in London and in Paris. While at the Slade he met his wife-to-be, Lily Margaret Graham Parry and together they spent many painting sojourns at Coole Park, his mother's house near Gort, and at Mount Vernon, his summer house on the Finavarra peninsula of the Burren. His paintings of this district show a poetic perception of this unique landscape

2

3

with its subtle shades of colour and ever-changing light.

During the early days of the Abbey Theatre he designed and painted sets for productions by such playrights as W.B. Yeats, Douglas Hyde, J.M. Synge and his own mother, Lady Gregory.

The selection of work published here shows the reader the quality of this under appreciated artist's work.

Lily Margaret Gregory (nee Graham Parry)
(1884-1979)
No title, Oil on canvas, 60 cm x 80 cm.

Derek Hill (b. 1916)
"The green road at Mullaghmore", 1978.
Oil on canvas, 20 cm x 46 cm.
(Private Collection)

Derek Hill was born in Southampton in 1916. Though now internationally recognised as a portrait artist, his early interest was in theatre design, which he studied in Munich, Paris, Vienna and Moscow. While living in Paris in 1938, he gradually abandoned stage design and turned to painting. In 1939 he returned to England and continued painting, holding many exhibitions.

In 1946 he came to the west of Ireland, painting in Galway, Mayo and Achill Island. During the following years he travelled and painted extensively and in 1954 bought a house in Donegal, where he now spends most of his time.

Barrie Cooke (b. 1931)
"Winter Knot", 1982
Oil on canvas, 150 cm x 245 cm.
(Collection of Stokes, Kennedy, Crowley & Co.)

Barrie Cooke was born in Cheshire, England, to an English father and an American mother. The family moved to the United States in 1947 and Barrie studied Art History at Harvard University. In 1954 he came to live at Kilnaboy in the heart of the Burren where he painted extensively for a number of years. His work is steeped in nature and his vision of the landscape is dynamic, restless and fluid. He constantly looks beyond surface appearances for the patterns in apparent chaos, lending his paintings and sculptures a rare breadth and thoughtfulness.

Anne Madden
"Mountain Structure", 1964
Watercolour and pigment on paper, 50 cm x 65 cm.

Anne Madden was born in Chile where she spent her first four years until her parents moved back to England. A naturally rebellious nature led her to an early passion for horse-riding and life outdoors, and she spent much of her teens on horseback in the Burren, which became for her a kind of spiritual home. Her father was killed in a car crash when she was 14, the first of several tragic deaths of those close to her, losses that have substantially shaped her tragic view of art and life, and have sharpened her realisation of the high stakes involved in art. In the 1950s she spent three years recovering from a spinal injury and during this time she met the painter, Louis le Brocquy, who she married in 1958. Since then they have divided their time between Ireland and the south of France. Madden works in large series of paintings, including the rocky landscapes of the 1960s and the Elegies and Megaliths of the 1970s, both largely inspired by her memories of the Burren.

Brian Bourke (b. 1936)
"The Tree".
Oil on paper, 76 cm x 56 cm.

Brian Bourke was born in Dublin. He has lived for periods in London, Germany and Switzerland and, in Ireland, in Connemara, Kilkenny and Co. Clare. He is now based near Moycullen in Co. Galway. He is a landscape and figure artist of the old mould, applying himself to these enduring themes with verve, wit and intelligence. His Burren landscapes are typical of his output, with their lightness of touch and colour, his liking for following a region throughout the seasons and his technical ease. Bourke, acutely sensitive to the drama of landscape, is completely at home in the West, with its big, restless skies and its ever-changing light.

Catriona O'Connor (b. 1945)
Atlantean Series, "Hostage", 1990
Acrylic on canvas, 86 cm x 76 cm.

Born in Killarney, Catriona O'Connor studied art in Dublin, Florence and Urbino. She has exhibited widely in Ireland and on the Continent and at present lives and works in Bunratty, Co. Clare. Commenting on her Milan exhibition "A coming to terms", Samuel Walsh wrote: "O'Connor's paintings of the Burren are cold to the bone and are correctly atlantean in feeling. The greys, browns and blues evoke an atmosphere only present in Ireland; the meeting of northern and southern worlds through the European Irish eye".

Joseph Quilty (b. 1914)
"Marhy Land".
Oil on paper, 32 cm x 32 cm.

Born in Limerick, Joseph Quilty emigrated to England with his family when he was a young man. There he studied at Arthur Segal's School of Painting and later under Gerard Dillon and Walter Messler. Much of his work is inspired by the strange, sad, beautiful Burren region.

Hugh McCormick (b. 1943)
"The Burren"
Oil on canvas, 168 cm x 122 cm.

Hugh McCormick was born in Dublin. He
graduated from Belfast College of Art and
Hornsey College of Art (London) in 1965.
Initially an abstract painter, he has returned to
more image based work which is thematic in
approach. Over the years such themes as
docks, water, musicians, the urban environment and the nude have formed these themes,
but he is primarily a landscape painter. In 1975
he first visited the Burren and that area, while
forming the basis for one major exhibition, has
been a recurring subject in his work. Being an
expressionist painter, the Burren had an immediate attraction for him with its "organised
chaos". For McCormick, the Burren is not a
bleak, ravaged and grey place but an area with
which he has an immediate affinity. To him it
is vibrant, mystical and romantic and allows
him to explore his own attitudes and feelings
with strong colour and free brush strokes.

Manus Walsh (b. 1940)
"Out of the Burren"
Oil on board, 60 cm x 60 cm.

Manus Walsh loves music in all its shapes and forms and loves the Burren in all its moods and lights. He incorporates the rhythms and colours of both into his paintings. There is an energy and excitement in his work which permeates even the night time stillness of the Burren. Manus uses many different media; collage, oils, watercolours and sometimes glass. He designed fine windows for Galway Cathedral. He lives and works at Bally-vaughan, Co. Clare.

Anne Korff (b. 1944)
"The Pooka's Defence", 1987
Acrylic on canvas, 90 cm x 90 cm.

Anne Korff was born in Germany and studied Fine Art and Graphic Design, in Berlin. Her professional career in Germany included design work for films, publishers and government departments.
She came to live in Ireland in 1977 and worked freelance with various agencies.
Anne Korff moved to Kinvara, Co. Galway in 1982 and continued to work freelance. She grew vegetables (organically, of course!) and explored and painted in the Burren region. In 1985 with Jeff O'Connell she produced "Kinvara, A Ramblers Map and Guide" which led to the production of five further Guides and Maps covering the Burren region and South Galway. In 1988 she co-founded Tír Eolas with Jeff O'Connell.

Carl Vetter (b. 1949)
Photographs, 1981

Carl Vetter was born in Weimar Germany. In 1967 he moved to Hamburg where he studied Art. In 1979 he was awarded a one year scholarship to Ireland which he spent at Aughinish, Co. Clare. Since then he has been a regular visitor to the Burren.

Carl Vetter's aim is to become part of the natural environment, to work together with nature, not against it, reacting by using the natural materials, different single pieces forming a unit. The pieces shown in the photographs are all in the townland of Poulcoin.

Thomas Quinn
Photograph

Thomas Quinn is a native of Kinvara. He attended Limerick School of Art and Design where he studied painting and photography graduating in 1978 with a diploma in Fine Art.

Acknowledgements
I wish to thank Thomas Quinn, Geraldine Quinn, Aidan Dunne, Colin Smythe and Séamus O'Reilly in helping me to show "The Artist's Eye".

12.1 *"Sancta Maria de Petra fertile", Corcomroe Abbey, drawing by T. J. Westropp. Courtesy of the Royal Irish Academy.*

The Fertile Rock: The Burren as Desert

Patrick Sheeran

In 1986 the Australian artist Sir Sidney Nolan presented fifty of his paintings to the Irish people. It was a gesture of commemoration and celebration - his mother's people came from Galway, his father's from Clare. To complete the act of filial and geo- piety he announced his intention to paint the orchids of the Burren just as he had earlier painted the desert flowers of the Australian outback. Echoes and associations were as important as the place and its flora. For him the Burren and Australia were antipodes. They roused the same apprehension of being "on the edge of the world". "The people sent out from Clare", he surmised, "went from one edge of the world to the other edge of the world. I sometimes wonder if built into me there's a funny kind of memory of this edge to edge. Maybe the Burren is just the other edge, the polar oppo- site of the edge I was born into"[1].

Sir Sidney's sense of the Burren as a terminus and his annexation of North West Clare to a far off desert is not unprecedented. Other men in other times thought of "the rocky place" in equally exotic terms - as cognate with the wildernesses of Sinai, the Thebiad and Palestine. Indeed all through the written record, from a mysterious entry in the Dindsenchas (9 - 12 C.) to John Ennis's picaresque poem The Burren Days (1985) the region has been imaged as a remote limen, a refuge and a wilderness.2 Beyond the facts of geographical location and topography it has been constituted, in a variety of discourses, as a desert. What are the sources of this image? What are its variants? Is it a serviceable way of apprehending the place today?

Central to the Burren-as-desert is a paradox. The apparent contradiction is most powerfully compressed in the dedication of the Cistercian monastery of Corcomroe to Sancta Maria de Petra Fertilis, to, in a tensile phrase, Holy Mary of the Fertile Rock. Our task is to unpack that paradox of fertility and barrenness.

I

There are literal, palpable ways (geological, ecological, botanical and habitational) in which the Burren may be seen as both barren and fertile. Most obvious is the contrast between the naked karst of the uplands and the verdure of valleys rich in glacial drift. The bleak physiognomy of the hills and their shattered rock surfaces have all too often invited the epithet "lunar" and - more promisingly - a comparison with "the stricken hills of Judea". Bleakness, however, is an impression created by distance. Up close, the recesses of the pavements are dense with rank grass and hazel scrub. Closer still and the pewter-grey

cicatrices in the hide of limestone show themselves crammed with vegetation. It is these teeming clefts and crannies that have inspired that other common epithet for the Burren: it is a "rock garden". The collocation of desert and garden, as we shall see, has a venerable precedent.

For the pastoralist no more fertile rock than the Burren could be imagined. Not only is fodder abundant but cattle can graze on the hills all the year round. Elsewhere in Ireland the herds were driven to mountain pasture in Spring in accordance with the normal transhumance practice. In the Burren, as befits its contrary nature, they were moved to the uplands for the Winter. Part of the explanation lies in the way in which the exposed tabular limestone acts as a huge storage heater, soaking up warmth in summer and slowly emitting it in winter. Hence the growing season is much longer here than elsewhere and the herbage is extraordinarily rich in calcium. The Burren, despite its inhospitable appearance, is, in many respects, a cattleman's dream.

This is but one conspicuous example of the combination of fertility and barrenness on the Burren. The question arises then: does the dedication of Corcomroe Abbey to Mary of the Fertile Rock allude, graciously if simply, to the surrounding locality and its most salient feature? Or is there more to the dedication? Is the "fertile rock" perhaps less a description and more a symbol?

There is some evidence to support the latter contention. Wherever Cistercian monks built an abbey they were accustomed to give the location a new name to signify a new birth. Thus in 1115 an early colony from the mother house of Citeaux changed the name of the Valley of Wormwood in the French diocese of Langres to Clairvaux (Clara Vallis), the Valley of Light. The Fertile Rock was itself the great-grandaughter of Mellifont (Fons Mellis, the Fountain of Honey) in Co. Louth. Perhaps the title of Corcomroe Abbey also reveals a meta-physical rather than a naturalistic reading of place?

The very distinction between the physical and metaphysical is unwarranted in this case. In a traditional society, such as that of medieval Christendom, the natural was not yet fully divorced from the supernatural just as nothing was made for use that had not also a mean ("The needs of the body and the spirit were satisfied together"). The Burren could function both as a habitat for herdsmen and a support for contemplation. More, the whole region could be thought of as not merely a geographic entity but a sacred place with a special vocation. In naming their abbey the fertile rock the Cistercians were alluding to a long established way of reading these penitential-paradisiacal hills.

12.2 "Bóthar na Mias" at Keelhilla. Photo, T. Quinn.

We discover the Burren code in the bits and pieces of hagiography accumulated around Colman mac Duach, the 7th century saint whose name, as Lady Gregory noted, is every-where in the region. He was the first, so far as one can tell, to render this place "susceptible to the presence of heaven" and to place the Burren under the law of quality.[3] That law states that, for the believer, the more energy one draws from a sacred place or relic, the more it becomes capable of bestowing. The rocks metaphorically break into flower and their efflorescence is a symbol of spiritual favour. (The law of quantity, on the other hand, posits an inverse relation between energy deposited and energy consumed. Rocks, in our ordinary, everyday secular experience, are rarely fertile.)

II

S. Colman ma Duach belonged to the Third Order of Irish saints, to those qui in locis desertis habitabant et oleribus et aqua et eleemosynis uiuebant - "who lived in deserts and lived on herbs, water and alms". He spent some years on Inishmore but the island, it seems, was too populous and not sufficiently remote for the holy man. He sought a still deeper solitude in which to practice his austeri-ties and hence, sometime in the last decade of the sixth century, he entered the dítrub ("unin-habited place") of the Burren."
Colman chose as the location of his cell a place which was furnished with all the natural symbols for which a hermit anywhere from Mount Nitria to Mount Meru might wish. There was a high escarpment ("Cinn Aille"), a spring well, a cave, and a thicket of oak and hazel.

That Colman went into a hermitage in Boirenn of Connaught
and a single young cleric with him. In the time of Guaire
of Aidne they went. A pot and an axe they had. For seven
years they were in the hermitage without nourish-ment
of food from anyone, without converse with other human
beings. They had a church and a refectory in the forest.
The raiment they wore was the skin of deer. Cress and water
and the herbage of the forest was what they used to consume
during that time.[4]

12.3 *Section of stained glass window at Tirneevin Church by George Walsh, 1975. Photo, A. Korff.*

In a version of the saint's legend recorded by Keating, Colman is accompanied in his desert solitaire, not by a young cleric, but by a cock, a mouse and a fly. The cock wakes him for matins, the mouse scratches his ears if he sleeps more than five hours in twenty-four and the fly marches along the lines of his psalter to keep the hermit's attention rivetted to the text.[5]

Colman's best known miracle irresistibly calls to mind the apports and prodigies effected by the contemporary Hindu holy man, Satya Sai Baba.[6] Having observed the forty days of the Lenten fast and celebrated the Mass of Easter morning the hermit and his steward sat down to a very modest meal. At the same time King Guaire and his retainers in Durlus were about to feast from the "Cauldron of Guaire" which contained a roast pig and a bull-calf. "'Well then', says Guaire, 'I should be grateful to Christ if there was some friend of God who would like this to help him, or who would consume it, for I shall get the equivalent again.'" (Guaire, too, observed the Law of Quality). With that, the cauldron rose from the table and, escorted by two angels, headed west over the crags until it stopped in front of Colman's hermitage

'Well', said the clerk, 'here is the reward of thy abstinence; eat therefore what God has sent thee.'
'Not so', said he, 'until we know from whom it has come;'
and then looking at the bowl, he said:

'O little bowl,
What brought thee over Luaine?'

(That is, over the wood, viz. Luaine is the name of the wood.)
'The prayer thou makest for it', said the angel, 'has
brought it and the liberality of Guaire.'[7]

The nineteenth century historian of the diocese of Kilmacduagh, Fr. Fahey, was a little embarrassed by this legend. To some it would appear incredible, to others purerile. Nonetheless he went on to make a valiant defence of it on the grounds that neither modern science nor modern modes of thought can regulate God's ways with His Saints.[8] Granted: but there are other ways of saving the appearances. Today, after the work of such metaphysicians and iconographers as Coomaraswamy and Guenon it is possible to see in legends and folktales of this kind, "the form in which metaphysical doctrines are received by the people and transmitted by them."[9] Images are the proper linguistic of metaphysics. It is in the "marvels" that the deepest truths of legend inhere. Miracles are to be understood, not so much as breaks in the laws of nature as signs of the power of heaven. God, they affirm, continues to act through the saints of the desert as he once acted through the apostles and prophets.[10]

The episode in which Colman is assisted by the friendly cock, mouse and fly is an image for the re-establishment of a provisional paradise on earth: Colman has returned, by means of prayer and fasting, to the Adamic state where man and beast live in fruitful harmony with one another. The bounty of Guaire is "manna from Heaven" with which the faithful servant of God is nourished. Colman himself, in fasting for forty days and forty nights is engaged in an imitatio Christi - this part of the story, at least, is readily intelligible. What links all of these episodes together is the Biblical motif of the desert. Colman is a type of Israel, the Burren a type of Sinai.

In the Old Testament the desert is regarded as a place of paradox: it points to both punishment and salvation. Negatively it is the "howling waste" through which Israel was condemned by Yahweh to wander for forty years. Positively, it was the means by which the Israelites escaped from bondage in Egypt. God's Holy Mountain was there and the people were fed with manna from heaven. The prophet speaks of the relationship between God and his people in the desert as the love of the bridegroom for his bride (Jeremiah 2:2). Many passages in Deutero-Isaiah envisage a second exodus when the desert will become a garden.

In the New Testament Jesus re-enacts the wilderness experience of Israel when, after being baptized in the Jordan by John, he was led by the spirit into the desert for forty days and was tempted by Satan. As Mark explains (1:2f.), to be in the wilderness is to be confronted with temptation, to live with companionable beasts and to be ministered to by angels. Finally, at his transfiguration, Jesus is seen in conversation with the two great veterans of the desert, Moses and Elijah. The mountain of theophanies (Sinai, Horeb, the Mount of Transfiguration) is a wilderness mountain.

Post-biblical Christian imagining of the desert,

then, endlessly combined four main concepts. It was a moral waste but a potential paradise. It was a place of testing and punishment but also the site of nuptial bliss. It was both a refuge from the world and the locus of ultimate revelation.[11]

These antitheses found their fullest expression in the lives and writings of the Desert Fathers, those athletes of God (athletae Dei) who trained for paradise in the wastelands of Egypt and Palestine. Thence, as Christianity moved northwest into Europe, the desert and its ascetic traditions moved with it. By the sixth century even "the Burren of Connaught" could be seen in its image and likeness. This metaphoric "dessertification" is the root metaphor from whence, centuries later, a myth of the West of Ireland as a timeless, chaste, and spiritual place would be constructed.

It is not only a myth however. In 1990, thirteen centuries after Coleman retired to his cave under Cinn Aille, a young woman was professed as a hermit by the Archbishop of Tuam. She lives in a caravan at the edge of the sea near Colman's oratory on Inishere, rises at five a.m. for prayer and subsists on a vegetarian diet. The desert is still inhabited.

III

If this is the general, traditionally sanctioned reading of the Burren landscape, is it possible to be more precise? After all there are many "dyserts" up and down the country. Further, the desert as an image was woven of multiple strands and had many lines of transmission over the centuries. Was there anything specific about the application of the image to the Burren?

The dedication of Corcomroe Abbey holds the key to an answer. "The Fertile Rock" is a variant of one of the commonplaces of medieval thought expressed in the oxymoron *dessertum floribus vernans*, "the flowering desert". It was first used by St. Jerome (d.? 420), author of the life of Paul the Hermit, when he contemplated the great number of monks who lived in the wilderness: *O dessertum Christi floribus vernans* (Ep. 14, 10). Thereafter the theme was taken up by St. Eucherius of Lyons (d. c. 449) who wrote the definitive work on the subject, *De Laude Heremi* ("The Praise of Solitude"). Eucherius's ascetic treatise is the most ample - and precise - statement of the meaning of the fertile rock.

12.4 Church of St. Colman MacDuada at Keelhilla. Photo, T. Quinn.

The desert, says Eucherius, is the special dwelling place of God. He lives in silence and in secret places and has shown himself to human beings more often in the desert than anywhere else. When God created everything in his wisdom he made each thing suitable for future use. The purpose of the desert was to act as a hermitage for His saints. Other places were rich in fruits, here he gave an abundance of saints so that "the region of the desert drips richness". He who desires life cultivates the desert.

God made known the sacredness of the desert to Moses when He appeared to him in the burning bush and told him to take off his sandals: "The place on which you stand is holy ground". Moses himself drew sweet water from the rock and manna, the bread of angels, covered the sands of Sinai like a white cloud. Christ, too, fed the multitude in the desert with bread as a sign. More, he went into the desert to pray and showed by this that "prayer can more easily penetrate the heavens with the help of desert surroundings because they have been honoured in a mysterious manner." Again: "a chorus of rejoicing angels visits the beauties of the desert, and, coming and going by Jacob's ladder, they honour the hermitage by the frequency of their visits".

In sections 39 and 40 of the treatise comes a great rhetorical passage celebrating the fertile rock (in the immediate case Eucherius is thinking of the hermitage near Lerins in France where his friend Hillarius is resident). It is introduced by an allegorical interpretation of the parable of the sower and the seed (Matt. xiii.):

[39] The earth of the desert is not - as I believe - unfruitful or barren. Nor are the rocks of the arid desert infertile; there the manifold seed gives back a hundred-fold for the cultivator. Not easily do the seeds cast there go astray from the right path for birds to eat, nor do they easily fall into stony places ... In that place the cultivator will reap the harvest with its rich crop; corn is brought forth from those rocks by means of which the innermost being is nourished ... There break out on those rocks refreshing fountains and living waters which are able not only to satisfy but to bring about salvation. Here is the meadow and pleasure of the inner man, here is the unculti-vated desert ...

[40] No land, however fertile, shows itself comparable to the land of the desert. Is there any other land richer in fruits? In this land above all there grows that corn which satisfies. Is there another land rejoicing with heavily-laden vineyards? - In this land there is produced that wine which makes the heart of man most joyful. Is there another land outstanding for its pas-tures? In this land those sheep can graze about which it

is said
'feed my sheep'. Is there another land adorned with
flourishing flowers? In this land above all there
shines that true flower of the field and lily of
the valley...[12]

It is these flowers, flos campi et lilium conual-lium, which are carved on the pillar capitals of the chancel of Corcomroe Abbey.

12.5 Carved flowers on capitals at Corcomroe Abbey. Photo, A. Korff.

IV

How relevant are these images for us? Can they suggest a way of caring for the Burren? The answer must be: probably not. The desert as Eden or as a demonic land has never been valued in and for itself. It was more of a vacuum. If it was idealized, it was because it was conducive to revelation or purification or sometimes both together. In many respects the desert image, as employed by western religion, signified an extreme estrangement from nature. As such, it can hardly inspire a relevant environmental ethic. For the latter we must cultivate those earthly powers - the spirits of place - so unjustly demonized by the saints of the desert.[13] But wherever we look, the Burren belongs to S. Colman mac Duach if only because, as Joan Didion puts it in The White Album, "a place belongs forever to whoever claims it hardest, remembers it most obsessively, wrenches it from itself, shapes it, renders it, loves it so radically that he remakes it in his image."

Notes, References and Further Reading

The Rocks and Landforms of the Burren - John Feehan

Further Reading:

Aalen, F.H.A. 1978. Man and the Landscape in Ireland, Academic Press.

Davies, G.L. & Stephens, N. 1978. Ireland, A Geomorphology, Methuen.

Dillon, Emma & Drew, David. 1981. Jacko McGann and Aillwee Hill, A Forgotten Way of Life, Burren Heritage Series No. 1, Aillwee Cave Co.

Evans, E. 1981. The Personality of Ireland, Habitat, Heritage and History, Blackstaff, Belfast.

Feehan, John. 1979. The Landscape of Slieve Bloom, Blackwater, Dublin.

Holland, C.H. (ed.). 1981. A Geology of Ireland, Scottish Academic Press.

Jennings, J.N. 1980. Karst Geomorphology, Basil Blackwell.

Mitchell, Frank. 1986. Shell Guide to Reading the Irish Landscape (incorporating The Irish Landscape), Wild Ireland Library, Country House.

The Burren Flora - Cilian Roden

Notes:

1.   Ivimey-Cooke, R.B. & Proctor, M.C.F. 1966. The Plant Communities of the Burren, Co. Clare. Proceedings of the Royal Irish Academy 64B, 211-301.

2.   Foot, F.J. 1864. On the Distribution of Plants in the Burren, County of Clare. Proceedings of the Royal Irish Academy 24, 143-60.

3.   Corry, T.H. 1880. Notes on a Botanical Ramble in the County of Clare, Ireland in 1879. Proceedings of the Belfast Natural History and Philosophical Society, 1879-80, 167-94.

4.   Praeger, R.L. and Carr, J.W.M.1895. Report of the Field Club Union Conference of Galway. Phanerograms, Ferns, etc., Irish Naturalist 14, 246-52.

5.   Praeger, R.L. 1905. Notes on the Botany of Central Clare, Irish Naturalist 14, 188-94.

6.   Praeger, R.L. 1934. The Botanist in Ireland, Hodges, Figgis, Dublin.

7.   Webb, D.A. & Scannel (eds.). 1983. Flora of Connemara and The Burren, Cambridge.

Further Reading:

Curtis, T.G.F. & McGough, H.N. The Irish Red Data Book, 1 - Vascular Plants, 168p, Government Stationary Office

Praeger, R.L. 1937. The Way That I Went, Hodges, Figgis, Dublin.

The Wildlife of the Burren - Gordon D'Arcy

References:

D'Arcy, G. 1981. The Guide to the Birds of Ireland, Irish Wildlife Publications, Dublin.

D'Arcy, G. 1987. Pocket Guide to the Animals of Ireland, Appletree Press.

D'Arcy, G. and Hayward, J. 1991. The Natural History of the Burren. Immel Publications.

de Buitlear, E. 1984. Wild Ireland, Amach Faoin Aer, Dublin.

The First People, The Prehistoric Burren - John Waddell

References:

Burgess, C. and Gerloff, S. 1981. The Dirks and Rapiers of Great Britain and Ireland. Praehistorische Bronzefunde, Munich.

Cahill, M. 1983. 'Irish Prehistoric Goldworking'. Treasures of Ireland. Irish Art 3000 BC - 1500 AD. Dublin. pp. 18-23, 92.

Coffey, T. 1984. 'Fulachta fiadh in the Burren'. The Other Clare 8: 160-164.

Coffey, T. 1985. 'Field Notes'. The Other Clare 9: 27-31.

Crabtree, K. 1982. 'Evidence for the Burren's forest cover'. In: Archaeological Aspects of Woodland Ecology, British Archaeological Reports (International Series)146. S. Limbrey and M. Bell (eds.), Oxford. pp. 105-11.

De Valera & O Nualláin, S. 1961. Survey of the Megalithic Tombs of Ireland. Vol. 1. Co. Clare. Dublin.

Eogan, G. 1965. Catalogue of Irish Bronze Age Swords. Dublin.

Gleeson, D.F. 1934. 'Discovery of Gold Gorget at Burren, Co. Clare. Journal of the Royal Society of Antiquaries of Ireland, 64: 138-139.

Harbison, P. 1989. The Axes of the Early Bronze Age in Ireland. Praehistorische Bronzefunde. Munich.

Hencken, H. O'N. 1935. 'A Cairn at Poulawack, County Clare'. Journal of the Royal Society of Antiquaries of Ireland 65: 191-222.

Lucas, A.T. 1970. 'National Museum of Ireland: Archaeological Acquisitions in the year 1967'. Journal of the Royal Society of Antiquaries of Ireland 100: 145-166.

Lynch, A. 1988. 'Poulnabrone - a stone in time...'. Archaeology Ireland, Vol. 2(3): 105-107.

MacMahon, M. 1982. 'Bronze Age ritual monuments(?) in the Burren', The Other Clare 6: 5-7.

O Drisceoil, D. 1988. 'Burnt mounds: cooking or bathing?'. Antiquity 62: 671-680.

O Nualláin, S. 1989. Survey of the Megalithic Tombs of Ireland. Vol. V, County Sligo. Dublin.

Raftery, B. 1983. A Catalogue of Irish Iron Age Antiquities, Marburg.

Raftery, B. 1984. La Tène in Ireland, Marburg.

Robinson, T.D. 1977. The Burren. A map of the uplands of North-West Clare, Eire.

Rynne, E. 1982. 'The Early Iron Age in County Clare'. North Munster Antiquarian Journal 24: 5-18.

Watts, W.A. 1984. 'The Holocene vegetation of the Burren, western Ireland'. In: Lake Sediments and Environmental History. E.Y. Haworth and J.W.G. Lund (eds.), Leicester. pp. 359-376.

Westropp, T.J. 'Prehistoric Stone Forts of Northern Clare'. Journal of the Royal Society of Antiquaries of Ireland 27: 116-127, 1897

Westropp, T.J. 1915. 'Prehistoric Remains (Forts and Dolmens) in Burren and its south western border, Co. Clare'. Journal of the Royal Society of Antiquaries of Ireland 45: 249-274.

The Burren in Early Christian Times - Paul Gosling

References:

Binchy, D. A. (ed.). 1941. Críth Gablach, Mediaeval and Modern Irish Series Vol. 2, Dublin.

Byrne, F. J. 1973. Irish Kings and High-Kings, B. T. Batsford Ltd, London.

Fleming, A. 1987. 'Coaxial Field Systems: some questions of time and space', Antiquity, 61, 188-203.

Gibson, D. B. 1988. 'Agro-Pastoralism and Regional Social Organization in Early Ireland', in Gibson, D. B. and Geselowitz, M. N. (eds.), Tribe and Polity in Late Prehistoric Europe, Plenum Press, New York, 41-68.

Hodkinson, B. 1987. 'A Reappraisal of the Archaeological Evidence for Weaving in the Early Christian Period', Ulster Journal of Archaeology, Vol. 50, 47-53.

Kelly, F. A. 1988. Guide to Early Irish Law, Dublin Institute for Advanced Studies, Dublin.

Mac Niocaill, G. 1972. Ireland Before the Vikings, Gill and MacMillan Ltd, Dublin.

Ó Corráin, D. Ireland before the Normans, Gill and Macmillan Ltd, Dublin, 1972

Ó Cillín, S. P. (ed.). 1977. Travellers in Co. Clare 1459-1843, privately by the author and P. F. Brannick, Galway.

O'Neill Hencken, H. 1938. Cahercommaun: a stone fort in County Clare., Royal Society of Antiquaries of Ireland, Dublin.

Robinson, T. 1977. The Burren: a map of the uplands of North-West Clare, Éire, Cill Rónáin, Árainn.

Rynne, E. 1982. 'The Early Iron Age in County Clare', North Munster Antiquarian Journal, Vol. XXIV, 4-18.

Watts, W. A. 1984. 'The Holocene vegetation of the Burren, western Ireland', in Haworth, E. Y. and Lund, J. W. G. (eds.), Lake Sediments and Environmental History, Leicester, 359-76.

Westropp, T. J. 1900-02. 'The Cahers of County Clare: Their Names, Features and Bibliography', Proceedings of the Royal Irish Academy, Vol.22, 415-99.

Stokes, W. 1894. 'The Prose Tales in the Rennes Dindshenchas', Revue Celtique, Vol.15, 272-336.

The Churches, Monasteries and Burial Grounds of the Burren - D.L. Swan

Further Reading:

Barry, T.B. 1987. The Archaeology of Medieval Ireland, Methuen, London & New York.

Gwynn, Aubrey & Neville Hadcock, C. 1988. Medieval Religious Houses, Ireland, with an Appendix to Early Sites, Irish Academic Press.

Hughes, K. & Hamlin, A. 1977. The Modern Traveller to the Early Irish Church, SPCK.

Swan, D.L. 1983. Enclosed Ecclesiastical Sites and their Relevance to Settlement Patterns of the First Millenium AD, in Reeves-Smyth, T., & Hammond, E., (eds) Landscape Archaeology in Ireland, Oxford, 269-94.

Swan, D.L. 1991. Some Ecclesiastical Sites in County Clare, in The Other Clare, Vol. 15.

Westropp, T.J. 1900-02. 'The Churches of County Clare, and the Origin of the Ecclesiastical Divisions in that

County', Proceedings of the Royal Irish Academy, Vol. 22, 100-180.

The Burren in Medieval Times - Paul Gosling

References:

Barry, T. B. 1987. The Archaeology of Medieval Ireland , Methuen & Co. Ltd., London.

Graham, B. J. 1977. 'The Towns of Medieval Ireland', in Butlin, R. A. (ed.), The Development of the Irish Town , London. pp. 28-60.

Gwynn, A. and Hadcock, R. N. 1988. Medieval Religious Houses: Ireland , 1970; reprinted by Irish Academic Press, Co. Dublin.

Kelly, F., A. 1988. Guide to Early Irish Law , Dublin Institute for Advanced Studies.

Leask, H. G. 1951. Irish Castles and Castellated Houses , Dundalgan Press Ltd. Dundalk (reprinted 1973).

Meyer, K. 1906. Contributions to Irish Lexicography , Volume 1, Part 1: A-C, Halle.

Nicholls, K. 1972. Gaelic and Gaelicised Ireland in the Middle Ages , Gill and Macmillan Ltd., Dublin.

O'Donovan, J. (ed. & transl.). 1851. Annals of the Kingdom of Ireland by the Four Masters , Vol.VI (1589-1616), Dublin.

O'Flanagan, M. (ed.). Letters Containing information relative to the Antiquities of the County of Clare Collected during the progress of the Ordnance Survey in 1839 , Bray 1839, three trypescript volumes, College Library, UCG

O'Grady, S. H. (ed. & transl.). 1929. Caithréim Thoirdhealbhaigh , Irish Texts Society; Vol. 1: Introduction and Text; Vol. 2: Translation and Index. Reprinted by Elo Press Ltd., 1988.

Robinson, T. 1977. The Burren: a map of the uplands of North-West Clare, Éire , Cill Rónain, Árainn.

Stalley, R. 1987. The Cistercian Monasteries of Ireland , Yale University Press.

Watts, W. A. 1984. 'The Holocene vegetation of the Burren, western Ireland', in Haworth, E. Y. and Lund, J. W. G. (eds.), Lake Sediments and Environmental History , Leicester. pp. 359-76.

Westropp, T. J. 1890-1. 'The Normans in Thomond', Journal of the Royal Society of Antiquaries of Ireland., Vol. 21: Part I., 1275-1287, 284-93; Part II., 1287-1313, 381-7; Part III., 1313-1318, 462-72.

Westropp, T. J. 1899. 'Notes on the Lesser Castles or "Peel Towers" of the County Clare", Proceedings of the Royal Irish Academy   Vol. 20: pp. 348-65 and Plates XVI-XVII.

Westropp, T. J. 1908-09. 'The Forests of the Counties of the Lower Shannon Valley', Proceedings of the Royal Irish Academy   Vol. 27: pp. 270-300.

Leamaneh - An O'Brien Castle and Manor House - J.W. O'Connell & Paul Gosling

Further Reading:

Mac Neill, M. (ed. by M. Murphy). 1990. Maire Rua, Lady of Leamaneh, Ballinakella Press.

Ua Croinin, R. & Breen, M. 1987. "Interesting Remains at Leamaneh", in The Other Clare, Vol. XI.

Weir, Hugh, W.L. 1988. O'Brien People and Places, Ballinakella Press.

Post Medieval and Early Modern Times in the Burren - J.W. O'Connell

References:

Aalen, F. 1989. "Imprint of the Past", 83-119, in The Irish Countryside, Gillmore, D. (ed.), Wolfhound Press.

Boyne, P. 1987. John O'Donovan (1806-1861), a Biography, (Studies in Irish Archaeology and History), Boethius: Irish Studies.

Coen, M. Rev., unpublished notes compiled from material in the Diocesan Archives in Galway Cathedral

Corish, P. 1985. The Irish Catholic Experience, A Historical Survey, Gill and Macmillan.

de Lourdes Fahy, Sr. M. 1986. Origin and Growth of Lisdoonvarna 1750-1900, unpublished talk delivered at the Merriman School.

de Paor, Liam. 1986. The Peoples of Ireland, From Prehistory to Modern Times, Hutchinson & Co. Ltd.

Dinan, B. 1987. Clare and its People, The Mercier Press.

Evans, E. 1957. Irish Folk Ways, Routledge & Kegan Paul.

Foster, R.F. (ed.). 1989. The Oxford Illustrated History of Ireland, Oxford University Press.

Foster, R.F. 1988. Modern Ireland 1600-1972, Allen Lane.

Frost, James. 1983. The History and Topography of County Clare.

Murphy, F. (ed.). 1987. The Bog Irish, Who They Were and Where They Lived, Penguin Books.

Murphy, I. 1988. "Tenant Rights in County Clare in the 1850's", in The Other Clare, Vol. 12.

O Tuathaigh, G. 1972. Ireland Before the Famine, Gill and Macmillan.

Power, J. 1986. Terry Alt and Lady Clare, in The Other Clare, Vol. 10.

Spellissey, S. (Text) & O'Brien, J. (Photography). 1987. Clare, County of Contrast, Spellissey & O'Brien.

Swinfin, A. 1986. Kilfenora Cathedral, privately published.

Wall, M. 1989. Catholic Ireland in the Eighteenth Century, O'Brien, G. (ed.), Geography Publications.

Weir, Hugh, W.L. 1986. The Houses of Clare, Ballinakella Press.

White, V. Rev. P. 1983. History of Clare and the Dalassian Clans of Tipperary, Limerick and Galway.

Lore and Cures and Blessed Wells - Lelia Doolan

References:

Arensberg, Conrad, M. and Kimball, Solon, T. 1968. Family and Community in Ireland, Harvard.

Bord, Jane and Colin. 1986. Sacred Waters , Paladin.

Curtin, Chris and Varley. 1987. "Tony - Marginal Men? Bachelor Farmers in a West of Ireland Community", in: Gender in Irish Society , UCG Press.

Foot, F.,J. 1862. On the Distribution of Plants in Burren, County of Clare, Trans. RAI, XXIV, Science, Part II.

Irish Folklore Commission - Schools Collection 1937 - 1938, in Archive Department, Clare County Library, Ennis

Logan, Patrick. 1972. Making the Cure, Talbot Press.

 - 1980. The Holy Wells of Ireland, Colin Smyth.

MacNeill, Máire. 1962. The Festival of Lughnasa, OUP.
 - 1990. Máire Rua, Lady of Leamaneh, Ballinakella.
- The Folklore of the Burren, Unpubl. talk given to Clare Archaeological and Historical society, April 1979

O Catháin, Séamus. Súil Siar Ar Scéim na Scol (1937 - 1938), In: Sinsear 5, The folklore journal

O Céirín, Cyril. 1991. Making the Cure in Clare. In: Dal gCais.

O Duilearga, Séamus. 1965. The Oral Tradition of Thomond, JRSAI 95.

Webb, D.A. 1977. An Irish Flora, Dundalgan.

Weir, Grania and Brew, Frank. Rural Medicine in Former Times, Two articles in The Other Clare, Vol. 14

The Bardic Connection - Charlie Piggott

Notes:

1.   Private Communication: Bob Quinn, An Cheathru Rua, Conamara, Co. na Gaillimhe

2.   de Blácon, Aodh. 1973. "Gaelic Literature Surveyed". Talbot Press.

3.   Mac-White, Eoin. 1945. "Irish Bronze Age Trumpets". J. Royal Soc. Antiq. of Ireland, 75: 85 - 106.

4.   "Treoir". 1979. 11, No. 4, 10.

5.   Graves, Robert. 1959. "The Crowning Privilege". Penguin Books, 1959

6.   Graves, Robert , "The Crowning Privilege". Penguin Books.

7.   Private Communication: Mr. P.J. Linnane, Bell Harbour, Co. Clare

8.   Flood, W.G. Grattan. 1970. "A History of Irish Music". Dublin. (Reprinted, Irish University Press.

9.   Russell, Miko. 1989. "The Pipers Chair. A collection of tunes, songs and folklore". Ossian Publications.

10. Private Communication: Mr. Tom Munnelly, Miltown Malbay, Co. Clare

11. Mongovan, J., "Clare Music. Old and New". Quinn, Co. Clare.

The Artist's Eye - Anne Korff

Further Reading:

Crookshank, A. and the Knight of Glin, The Printers of Ireland 1660-1920, Barrie and Jenkins, 1978

The Fertile Rock - The Burren as Desert - Patrick F. Sheeran

Notes:

1.   "Art of the Outback": interview with Sidney Nolan in The Sunday Tribune, 6 April 1986.

2.   Whitley Stokes, "The Prose Tales in the Rennes Dindsenchas: Second Supplement", Revue Celtique 16: 282, 1895 See under "Emáin Macha"
    Two mythical accounts, in particular, contain instructive references to what we might think of as the "pagan" version of the Burren. In the first, the five sons of Dithorba ("without patrimony") whose names may be roughly translated as Proud, Rash, Evil Deed, Foolish and Thick are banished into "the deserts of Connaught" by Macha. "...Macha went to seek Dithorba's sons in the guise of a lepress - that is, rye dough and red bog-stuff were rubbed over her - and she found them in Boireann

Connacht (around a fire), cooking a wild boar. The men ask tidings of her, and she tells them (the news), and they give her food by this fire. One of them says: "beautiful is the hag's eye! let us lie with her." He carries her off through the wood. She binds that man by dint of her strength and in the wood she leaves him. She comes again to the fire. "Where is the man who went away with thee?" say they. "He is ashamed," quoth she, "to come to you after lying with a lepress." "'Tis no shame," say they, "for all of us will do the same." So each of them carries her through the wood, and she binds each of them by force, and brings them in one bond to Ulster..."

Macha is clearly a figure of the sovereignty of the land whom these outlaws attempt to rape. Because they are unworthy of her she takes them captive instead and brings them back to Ulster as slaves. What is especially interesting about the story in our context is the implication that the Burren in pre-Christian times was seen as a wasteland fit for outcasts, wild men and lepers. Perhaps there is an analogy to be drawn between the sanctification of the pagan dithreb and the appropriation of wells for Christian purposes?

The second account is even odder and comes from a non-canonical Fiannaiocht lay, Seilg mhór Bhoirinn Uí Lochlainn which recounts the conception, birth and early years of Fionn's son Oisin in the Burren.

Fionn and his companions were out hunting in "O'Lochlainn's Burren" when they discovered a beautiful doe in a covert. Fionn catches the doe and will not allow the others to harm her:

Having calmed the doe's fear
He was struck by male lust and love
Scandalous to relate
He made her take a woman's place.

Instead of a fawn the doe gives birth to Oisin. She suckles him for twenty one years. Oisin grows up to be the "wild man" (geilt) of legend - the Burren's very own Yeti:

In moving quickly
Through woods and bushes
The skin of my feet became wrinkled
From the tufts of grass and thorn.

With on one looking after me
Among the stones and grasses
For lack of care, my hair grew
From the crown of my head to the ground

The Fianna eventually discover Fionn's long lost son and Oisin is taught to speak human language by the poets. Notice that in all the early descriptions of the Burren it is described as a wooded place. For Oisin see Mairtin O Briain, "Some material on Oisin in the Land of Youth" in Sages, Saints and Storytellers, eds., O Corrain, Breatnach and McCone, Maynooth, An Sagart, 181-199, 1989. The verse translations above are by Maire Ni Fhlathuin.

3.   See the propositions on the nature of sacred place advanced by Valentine Tomberg in Die Grossen Arcana Des Tarot, Herder: Basle, 1983

4.   Whitley Stokes, "Three Legends from the Brussels manuscript 5100-4", Revue Celtique 26: 373, 1905

5.   Geoffrey Keating, History of Ireland, 4 vols, London: Irish Texts Society, 3: 65-67, 1908

6.   See, for example, Howard Murphet, Sai Baba Avatar, London: Frederick Muller, 1979

7.   J.G. O'Keeffe. 1904. "Colman MacDuach and Guaire" Eriu 1: 47.

8.   J. Fahey. 1893. History and Antiquities of the Diocese of Kilmacduagh, Dublin: Gill.

9.   Roger Lipsey (ed.). 1977. Coomaraswamy: Selected Papers, Princeton at the University Press, 306.

10. Benedicta Ward SLG has written extensively on miracles and the Desert Fathers. See her introduction to The Lives of the Desert Fathers (London: Mowbray), 1980), especially the section entitled "A Sense of Wonder: Miracles of the Desert". Also "'Signs and Wonders': Miracles in the Desert Tradition" in Studia Patristica 18 (1982): 539-542 where she writes on signa, signs of the kingdom. "They are events which illustrate the action of God in the world, in the new age, through these men. They affirm that God is acting now, that he has not been left behind with the apostles and prophets. These stories link the saints of the desert with the saints of the most authenticating text possible, the Bible, and parallels are drawn or implied: it was said that for Patermuthius, the sun stood still, as it did for Gideon, and Biblical texts are supplied to confirm the mean of this...The saints of the desert are those through whom God acts now; it is not a question of authority or succession but of present charismata." (p. 540). There are relevant considerations - especially the notion of "explanatory intellect" in W.B. Yeats's essay "An Indian Monk" in Essays and Introductions (London: Macmillan, 1961) 429.

11. See George H. Williams, Wilderness and Paradise in Christian Thought (New York: Harper, 1962); Alexander Altman, Biblical Motifs (Cambridge, Mass.: Harvard University Press, 1966) and Ulrich Mauser, Christ in the Wilderness, (London: S.C.M. Press, 1963)

12. There is no English translation of De Laude Heremi. The Latin text may be found in Carl Wotke, ed., Corpus Scriptorum Ecclesiasticorum Latinorum (Vienna, 1894) 31: 177-194. Present translations by Candellaria Von Strien-Reney.

13. Vine Deloria's God is Red (New York: Grosset and Dunlap, 1975) and Paul Shepard's Nature and Madness (San Francisco: Sierra Club, 1982) suggest some alternatives. The "red" of Deloria's title refers, not to Marxism, but to Amerindian polytheism.

Notes on the Authors

Jeffrey O'Connell is a freelance writer, journalist and historian. Born in the United States, he came to Ireland twenty years ago. He took his Arts Degree at U.C.G. and taught at a Rudolf Steiner School outside London for six years. His interest in archaeology was stimulated by the excavations carried out in the grounds of the school in Kings Langley, site of one of the Royal Palaces belonging to Richard II.

Since returning to Ireland, he has lived outside Kinvara. He is editor of "Tracht", the Kinvara parish magazine, and has published two books devoted to aspects of Kinvara history. "St. Colman's Church" is a study of a unique, pre-Emancipation church, making use of original manuscript material from the papers of Dr. Nicholas Archdeacon, Bishop of Kilmacduagh and Kilfenora from 1800 to 1823. He is presently preparing a feature article on Dr. Archdeacon for the Journal of the Galway Archaeological and Historical Society. His other publication, "Kinvara History: A Family Affair", is based on the research he conducted into parish family history. Since 1985, he has collaborated with Anne Korff on six Ramblers Guides and Maps to the Burren, South Galway, Kinvara, and Medieval Galway. He is, along with Anne Korff, one of the directors of Tír Eolas.

Mr. O'Connell is married, with four children, and edits the Arts section of The Galway Advertiser.

Anne Korff was born in Germany and studied Fine Art, Visual Communication, Graphic Design, and Publishing in Berlin, taking a Masters Degree in Fine Art. Her professional career in Germany included design work for films, publishers, and government departments.

She came to live in Ireland in 1977 and worked freelance with various agencies. She also taught at the National School of Art and Design.

Ms. Korff moved to Kinvara, Co. Galway in 1982 and continued to work freelance. She grew vegetables (organically, of course!) and explored and painted in the Burren region. In 1985 with Jeffrey O'Connell she produced "Kinvara, A Ramblers Map and Guide" which led to the production of six further Guides and Maps covering the Burren region. In 1988 she co-founded Tír Eolas with Jeffrey O'Connell.

John Feehan is an environmental scientist and historian whose work is largely concerned with the conservation of environmental heritage and widening people's awareness of its importance. He has been described by Kevin Myers as "one of life's great communicators", and is perhaps best-known for his TV series "Exploring the Landscape", for which he won a Jacobs' Television Award in 1988. The third series of "Exploring the Landscape" is due for transmission in Winter 1991. The Burren has featured strongly in all of these television series.

As a post-graduate student at Trinity College, he was involved for many years in research on the geology of the Slieve Bloom and Devilsbit Mountains in Central Ireland, on which he has written many articles and papers as well as a book, "The Landscape of Slieve Bloom", which Peter Harbison described as "setting a new standard in local history studies". He has also published an environmental history of County Laois, and several papers on the pollination biology of tropical mistletoes. He is at present working on a major book on the boglands of Ireland.

Dr. Feehan was born in Birr in 1946, and worked as a teacher in Ireland, England, Malawi in Central Africa, and in Southern Africa before moving into broadcasting. He is married, with two children, and now works with the Natural Resources Centre at Trinity College on environmental heritage resource development.

Patrick F. Sheeran is Director of the Centre for Landscape Studies at University College Galway. The Centre promotes the interdisciplinary study of the natural and cultural landscapes in the region. Relevant publications by Dr. Sheeran include:
"Genius Fabulae: the Irish Sense of Place" in Irish University Review, Vol. XVIII (1988).
"Sacred Geography" in Eire-Ireland, Vol. XXIII (1988).
"The Idiocy of Rural Life Reviewed" in The Irish Review, No. 5 (1988).
"The Ideology of Earth-Mysteries" in Journal of Popular Culture (Ohio), Vol. 23 (1990).
"Place and Power" in ReVision, California (Winter, 1990).

Dr. Sheeran is currently editing a volume entitled "Decoding the Landscape", the proceedings of the inaugural conference of The Centre for Landscape Studies, held at U.C.G. in November 1990.

Lelia Doolan has worked in television, theatre, film and journalism, for RTE, the Abbey Theatre, The Irish Press, and many other leading national newspapers and magazines. She has lived and worked in Belfast and Mayo and settled in South Galway some years ago, where she now freelances as a writer, teacher, and film-maker. She has a primary degree in Modern languages from University College, Dublin and a Ph.D. in Social Anthropology from Queens University, Belfast.

Her parents were both from County Clare, her father's family coming from Kilshanny on the edge of the Burren where she spent her childhood summers. Since 1987, an interest in herbal medicine and nutrition has expanded through explorations of folk cures and belief systems in North Clare.

Gordon D'Arcy has an M.Sc. in Environmental Science from Trinity College, Dublin. He has published four books, including "Guide to the Birds of Ireland" (1981); "Pocket Guide to the Birds of Ireland" (1986); "Pocket Guide to the Animals of Ireland" (1987). In addition, he has contributed numerous articles to various journals, including The Irish Naturalists' Journal; The Irish Wildland Conservancy News; and The "Badger" (I.W.F. Journal).

Mr. D'Arcy has a particular interest in the Burren and has compiled over the last five years detailed notes on all aspects of the wildlife of the area. During this same time he has led numerous field trips into the Burren and has organised courses for teachers and other interested groups. Since 1982 he has been running natural history courses on the Burren for National School teachers.

Mr. D'Arcy's knowledge of the wildlife of the Burren has been widely recognised and his book on the birds of Ireland was a landmark event in that it was the first such publication to consider Irish birds exclusively.

Cilian Roden took his degree in Botany at University College Dublin and subsequently studied marine and freshwater algae at University College Galway and at University College Dublin, where he obtained his Ph. D. in 1979. Since 1980 he has worked on the West coast of Ireland, firstly at the Shellfish Research Laboratory in Carna, Co. Galway and, since 1987, at Redbank Shellfish, New Quay, Co. Clare.

Throughout his working life he has been attracted to two very different types of plant: the marine plankton of the Atlantic coast and the flowering plants of the West coast of Ireland. The first interest started with studies of seaweeds on the coast of Clare under the direction of the late Prof. Mairin De Valera. This interest has now led to participation in a commercial project to restore Redbank Oyster Beds in Aughinish Bay on the North shore of the Burren.

Dr. Roden's interest in the flora of the Burren dates from an undergraduate field trip led by Prof. J.J. Moore, then Professor of Botany at University College Dublin. Since then he has climbed and walked throughout the Burren, and discovered new locations for several of the rarer plants. He has a particular interest in the arctic alpine flora and has written an account of the mountain plants of Galway and Mayo, as well as contributing records to "The Flora of Connemara and the Burren" by Prof. D.A. Webb and Ms. M.T.P. Scannell. While much of his published work centres on the ecology and growth of marine algae, he has also written a number of papers dealing with the plants, both terrestrial and marine, of the West of Ireland, e.g. "The Vascular Flora and Vegetation of Some Islands in Lough Corrib" (Proceedings of the Royal Irish Academy 79B, 223-236); "A Survey of the Flora of Some Mountain Ranges in the West of Ireland" (Irish Naturalists Journal 22, 52-59).

Daniel Leo Swan was born and brought up in Co. Meath, near Slane, and from an early age was familiar with the many historic and prehistoric sites and monuments in the area. In the course of a busy career, which included a period as Headmaster of a large suburban school in Tallaght, a period as a lecturer in St. Patrick's College, Maynooth, and since 1987, lecturing in Archaeology in the Dublin Institute of Technology, he has continued and considerably extended his original field of research through aerial survey as well as by more orthodox methods. His five years in commercial aviation, where he spent time with the famous Flying Tiger Line, his duties as despatcher and navigator bringing him to Africa and Asia as well as Europe and the U.S., have been put to use in the aerial surveys he has made of ecclesiastical sites around Ireland.

Mr. Swan commenced formal study of archaeology under Prof. Ruairi De Valera at University College Dublin, and was awarded a Master's Degree with First Class Honours. His research topic involved the application of aerial reconnaissance and air photography to archaeology, and marked a new departure in this technique in Ireland. He is an acknowledged expert on Early Medieval Ireland, in particular the ecclesiastical settlement of that period, and has lectured and published extensively, both at home and abroad, on this topic. He is a regular contributor to historical and archaeological journals, and has edited "Here Lyeth", a study of a number of early church sites in North Dublin.

Paul Gosling was born in Dundalk, Co. Louth, and studied Archaeology and History at University College Dublin (1973 - 76) and The Queen's University of Belfast where he was a Junior Fellow in the Institute of Irish Studies (1979 - 80). He subsequently spent two years as Archaeological Officer with Dundalk Urban District Council before taking up his present position as Director of the OPW/UCG Archaeological Survey of County Galway, in 1983.

His principal research interests are Early Historic Settlement (A.D. 400-1200) and the origins and development of urban life in Ireland. He has carried out a major survey of souterrains in Counties Louth, Armagh and Monaghan for an M.A. thesis and has published a detailed survey of the topography of medieval Dundalk.

Since moving to Galway he has taken a particular interest in the Burren in north Clare, where he has been a tutor on summer schools for the past five years. Current research interests include his thesis, the topography of early Tuam, Co. Galway, a survey of the archaeological remains on Turlough Hill in the Burren, and distributional analysis on medieval castles in north Clare. His most recent publication was as joint editor of Volume 41 of the Journal of the Galway Archaeological and Historical Society, published in 1989. This was a special issue devoted to archaeological excavation and research in the West of Ireland.

John Waddell is a lecturer in Archaeology at University College Galway. He received his Doctorate from U.C.G. and he has also studied at the University of Glasgow. Dr. Waddell was also on the staff of the National Museum of Ireland for a number of years.

Dr. Waddell has a special interest in the Prehistoric archaeology of Western Europe and has done extensive research on Bronze Age pottery and burials. His field survey work includes the Aran Islands and the Burren, and he has been involved in field excavations of burial mounds in Wales and at the important royal site of Rathcroghan in Roscommon. Dr. Waddell has published numerous papers on different areas of archaeology, including the influence of Ireland's position as an island on the question of cultural development and diffusion. His most recent publication is "Bronze Age Burials of Ireland".

Charlie Piggott was born in Cork and received his Ph. D. at University College, Cork in Biochemistry. After moving to County Galway, he spent several years teaching, as well as carrying out and publishing post-doctoral research on digestion. He played traditional music from an early age and was a founder member of the traditional group, De Danann, which also involved recording several LP's with the group.

Charlie now lives in Kinvara, Co. Galway, where he maintains a healthy interest in Irish folklore, traditional crafts (he has thatched his own house) and the performance of traditional music. He has published several articles on themes relating to these topics.

One of his main interests is diet and he is at the moment preparing a guide to the edible sea vegetables of the North Atlantic. He is also involved in a study of the relationship between Irish traditional music and early church music.

Caoilte Breatnach was born in Dun Laoire and move to Kinvara, Co. Galway in 1985. He has always had a deep interest in Irish folklore as part of the wider cultural heritage of Ireland and has researched the folklore of the Kinvara area and North Clare. He is the author of "A Word in Your Ear - Folklore from the Kinvara Area", published in 1991 by Kinvara Community Council.

Tír Eolas is a publishing firm based in Kinvara, Co. Galway. Since it was established in 1985, Tír Eolas has published six Guides and Maps, covering the Burren, South Galway, Kinvara, and, most recently, Medieval Galway. Its two Directors are Anne Korff and Jeff O'Connell.

Ten Years On

1. Photo, Veronica Nicholson.

Contents

Ten Years On

By Richard Broad

The first edition of this book ten years ago was an eloquent and passionate affirmation of the importance of the Burren – a hymn to its diversity and beauty. Then, its editor wrote, 'a landscape can be "used up". The Burren is not a "theme park"'. That remains the case, but by and large, it has been quite a good decade for the Burren.

In the early 1990s the Burren's prospects looked bleak. The authoritative 'Atlas of the Irish Rural Landscape' edited by F.H.A. Aalen, Kevin Whelan and Matthew Stout spelt it out. 'Almost all the natural flora is confined in patches surrounded by unvegetated limestone or rubble fields. These patches are inexorably shrinking. Ecological diversity is one of the great attractions of the Burren – its gentians and orchids, its otters and pine martins, its wheatears and stonechats, its pearl bordered fritillaries – a remarkable profusion that is now under intense pressure'. 'Land reclamation has', it continued, 'converted more than 4 per cent of the Burren from rocky pasture, pavement and scrub land into large fields of seeded pasture, often used for silage and of no difference in appearance or ecology to any area of lowland Ireland'.

But change was on the way. Today, for the first time in the Burren's history, some of its wildlife is protected. The most important development was the establishment of the Burren National Park in an area covering about one tenth of the greater Burren area in the south east, providing 'rock solid' protection for one of the most vulnerable habitats in the whole region. This, along with the Special Areas of Conservation and Statutory Nature Reserves, should ensure that some of the natural heritage is preserved for future generations. In this context, Cilian Roden's and Gordon D'Arcy's updates on the state of the Burren's flora and fauna are very reassuring.

Ecology is often seen as something 'nature' does. Plants, animals, climate interrelating changing while remaining self-sustaining. We can easily forget that humanity is part of all that. The Burren's natural heritage depends on traditional farming practice. Its ecology is not 'natural'; it is the result of the interaction of its people, in this case farmers, and nature over the centuries. This is something that has only recently been properly understood, as Brendan Dunford explains.

He points out that the Burren is best seen as a series of different ecological systems, rather than a single one, all intimately connected to local traditional farming practices. The introduction of the Rural Environmental Protection Scheme (now supported by the majority of Burren farmers) is encouragingly sustainable; environmentally-friendly land use which, hopefully, will ameliorate the impact of the more intensive agriculture of the last 25 years. However, as he points out, it does not address a new and important problem in the Burren, the invasion of scrub on land being left ungrazed and uncultivated. So there is still much to do.

In planning terms, the Burren is neither seen nor protected as a whole. There is still no effective landscape management. It is to be greatly regretted that it never came under the protection of the Environmentally Sensitive Designation scheme, now in abeyance. This has been very effective in protecting areas with a similarly clear regional identity - such as the Mourne Mountains and the Glens of Antrim. The Burren needs to be managed as a whole in the context of a broad topographical framework that this scheme could provide. It is not too late for the government to do that, and future legislation should give farmers a leading role and appropriate incentives in managing the natural heritage. Arguably, there is more knowledge of the Burren in its farmsteads than in Ireland's Universities – a knowledge that needs to be respected and tapped.

For people are part of the ecology of the Burren too. The Burren needs all its people to be involved in the

2. Muckinish Castle in 1885 as drawn by T.J.Westropp. Beside the castle is a small thatched farmhouse with chimneys on both gables and a thatched outhouse, surrounded by trees.

3. This photograph circa 1915, from the Laurence Collection, shows that the farmhouse had been extended and slated although the outhouse is still thatched. By 1991, the scene had hardly changed. (See page 131)

4. Recently, the farmhouse was demolished and the terraces of town house style holiday homes, built. Originally painted a luminous green, the colour was later changed in an attempt, presumably, to 'whitewash' this intrusive and insensitive development.

Shane-Muckinish Burren.

development of coherent, viable, socially mixed communities in the context of preserving one of the most extraordinary places on earth. During the decade, development continued to be ad hoc without an overall vision of, and proper respect for, the Burren's heritage. Some decisions have been extraordinary. At Muckinish, the 'planners' allowed terraces of town houses to be built alongside a late medieval castle on a prime scenic site.

But there is good news here too. People are beginning to take these matters into their own hands. Community-based development plans have been drawn up in Corofin and Ballyvaughan and one is in progress in Kinvara. Richard Broad's article looks, in the context of Ballyvaughan, at some of the problems these plans are addressing.

On the archaeological front, the government's decision to purchase land in order to access and protect the Poulnabrone dolmen and the Cahercommane ringfort, two of the Burren's most important monuments, is very positive. Carleton Jones reports on the most important archaeological excavation done in the last decade.

Jessie Lendennie shows us how poetry and art continues to be inspired by the Burren and Maria Kerin points out that 'tradition' is an ongoing process. Anne Korff has selected three outstanding artists working with the Burren's nature and landscape.

The single most important event of the decade was the long drawn out and often bitter dispute over the proposed Visitor's Centre in the very heart of the Burren at Mullaghmore. This crass and insensitive scheme, akin to suggesting that the information pamphlets in a cathedral should be distributed from the high altar, was finally defeated by a sustained campaign by the Burren Action Group. Lelia Doolan's article is a personal account of that battle from one of those involved from the start. The brief chronology of the dispute tries to convey how persistent, dedicated, patient and determined the protestors had to be.

In the early nineties, *'The Atlas of Irish Rural Landscape'* had concluded: "The situation is now precarious; without coherent policies, landscape and general environmental quality will rapidly deteriorate'. That does not appear to have happened. They went on, 'above all local communities need to become actively involved in sustaining their magnificent landscape'. That seems to be happening. Complacency would be foolish and vigilance is essential. Those of us who live here are the custodians of one of the most vulnerable and rare habitats in Europe with some of its turloughs, karst, limestone grassland existing on the Burren in pristine condition. The constraint of crass commercial interests masquerading as 'development' or 'modern farming practice' that was threatening the Burren a decade ago needs to be unremitting. Those who saved Mullaghmore showed the way. For heritage is a non-renewable resource. When the gentian and the stone wall have gone, they have gone forever.

Our planet is not a 'theme park' for the exclusive use of human beings to be 'used up'. If all local communities everywhere looked after their own natural heritage, it would go a long way to solving the environmental crises confronting our world.

Beyond the Tourist Boom

By Richard Broad

The small towns and villages of the Burren are enjoying far better times than were imaginable in the grim post-war years, when the West of Ireland was impoverished and being drained of its young and vigorous by emigration. But the new prosperity, largely based on tourism, has brought with it new and different problems. Take Ballyvaughan, for example.

Ballyvaughan sits at the foot of the Burren beside Galway bay. Originally an important trading port with a significant fishing industry, it began to go into decline at the end of the nineteenth century. As well as suffering from the general economic decline of the West, the improvement of the roads in the last century and development of motorised transport took trade from the harbour and deprived Ballyvaughan of its 'raison d'être'. Even today, the population of the village is only a third of what it was in 1870. By the 1950's, its decline seemed terminal.

In the mid sixties a small group of people set up a Development Association. Such was their enthusiasm that Shannon Development decided to start the original 'Rent an Irish Cottage' holiday scheme in Ballyvaughan. Twenty per cent of the money had to be raised locally – an extraordinary achievement for such a small village suffering such hard times. The first visitors arrived at Easter in 1968. Ballyvaughan's development as a tourist centre had begun.

In 1972 Hyland's, originally a shop and bar, was operating as a fully functioning hotel. In the summer of 1976 the Aillwee caves opened and was such a success that it is now one of the biggest tourist attractions in the mid-west. The pubs and shops modernised; guesthouses were built, a nationally acclaimed restaurant opened and more holiday homes were built. People began to buy second homes in and around the village.

The local community continued to rebuild. The ladies' club raised the funds to restore and restructure the old school as a community centre and the GAA, also raising money locally and with the help of modest grant from the Lotto, provided the village with playing fields and changing rooms. In the early nineties, Newtown Castle was restored as part of the development of the Burren College of

Art, followed by the establishment of a Language centre nearby. Academics, other than the botanists who had long understood the unique nature of the Burren, began to come to Ballyvaughan. In summer, by the turn of the millennium, Ballyvaughan had become a bustling tourist centre.

But there was a downside. Tourism provided work but mainly for women and largely in the summer. There was a shortage of housing for local people for whom property and building land prices had put home ownership beyond their means. Nor was there affordable rented accommodation in the summer for those who came to help service the tourist industry.

There was little local industry, the shopping was limited; professional and commercial services were virtually non-existent. Public transport was poor, making the ownership of a car essential. There was serious traffic congestion during the tourist season and the water services and sewage system were proving to be inadequate. The village was very quiet in winter with many of its businesses closed and its holiday cottages and second homes, which accounted for about 40% of the houses in the village, standing empty.

It was a pattern that could be seen in villages across the Burren. Tourism had revitalised the region, but created unbalanced communities that were potentially divisive with economies only really viable in the summer. Commuters from Galway or Ennis and those from further afield looking for a 'weekend cottage' bought existing properties or built themselves new houses. Meanwhile there was a real housing shortage for both local people and the lower paid workers who came to work in the tourist industry as, across the decade, the price of a three-bedroomed house quadrupled and that of a half acre site quintupled. This, in turn, led developers to build denser often 'suburban-style' estates, seen by many as unfortunate additions to the Burren landscape and its nineteenth century architecture

These developments stressed the sewage and water systems. In some cases they are becoming a threat to public health. In Ballyvaughan and Kinvara for example, the communities' untreated sewage goes directly into their respective bays. In some places in the Burren, the ground water is polluted and unsafe to drink. How far this is due to agricultural practices and how far to poorly designed and maintained domestic septic tanks is a moot point. It could be argued that the system of percolation and septic tanks used by most houses in the Burren is inappropriate on a limestone pavement. The sewage problem can, of course, be solved. All you need is sewage works and the political commitment to find the money. The ground water is another matter and may prove to be the Burren's most intractable problem in the coming years.

So, market forces, unconstrained by a coherent vision of the real, long-term potential of the Burren and the needs of its local people, threaten its charm and beauty – the very heritage that had attracted the tourists, the second homers and the commuters in the first place.

But all is not gloomy on this front either. Recent government legislation compels developers of estates of more then four houses to include an element of cheaper 'social housing'. Ballyvaughan will soon have a sewage works although Kinvara is on the long finger. Local communities are becoming involved too, as they realise the need for planned development designed to create socially mixed communities with viable year-round economies.

Recently development plans have been drawn up in consultation with the residents in Ballyvaughan and Corofin. Kinvara is currently involved in a groundbreaking scheme designed to produce a town plan that reflects the views and aspirations of everyone in its community. This involvement of local people may well stop the drift of communities, integral to the Burren, from becoming dormitories with a summer tourist trade and revitalise them as places where many people live and work.

So to return to the story of Ballyvaughan. It was in 1998 that the Ballyvaughan Development Committee saw the need to address these problems. Supported by Clare County Council, they commissioned Michael Leahy and Paul Conway, architects and planners from Ennis to draw up a development plan based on a survey of the views of the people living in the village. A preliminary draft was produced in March 2000 which is still in the process of being discussed and refined by the local community.

Thanks to Patsy Mullen and Jim Hyland for their kind help.

Richard Broad is a retired TV documentary maker now living in Kinvara. Among his sixty or so major documentaries are a number on social and ecological matters. His series "Palestine" an account of British rule there before the establishment of the State of Israel won an international Emmy and he was responsible for "The Troubles" a five part series analysing the historical roots of the conflict in Northern Ireland.

Summary of the Survey conducted in Ballyvaughan

1. The main concern was the protection of the natural surrounding environment.

2. There was a need to create non-tourist based local employment. The preferred options being service and E businesses, craft and light manufacturing industry.

3. Residents wanted a solution to the town's traffic and parking problems.

4. The provision of designated walkways and indoor sports facilities as well as public parks and toilet facilities was considered to be important.

5. The consensus was that a population of between 500 and 1000 was desirable but that no more than 10 new houses should be built in any one year.

6. There was a strong feeling that the number of holiday and second homes recently constructed in Ballyvaughan has had a negative impact. Few wanted the provision of more tourist accommodation.

5. Mick Carrucan, Ballyvaughan. Photo, Veronica Nicholson.

Agricultural Practices and Natural Heritage
By Brendan Dunford

Reviewing the extensive literature on the Burren's geological, ecological and archaeological heritage, one is struck by the scant reference to, or acknowledgment of, the contribution of the indigenous farming community to this heritage. Even in recent years when farming in the Burren has been mentioned, it is usually in a negative context - seen, for example, in terms of the damage caused through land reclamation or pollution.

Unfortunately this misrepresents the overwhelmingly positive role that farmers actually play in sustaining the diversity of the Burren. It ignores a fascinating and unfolding history of how farming helped to create this unique environment. It also ignores a fascinating, ever unfolding, history of how farming adapted to, evolved with, and deeply influenced this unique environment.

To fully understand the Burren, we must look to farming. It has relevance to every aspect of the landscape. Even the bare skeletal hills are now thought to originate from prehistoric forest clearances by farmers. The ring forts that pepper the Burren reflect the laborious efforts of farmers to protect their livestock from the many raiding parties intent on plundering the region's considerable agricultural wealth.

Long before the Burren's repute as a botanical and cultural haven was established, the quality of its agricultural produce was widely recognised. In 1681 Thomas Dineley noted that the Burren 'raises earlier beef and mutton ... than any land in this kingdom, and much sweeter by reason of the sweet herbs intermixed and distributed everywhere.' Forty years earlier, in the Book of Survey and Distribution, some fourteen different classes (and 69 subdivisions) of pasture were recorded in the Barony of the Burren, reflecting the diversity of this landscape and the prevailing perception of it in purely agricultural terms.

Today, however, visitors to the Burren are often amazed to learn that farming exists at all when confronted with what is, ostensibly, an unrelentingly harsh landscape. Yet several hundred farming families are based in the Burren, wresting a livelihood from the land using the skills and knowledge accumulated by their predecessors over countless generations.

The unique natural attributes of the Burren uplands evoke an equally distinctive response in terms of how these areas are farmed. This is nicely captured

in the unusual and ancient practice of 'reverse transhumance', known locally as winterage, whereby many (but not all) upland grasslands are grazed between the months of October and April. The limestone bedrock retains sufficient heat to facilitate a long growing season and a dry lie for livestock, while the thin soil cover and tough vegetation is naturally resistant to poaching or muddying. Water is also more widely available in the uplands over the winter period. The hardy native breeds of cattle traditionally stocked, mainly Shorthorns and Herefords, were well suited to the difficult terrain and the coarse calcium-rich foliage. Thus the uplands constituted a low cost, healthy way of wintering cattle, a considerable resource particularly in an era before alternative fodder sources were readily available.

Winter grazing fulfils a very important ecological function through the removal of potentially dominant grass species and 'dead plant material'. Gaps opened up by animal's hooves provide space for the colonisation of new plants, dunging helps to redistribute nutrients and plant species. During the subsequent growing season the rich herb element of

6. Grazers
Suckler cows grazing on an upland grassland patch, a common sight in the Burren over the winter period, are a critical factor in ensuring the species richness of these grasslands. Networks of long established serpentine pathways are employed by the animals traversing the often-treacherous surface, allowing them to access the most unlikely of the scattered grassland patches. Ample shelter from wind is provided by hollows in the undulating landscape or by pockets of scrub. Failing this, on particularly exposed slopes, distinctive abbreviated wall segments were erected for shelter. The traditional extensive low-input system of winter grazing, practised for many generations in the uplands though now much modified, continues to produce an animal of some considerable renown and distinctive quality.

7. Turf tiles
Scattered singly or in clusters in the Burren uplands, the parallel walls shown here are referred to locally as turf tiles. They were used primarily to dry out fuel – often turf, heathy sods, or even cow pats – utilising the strong upland breezes running through the deliberately porous walls. Some of these structures may have also been used to provide shelter for kids and lambs by adding a makeshift ceiling of sods, vegetation or rock to protect the inhabitants from rainfall. Other variations of this structure incorporate a corbelled hut at one end for the same purpose.

The past thirty years have seen a virtual revolution in Irish farming and the Burren was not exempt from what has been termed the 'industrialisation' of agriculture. In common with other, similar, traditionally managed landscapes in Europe, this has had serious implications for the area's landscape. Farmers have had to become more efficient and sensitive to market and political forces to ensure their survival. In the Burren, this has meant that the specialised production of high-quality continental breeds of young cattle has become the dominant farming system today. There is no longer any place for older, hardy native breeds of cattle, sheep or goats on the uplands, and these areas are ill suited to cater for the nutritional requirements and limited mobility of the pregnant suckler cows that now prevail. Supplementary feeding has become necessary, often using slatted houses, so the vital ecological role of traditional grazers is not being adequately fulfilled.

the flora, much of which is quite minute and lies dormant over winter, faces less competition for light and other resources and, because grazing is light or nonexistent in summer, they suffer minimal disturbance from livestock.

A recent study found that winter-grazed grasslands contained, on average, 25% more plants than those grazed primarily in summer. More importantly, many of the most distinctive plant species of the Burren are closely associated with winter grazing. Occurrence of characteristic Burren species such as blue moor grass (*Sesleria albicans*), mountain avens (*Dryas octopetala*), eyebright (*Euphrasia spp.*) and orchids diminish considerably with increased summer use at the expense of competitive agricultural grasses and weeds. The characteristic *Dryas-Hypericum* heath and *Centaureo-Cynosuretum* grassland communities are also closely associated with winter grazing and are rarely found on heavily summer grazed areas, where they are replaced by species-poor *Lolio-Cynosuretum* grassland.

Meanwhile the number of farmers continues to fall (by 8% in the last decade) and farm size increases (currently 100ha). Over half of all farm families now have another income source. All this has contributed to the marginalisation of uplands, as farmers focus their energies on the more accessible and productive lowland areas. The use of fertilisers to increase productivity on ryegrass-dominated lowland pasture and the introduction of the versatile wrapped round silage bale has greatly facilitated this shift in emphasis.

Reduced levels of grazing in upland grasslands inevitably leads to a loss of floral diversity. Research has found that plant species diversity was almost 26% less on under grazed grasslands (prior to scrub encroachment) than on their winter grazed counterparts, with less competitive herb species succumbing to the unchecked growth of grasses such as Sesleria and fescues (*Festuca* spp.). Scrub species, particularly hazel (*Corylus avellana*), soon follow on all but the most exposed of sites, and the microenvironment is gradually altered through the

236

build-up of organic matter and changes in light and humidity levels. A whole new, relatively impoverished, flora then develops. There are many examples of scrub incursion not just within the Burren, but in similar semi-natural karst landscapes in Britain, and mainland Europe, where land has been abandoned and costly restorative efforts have had to be put in place.

The Burren region sorely lacks a conservation strategy to inform would-be managers as to what is the desirable extent of individual habitats, particularly scrub. For farmers, increased scrub levels reduce the grazing capacity of their land and greatly complicate the herding, watering and feeding of animals. Hard-earned fields and well-built walls are being subsumed and could be destroyed should current protective environmental legislation ever wane. Scrub has been known to cause structural damage to ancient tombs and forts, and rendering sections of the landscape impassable. While constituting a wonderful habitat itself, we must decide whether scrub is more valuable than the characteristic, EU-designated 'priority' limestone grassland habitat which it displaces. Such issues must be addressed urgently before a consensus on action can be established and supported.

As scrub encroaches, and another generation of farmers pass on, the unique traditions of this land are becoming blurred. Tales of herdsmen, goat husbandry and epic droves to faraway fairs are losing immediacy and significance. The Burren is a landscape steeped in agricultural tradition, as a brief conversation with any elderly farmer will reveal. The assorted structures associated with this tradition litter the uplands, the creative use of limestone allowing them to melt effortlessly into the land, often invisible to all but the trained eye. Each structure tells its own story: the cahers and crós used for goat husbandry, folds and wickets to manage sheep, parallel walls called tiles used to dry out fuel, elaborate rainwater collection tanks to circumvent the limitations in water supply.

The fascinating legacy presented by these ubiquitous structures remind us of how intensively these areas were once farmed, how they were remorselessly and often ingeniously, exploited. The high labour requirement implicit in these systems is no longer feasible; much of the produce no longer valued. Farming has become homogenised, and before our very eyes the diversity of farm systems and the hard-earned knowledge that sustained them is being eroded. To quote John O'Donohue 'There is a world in the land, a farming world of the most sophisticated complexity and the most astute and rich memory that in the next ten years will have vanished completely. Isn't there something wrong with either our way of life or style of education that these huge ventricles of life, of memory or of perception are not being passed on?'

As traditional management systems lose their relevance to today's farming community, it is clear that a new paradigm will be necessary to encompass the revised dynamic that now exists between farming and the Burren. A new generation of

8. Goat Cró
Ostensibly ad-hoc arrangements of limestone slabs, goat crós such as the one shown on the top left of the photograph are commonly found on upland grasslands, reflecting the strong tradition of goat husbandry in the area.
These tiny huts, some of which are little more than a slab covering a hollow in the ground, were used to house young goat kids by day while their mothers foraged. By night the kids were released to suckle their mothers in the larger enclosure (shown), before being re-interned in the adjoining cró the following morning. The kids were thereby reared on a diet of milk only, rendering the meat more tender and sweet, preferable to the tough, strong tasting meat of the equivalent 'grass kid'. Traditionally kid meat was a very popular dish, closely associated with Easter.

9. Scrub incursion Reduced levels of grazing on upland grasslands invariably leads to a loss in plant species diversity, in many cases resulting in the encroachment of woody species such as hazel Corylus avellana, *blackthorn* Prunus spinosa *and hawthorn* Crataegus monogyna. *Local sources reveal that, over the past 20 years or so, the area on the right side of this field wall was very heavily grazed, while that on the left has been poorly grazed, with obvious effect. The abandonment of traditional, often labour-intensive methods of control, including goat browsing, pulling saplings by hand, harvesting of trees for firewood, and hazel rods (called scollops) for thatching, fencing and basketmaking, have also contributed to the recent expansion in hazel levels.*

farmers has arrived: well-educated and enterprising in realms beyond agriculture, efficient, pragmatic in their attitude to 'the land', not bound by loyalty to the ideals of family and community as were their predecessors, ambitious and well-informed.

The Burren Rural Environmental Protection Scheme agreement, introduced in 1995, acknowledges the unique attributes of farming in the region, and helps to keep many small-scale, traditionally based farmers in business. The scheme has limited the extent of summer grazing and feeding, but fails to realistically address the issue of scrub encroachment. Though many farmers complain that REPS does not recognise the individual traditions associated with each farm, the high uptake and general popularity of the scheme offers considerable hope for the future, and for the first time recognises and supports farmers in their role as custodians of the countryside. Any effective attempt to manage the Burren's extensive, unique

and diverse landscape must support, equip and encourage these farmers to become the main instigators and proponents in that process.

The situation regarding scrub encroachment offers a timely reminder of the important role of farmers in the Burren. We must respect the intimate multi-generational relationship that Burren farmers have had with this land, their unsurpassed knowledge of it through all seasons, and try to support them so that this bond is not broken and the area-specific traditions lost forever. The Burren is not a wilderness, nor is it a museum. When most of the visitors and flowers have left after the summer, it is then that the hills come alive from a farming perspective, in a manner that resonates over many centuries. It is only when this ancient order is seasonally restored that the pieces of the Burren jigsaw seem to come together and this beautiful, bewildering place somehow makes sense.

Brendan Dunford was born near Dungarvan, Co. Waterford and spent his formative years working on the family farm. Following completion of a BE in UCC, in 1988, he promptly abandoned a career in engineering and instead spent several years 'backpacking' the globe. Over this time he visited some of the world's more unusual and inspiring landscapes and met the local people that, for him, really brought these places to life. The visible despoliation of many of these places, and the erosion of indigenous communities and cultures through short-sighted development, led Brendan to return to university to pursue a Masters degree in Environmental Resource Management in UCD. Following this, he undertook a PhD study under the Teagasc Walsh fellowship scheme. This research, titled The impact of agricultural practices on the natural heritage of the Burren uplands, *allowed Brendan to revisit his favourite theme of the relationship between people and the environment within which they live, in one of Ireland's most precious landscapes. To address some of the issues identified through the research, Brendan co-founded burrenbeo (www.burrenbeo.com). He lives with Ann and their two children near Kinvara, Co. Galway where he continues to indulge in his complementary passions for exploring the Burren hills and the rich culture of the region.*

10. Site of the interpretative centre before the car park and the partially completed centre was built and as the now restored site will soon look. Photo, Nutan.

YES to conservation of Ireland's natural heritage and landscape
YES to management plan for the whole Burren
YES to a National Park
YES to jobs for the area
YES to a welcome for visitors
YES to payment for local farmers for their care of the Burren
YES to visitor facilities in the RIGHT LOCATION

NO to an Interpretative centre at Mullaghmore

From the Burren Action Group brochure,
"The Field that Watches the Mountain".

Ordinary People and the Mountain

By Lelia Doolan

In 1991 the Irish government presented plans to build an Interpretative Centre for the Burren National Park. The location chosen was at Mullaghmore. Opposition to this location was led by the Burren Action Group in a campaign which lasted ten years, resulting in momentous changes to Irish planning law and, in 2001, the complete restoration of the site. Lelia Doolan, a member of BAG, remembers the struggle.

To look back and reduce momentous happenings to a neat chronology is one matter. To be in the thick of things is another. The brief recital of these milestones hides the many emotions that fuelled a long journey.

First of all, there was a sense of disbelief:

how could intelligent people not see that their plan was daft? How could they risk polluting the very terrain they had acquired in order to protect it: endangering rare plant and wildlife species; risking contamination of the waters; altering the character of the area and its small country roads; providing a precedent for further building developments in an unspoilt region? Causing, in short, a man-made affront to the beneficient legacy of millennia of natural cataclysms. The gloriously eccentric symmetry of Mullaghmore invited wonder, indeed. Could it not be enjoyed without a large (no doubt tasteful) tourist facility in its foothills? Had alternative sites been properly

11. Protesters and supporters of the centre when the first sod was turned by local Fianna Fail T.D., Brendan Daly, November 1992. Photo, Nutan.

12. The first diggers move in, December 1992. Photo, Nutan.

considered? The Burren already had an excellent, community-based Display Centre in Kilfenora; Corofin had a locally-owned Heritage Centre. So why not put it in a nearby village where employment and education and enjoyment could be a year-round instead of a seasonal activity?

The response, where it was civil, was:

this unique landscape requires interpretation; this is part of the modern role of National Parks: protection and access. There is no danger to the environment - we are conservationists, like you, and we have a proven track record; visitors/tourists need to have a first-hand experience of the surroundings; they must be able to see the mountain; none of these plant or wildlife species is as rare as you claim; the sewage system we will install is foolproof and, in the unlikely event of failure, we will close the centre down or truck out the waste. The Park must have a management centre - how else can we protect it? As for Kilfenora, "the Display Centre and the one in the Park will complement each other ... especially in relation to the important question of interpretative themes". Think of the jobs and the economic spinoffs to a depleted community. And, no, we do not have to do an Environmental Impact Assessment nor do we have to apply for planning permission.

Where the response was not so civil, it consisted of some boycotting, occasional threats, anonymous poison-pen letters, insults hurled from passing cars: *yuppies, hippies, outsiders* etc, - the usual list. A fairly mild placard during one of BAG's annual Mullaghmore walks on New Year's Day read: **UCG and Dublin 4 vandals will not be let destroy our parish!**

There was plenty of energy flying about.

Nobody in the Burren Action Group denied the right of any visitor to enjoy the startling revelation of Mullaghmore nor the wide, windy acres of the surrounding park. We simply argued that their enjoyment and interest could be stimulated in a nearby village centre before travelling the few miles to the park.

The OPW and the Minister of the day accepted that there were concerns among conservationists and local people. These were, however, groundless. They would press ahead.

So the campaign began. Cyril and Kit O'Céirín's house in Lisdoonvarna became the hub in an accelerating whirl of activity. Sit down, keep calm, think out a strategy and some opening tactics: the government needs EU money; the EU has detailed environmental policies and criteria. Let's see if they realise our worries. Who to contact?

Very few of the group had knowledge of the EU and its Directives on Habitats, Special Areas of Conservation and other relevant matters. But soon there were people with that knowledge who heard of our need and offered their time and expertise. There were weekly meetings, in Kilfenora, Ballyvaughan, the Spa, Ennis; an immense letter-writing onslaught on the EU's Environmental Commission (DGXI) and on the Regional Commission (DGXVI) began. International environmental groups offered support.

At home, politicians of all parties were written to, visited in their clinics, presented with the arguments, vigorously lobbied. Newspapers and other media were kept informed. People learned how to write press releases, to take part in radio debates, to appear on the Late Late Show with members of the OPW's staff. People who had never done anything like that in their lives before discovered wellsprings of eloquence and stamina. Public meetings were organised and held. Wheezes to keep the issue alive in the public's mind were thought up and tried: a large and arresting poster, asking why the OPW should build without planning permission; postcards with similar messages; a house-to-house visitation in the Burren, seeking signatures requesting an Environmental Impact Assessment; a petition (it achieved 7,000 signatures from visitors and citizens) asking the Government to think again. We pushed a sizeable Burren rock (*papier maché*) from Ennis to Dublin and held a demonstration outside the Houses of the Oireachtas. Amidst all the activity, there were many glum moments; many moments of hopelessness and frustration; but we were also lucky in being able to celebrate the many, often unexpected, sources of encouragement and good humour that came our way. Cheerfulness kept breaking through.

There was fund-raising: a monster raffle; exhibitions and auctions; Sales of Work; musicians who gave their services for the cause in live concerts and in a CD, produced by P.J. Curtis; T-shirts and sweatshirts, Christmas cards, badges — and the big SAVE MULLAGHMORE banner.

Even though many of our members lived in or near Corofin, we never held a public meeting there. The National Park Support Association, who favoured the proposed location of the centre, did hold big meetings there. One such meeting, in February 1992, was reported in the Clare Champion under the headline "Appeal for Unity Among Mullaghmore Factions". Even though we had not felt much of a push for unity, the Burren Action Group called on the Champion to assist in the search for a mediator. None was forthcoming. At that time, all the TDs in Clare supported the planned siting of the Centre and only a handful of County Councillors, among whom Martin Lafferty was the most consistent, publicly called for another location.

The cry among the supporting politicians was: "Lose this once-in-a-lifetime chance and Clare will never get another penny". It was real fire and brimstone stuff, winding supporters up to paroxysms of rage and rancour. And it achieved its purpose of debasing discussion by characterising any alternative viewpoint as unpatriotic. It seemed as if only those who supported the location had the interests of the country at heart. Conflict was abnormal, pathological and perverse. Harmony was normal and good; it could only be achieved by toeing the party line — notably the Fianna Fail and Fine Gael line in Co. Clare.

It must be recorded, though, that Declan Kelleher who was Chairman of the NPSA, did come to Kinvara, as did Michael O'Donoghue of the Irish Farmers' Association (supporters of the OPW's plan), to debate with us on the issues. Unfortunately, they seemed to overlook the large areas of common ground between us and failed to accept that another site would bring greater benefits and fewer threats to the local community and its environment. We often felt that we had made some headway only to discover, the next day, that our arguments were discarded as irrelevant. Perhaps they felt the same about us.

When, by autumn 1992, all avenues of debate and argument with the OPW had proved fruitless, when the EU caved in (as we saw it), work on the site began and recourse to the law seemed the only path left, our spirits sank. Give up now, and all our work was for nought. Go on, through the courts, and risk serious financial loss or threat to livelihoods, especially for those farming and living in the immediate area. Seven members of BAG came forward to take up the legal case under the title HOWARD & OTHERS. Jim Shannon, our solicitor and supporter, laid out the ground fairly.

We decided to go on largely, I believe, because each one believed in the unshakeable solidarity of the other members of the group; that they would never abandon the seven plaintiffs.

They never did.

The years wrought on. Governments came and went, Ministers likewise. BAG members

13. *Members of the Burren Action Group outside the Dáil (Irish Parliament) 1992.*

14. *Oak tree planting, after BAG's annual New Year's Day walk. Now the group was into its eighth year of the campaign. Left to right: Patrick McCormack, who gave BAG the acre of land where the oak tree is planted, Father Sean McDonagh, chairperson of "Voice" and Kit and the late Cyril Ó'Céirín.*

learnt something about the way public power works; some of the intricacies of environmental law; the roads to the Four Courts; the titles of all sorts of organisations and people. And our own strengths and weaknesses.

As soon as the Supreme Court upheld the judgement requiring the OPW to be subject to planning laws (in 1993), the general public began to believe that the battle was over. As soon as Michael D. Higgins announced that the site would be re-habilitated (in 1995), the public already believed that it *was* over. But it was not over. When Fianna Fail Councillors lost the vote (in 1998) and Clare Co. Council finally had to refuse planning permission for the revised "entry point", there were three further years and two further major processes to be gone through. Many citizens had long ago lost track of the campaign.

In all of this, of course, our stamina and endurance were matched by the stamina and the might of the State. We had to find funds to pay our way and to accept that our taxes also paid the State's way (almost £3 million over the course of the struggle). That's democracy. We were glad that there were Courts and a Planning Board to hear arguments in an atmosphere of relative tranquillity. That's democracy, too, even though it's riskier and so more intimidating for a small group than it is for the State.

But it was an honour for us to be involved in this campaign; we were fortunate in the many talents of BAG members -- in writing and painting, in photography, music and performing -- and in a boundless capacity for hilarity and friendship. In an amazingly varied, unhierarchical group of people, there was always someone to undertake the job at hand and to spread the load so that everyone's contribution was equally useful and valued.

Many babies were born, cause for happiness. And some beloved members died untimely: Pat Healy and Cyril O'Céirín, lovely, passionate and generous men; cause for grief and woe.

They are remembered in trees planted in the acre that Patrick McCormack, BAG member and plaintiff, gave to the group to enable them to raise funds, known as The Field That Watches The Mountain.

And Gerrit van Gelderen, a big loss for his puckish humour and his multi-talented brush. Jim Kemmy of the Labour Party also died too young, one stalwart and faithful man. BAG was warily a-political; members may have been of all parties and of none, but we gladly welcomed support from any political quarter -- Mary Banotti and Pat Cox, alone among the MEPs; and BAG supported the Labour candidate for Co. Clare, Dr. Moosajee Bhamjee, in the General Election of 1992.

In those early days, (1992), we read a report about how the Director-General for Cultural Heritage in Florence and six of his senior officials had been taken to court by the Florentine magistracy because they had resurfaced a famous square, replacing the antique handworked stone blocks with machine-cut paving. Each one was sentenced to two months in prison. Fortunately for them, the sentence was suspended. In relation to the Irish Commissioners of Public Works, the thought often crossed our minds...

If there is any lesson to be learned here, it is that arguments about the environment are just one theatre where different values contend. Public authority and the power of money to force an outcome and to inhibit opposition: these are the challenges to action where different versions of 'good' stand in opposition to one another. In this case, local people and the larger population who wanted to keep a sense of proportion in human and environmental affairs formed unusual alliances and caused decisive change. It is not something, however, to get too starry-eyed about.

Ten years is just the apprenticeship.

The Ten Year Struggle for Mullaghmore

April 1991: Government plans unveiled for an interpretative centre at Mullaghmore in the Burren National Park.

December 1992: Planning permission not needed by the Office of Public Works (OPW) and construction begins on the project.

February 1993: Burren Action Group secures injunction to halt work. The High Court holds that it was unconstitutional for the OPW to be exempt from the Planning Acts. Works rendered illegal.

May 1993: Supreme Court upholds High Court ruling.

January 1994: Planning application lodged for centre with a reduction in size.

February 1995: Culture Minister Michael D. Higgins withdraws planning application after fall of Fianna Fail-Labour Government .

October 1996: Revised plan lodged by Minister Higgins for visitor facilities at Mullaghmore.

September 1998: Clare County Council refuses planning permission after a Council vote.

October 1998: Heritage Minister Síle De Valera appeals this decision to An Bord Pleanála (the Planning Board).

March 2000: An Bord Pleanala refuses planning permission on a number of grounds, among them: "... that nature conservation takes precedence when conflicts arise between different objectives for the management of the National Park".

July 2000: Burren Action Group secures High Court order to have Mullaghmore site restored to its original condition.

May 2001: Work is completed on demolition of the centre and restoration of the site at Mullaghmore.

I am indebted to the following members and supporters of BAG for photographs, newspaper cuttings, good ideas, editorial notes and other memorabilia: Martina O'Dea and family, Kit O'Céirín, Pat Wall, Joe Saunders, Betty McNamara, Éamon de Buitléar, Finola Macnamara, John Kelly, Jim Shannon, Comrade Hayes, Cheryl and Patrick McCormack, Gabriel Casey, Liam Kirwan, Michael Neylan, Ilse Thielen, Brigid Mullins, Thomas McCormack, Leo Hallisey, Suzanne Linnane, Brigid and James Howard, Phil Molony, John O'Donohue; and to Emer Colleran for her model for the (much shortened) chronology. I wish also to acknowledge the views of those in the locality who did not agree with us; in particular Pat Flanagan, Tom Burke, Michael McMahon and Seamus Kelly. I alone am responsible for all errors and omissions.

The Burren Flora

By Cilian Roden

In my original chapter on the Burren flora, I noted that naturalists interpret an island's flora as a balance between the immigration of new and the extinction of resident species. Today's environmental turbulence compels the thoughtful naturalist to evaluate any long known region in much the same manner. What new discoveries have been made and how are these to be balanced against environmental degradation? For the Burren the account is, more or less, in the black. True, many former rock strewn fields have been converted to monotonous managed pasture and the increasing use of artificial fertiliser is gradually raising the nutrient content of the Burren ground water but these very problems have resulted in state and EU legislation designed to halt such encroachments. Their introduction is a radical change in the relationship between man and nature in the Burren.

This changing relationship is reflected in people's attitudes too. More books have been published on the Burren flora in the last ten years, than in the preceding ten centuries! Charles Nelson and Wendy Walsh's book is a beautifully illustrated discursive account of the flora, while Gordon D'Arcy's Natural History of the Burren is a satisfying synthesis of our scientific knowledge of the area. Charles Nelson's photo guide of Burren Flowers is well worth its space in a rucksack on the way up to Cappanawalla or Eagle's Rock. For the serious botanist, Maura Scannell and Mattew Jebb of the National Botanic Garden in Dublin have prepared a supplement to Webb and Scannell's definitive Flora of Connemara and the Burren.

Thankfully I do not have to report the extinction of any Burren plant and new ones discovered include a rare species of Bellflower (*Campanula trachelium*)

15. Welsh Poppy (Meconopsis cambrica) growing on a limestone ledge in the large depression of Magheramaolan. This very attractive native wildflower is confined to the extreme west of Europe, where it is often found in upland woods and mountain cliffs. It grows in at least three locations in the Burren.

found by R. Goodwillie, previously thought to be confined to south east Ireland. The fact that it is a woodland species means that some hazel woods may have persisted for long periods of time. Research in turloughs has resulted in the discovery of a rare grass, *Alopecurus aequalis*, in Termon Lough, only known previously in Ireland in Co. Cork. Wild chives (*Allium schoenoprasum*), typical of wet limestone and already recorded from karstic limestone in Mayo and Galway, has recently been seen in the south east of the Burren but a herbarium specimen has yet to be collected.

Plants thought to have become extinct or to have small populations have been shown to be more widespread than suspected. E.M. D'Arcy discovered a large colony of the Welsh Poppy in the striking depression of Magheramaolan (east of Aillwee cave), while a second new station was found overlooking Fanore. The supposedly extinct Grass leaved Orache (*Atriplex littoralis*) is in fact well established on the shores of Aughinish Bay. Wild Calamint (*Clinopodium ascendens*) has been refound on limestone pavement in Deelinmore townland.

16. Fossil fragment of plant found in shale at the base of the cliffs at Doolin/Fisherstreet in August 1992 by Cilian Roden. The exact identity of this plant has yet to be determined but it is probably part of a seed fern- a now extinct group of plants. It appears that this plant was swept out to sea and then sank to the seabed where it was fossilized approximately 300 million years ago. Continual erosion results in new fossils being revealed from time to time at this site.

One recent study by T. Harrington of fungi growing in Mountain Avens communities has shed further light on the origins of the Burren's vegetation. He found species, not previously recorded in Ireland and Europe, such as *Cortinarius atrovirens*, *C. mussivus* and *C. odorifer*, typical of montane coniferous forest. Most were forest species. He did not find any of the large number of arctic alpine fungi associated with Mountain Avens abroad. He suggests that these fungi are relicts of the former Scots Pine forest that once covered the Burren. This association is unknown outside the Burren and demonstrates yet again that the Burren's ecology is unusual and poorly understood.

Micheal O'Connell and his team at NUIG have analysed the sediments of lakes and bogs for evidence of the Burren's former flora. Not unexpectedly they found that, unlike the mountain avens or spring gentians which still remain, many arctic alpine plants once present in the Burren have disappeared. The Burren's glacial history may also help to explain the presence of lime intolerant plants, such as heather on what seems to be a pure limestone. Based on cores taken throughout the Burren, Peter Vincent has concluded that parts of the Burren are overlaid by beds of loess, a wind-blown sandy silt, deposited just after the ice melted which today underlay many of the larger stands of heather.

Scholarship usually proceeds by small steps rather than spectacular leaps and the last ten years has been no exception. Our understanding of the Burren's flora has deepened rather than been revolutionised. Nevertheless time's flow does not cease. A botanist in the Burren should spend an afternoon along the cliffs and cobble beach at Doolin where fragments of the Clare shales litter the shore. These ancient rocks were laid down soon after the Burren limestone about 300 million years ago and one can occasionally find fossil stems, roots and even leaves of an earlier flora that grew, long ago, where we now hunt for rock roses and gentians.

Some recent botanical research has concentrated on an exploration of new habitats. Perhaps the most interesting new work has been the study of coastal lagoons by a team led by Dr Brenda Healy. Such lagoons contain a highly specialised and unique flora that is thought to be under threat in western Europe. Lough Murree at Finavarra, first studied in the 1970's by Colin and Miriam Pybus, has been found to be of international importance because it contains specialized algae known as *charophytes*. Two very rare species, *Chara canescens* and *Lamprothamnion papulosum*, are found there. Both species of Widgeon Grass (*Ruppia maritima* and *R. cirrhosa*) have been found in small lagoons north west of Kinvara.

Scannell, M.J.P. and Jebb, M.H.P. (2000) Flora of Connemara and the Burren- Records from 1984. Glasra 4: 7-45.

The Burren Wildlife

By Gordon D'Arcy

Ongoing research and observation continue to add to our knowledge of the Burren's wildlife and exciting new discoveries are regularly being made. Individual (often amateur) enthusiasts rather than institutions have been making the difference. Painstaking investigations by entomologists such as Ian Rippey have expanded our knowledge of the Burren's butterflies, moths and dragonflies. Formerly unknown aspects of insect lifecycles, range and even new species have come to light. The Irish annulet moth, *(Odontognophos dumetata)* otherwise unknown in Britain and Ireland, initially discovered at Mullaghmore (Forder, 1991), has been found since in several other locations. The Burren green moth *(Calamia tridens occidentalis)*, formerly also thought to be confined to the Burren, was discovered outside the region, in south Galway. Burren 'speciality' butterflies, the pearl-bordered fritillary *(Boloria euphrosyne)* and brown hairstreak *(Thecla betulae)* have demonstrated a wider range than was formerly thought and a new colony of the scarce, purple hairstreak *(Quercusia quercus)* was found in Garryland wood in August 2000. The most exciting discovery emerged from the examination of museum specimens of the wood white butterfly, in 2001. This showed clearly that Ireland has two very similar species. Moreover, the species, *(Leptidea sinapsis)*, (also found in Britain) is confined to the Burren, while the new one is found elsewhere in Ireland! The Burren's wood white is thus yet another Burren wildlife anomaly. The Burren with about 30 species remains the best place for butterflies in the whole of Ireland.

The discovery of several new dragon and damselflies brings the total for the region to 18 out of an Irish total of 22. Since other new dragonflies have been recorded elsewhere in the country (though not yet in the Burren) it is likely that continuing observation and investigation will be further rewarded. And who is to say that further concentrated work on less conspicuous invertebrates will not reveal similar groundbreaking results.

A symbol for the vulnerability of the Burren's 'mini-beasts' is to be found in the tiny snail, *Pomatias elegans*. It is restricted (in Ireland) to a kilometre or two of the land adjacent to the Flaggy Shore at Finavara. In 1995 the construction of an access road threatened the creature's highly restricted habitat. Thankfully, due to admirable cooperation between the landowner and conservationists, the colony and the habitat survives. It is nevertheless of the utmost importance to investigate the particular ecological requirements of this enigmatic land winkle and to look for hitherto undiscovered colonies elsewhere.

17. LAND WINKLE
(Pomatias elegans)
This elegant snail (also called the round-lipped snail) grows to about thumbnail size and is pinkish brown in colour. Its most distinguishing feature is the little shield (operculum) with which it closes off its shell entrance. This is a feature of shore winkles and points to Pomatias *having evolved to survive on land. Prehistoric remains of the land winkle have been found in many parts of Britain (and also in Ireland) suggesting that it has markedly declined - perhaps due to climate change. As far as is known, its entire present-day range in Ireland is a small coastal strip of the north Burren.*

18. HERALD MOTH
(Scoliopteryx libatrix)
The herald, named after the shape of its wings, (they resemble a shield or an heraldic symbol) is among the larger moths of the Burren. It is brownish with rust-coloured wing panels, relieved only by several pairs of tiny silvery spots. Though quite common in the Burren it is rarely seen, being nocturnal. It flies in autumn. Unlike most other insects which die off at the onset of winter, the herald moth hibernates. Investigation may reveal it in caves, souterrains or simply tucked into a crevice in masonry where it resembles a withered leaf. On emerging in spring it lays its eggs on willows or poplars, the foodplants of the caterpillar.

Within crawling distance of the land winkle's habitat is Carrickadda, a priceless habitat for marine invertebrates. A walk along this low limestone reef at low spring tide (preferably in the company of marine biologist Dave McGrath) is a magical experience. The intertidal rock pools, full of exotic sea weeds, support a bewildering variety of marine invertebrates – courgette-sized sea slugs, *(Aplysia modesta)* with wavy body flaps, squat lobsters *(Galathea)*, a dozen crab species from the tiny porcelain crab to the large (aggressive) velvet swimming crab *(Macropipus puber)* – and quaint fishes like scorpion fish *(Scorpaena porcus)*. Thankfully this remarkable reef is now designated a marine Special Area of Conservation which should ensure its future protection.

The spread of the slow worm *(Anguis fragilis)*, that strange legless lizard (which looks more like a snake), has been the subject of research (from 1996), by Ferdia Marnell. Apparently first introduced into the region around 1970 (perhaps inadvertently, as a pet) it has found the mild climate and fretted landscape of the Burren to its liking. Sightings of living and dead animals were reliably reported from places as far away as Corofin, Carron and Gleninagh: there can be little doubt that, barring climate change, disease or other radical factors, the slow worm is in the Burren to stay. In view of its harmlessness to humans most would adopt a *laissez faire* attitude and consider it simply another regional anomaly. Since the slow worm feeds on invertebrates, however, it is possible that it might adversely affect the diverse invertebrate population.

By 1997 Liam Lysaght had built up a detailed inventory of the birdlife of the Burren. Besides confirming findings of an earlier study, demonstrating the Burren's importance for cuckoos *(Cuculus canorus)* and yellowhammers *(Emberiza citrinella)* – birds generally regarded as being in decline elsewhere in the country – he noted the widespread abundance of wheatears *(Oenanthe oenanthe)*, ravens *(Corvus corax)* and other habitat-specific birds. Scarce breeding waders – snipe *(Gallinago gallinago)*, ringed plover *(Charadrius hiaticula)*, redshank *(Tringa totanus)*, and common sandpiper *(Actitis hypoleucos)* were found in the wetlands of the south and east Burren. Significant numbers of great-northern *(Gavia immer)* and black-throated divers *(Gavia arctica)* were found to winter along the Burren's protected north coast. Unfortunately the weird and wonderful nightjar *(Caprimulgus europaeus)* (now one of Ireland's rarest breeding birds), found in the Burren till 1990, seems to have disappeared. In contrast, the buzzard *(Buteo buteo)*, which became extinct throughout Ireland at the end of the 19th century, was seen in two localities on the edge of the Burren in summer 2000. It is surely only a matter of time before this magnificent raptor returns to nest in the ideal habitat of the Burren.

Whale-watchers like Simon Berrow have shown that cetaceans of many species are found off the west coast of Ireland, particularly in the summer and autumn. Regular watching throughout the 1990's from Black head at the Burren's north-western tip, revealed porpoises *(Phocaena phocaena)*, dolphins (including small pods of the large Risso's dolphin *(Grampus griseus)*, and even a Minke whale

(*Balaenoptera acutorostrata*) or two. A humpback whale (*Megaptera novaeangliae*) was seen on a number of occasions between Galway Bay and the Aran Islands. A pygmy sperm whale (*Kogia breviceps*) – only the fourth to be recorded in Irish waters – was washed up near Kinvara in June 1999. Since this is regarded as a tropical species its recent occurrences - like those of a number of tropical and sub-tropical fish - may point to changes in our marine fauna and the possibility of other exciting discoveries.

Otters (*Lutra lutra*) have long been known from the Burren coastline where there are a number of traditional holt sites. A current, ongoing investigation by Sabine Springer has confirmed much the data from a previous (1980) survey but has noted (initially) negative results from previously recorded inland sites. Whether this is due to less frequent use of these ephemeral sites (mainly turloughs) by the otters nowadays or to ecological change it is difficult to say at this stage. With increased use of artificial fertilizers close to wetlands and a suspected drop in the quality of the groundwater overall, a survey of this kind could be invaluable as an early-warning to more sweeping ecological impoverishment.

When the late Norman Hicken wrote about feral goats (*Capra hircus*) in his book Irish Nature (1980) he noted that 'only a few remain' in the Burren. In the interim, due to the protection afforded them in the reserves and national park, their numbers have burgeoned: there may now be as many as a thousand. As browsers they provide an important service - controlling the spread of the hazel scrub. In earlier times red deer (*Cervus elaphus*) acted in this capacity; is it time to consider re-introducing the red deer?

Despite the success of the feral goats the scrub continues to expand. In places this has permitted climax growth of ash, elm and scots pine to develop, favouring the beautiful pine marten (*Martes martes*) and the red squirrel (*Sciurus vulgaris*).

Though shaped by both natural and human forces for millennia, the Burren remains an internationally renowned wildlife habitat. It is, however, more vulnerable now to development than ever before. If it is to remain the wildlife haven it continues to be, at the start of the third millennium, it will need continued effort from the growing body of Burren enthusiasts and thoughtful, ongoing consideration from planners and decision-makers.

19. BUZZARD
(Buteo buteo)
The buzzard is a large bird of prey with a highly distinctive broad-winged profile and soaring flight. Its call is a cat-like mewing.
Buzzard bones have been found at a number of Irish archaeological sites indicating that it was once widespread here. Its decline and eventual extinction at the end of the 19th century has been linked to gamekeeping and to the laying of poisons for 'vermin control'. Since returning to the north of Ireland – in the 1930's – it has spread southwards and now nests in many counties in the Republic. Recent sightings at suitable nesting habitats point to the possibility of return to the Burren. Though it feeds principally on rabbits, rats and birds such as crows it has been maligned and remains vulnerable to shotgun and poison.

Excavation on Roughan Hill

By Carleton Jones

Since the first publication of The Book of the Burren in 1991 a programme of survey and excavation on Roughan Hill in the south-east Burren has recorded a remarkably complete prehistoric landscape. The unique environment of the Burren has ensured that alongside the very visible megalithic tombs, prehistoric settlements and field walls are visible as well. The Roughan Hill project has consisted of surveying ancient field walls and farmsteads along with excavations to establish a chronology for the various features on the hill. Dozens of trenches through ancient walls have been excavated, a Final Neolithic/Early Bronze Age farmstead was excavated and a Neolithic chambered 'court' tomb was excavated.

Most of the farmsteads, field walls and megalithic tombs on Roughan Hill date from the Final Neolithic/Early Bronze Age (late 3rd - early 2nd millennia B.C.). This is a period which in Ireland and in Britain is generally characterised by a lack of definite and substantial settlement sites. Roughan Hill, however, appears to have been a thriving community where several related families farmed and worshipped.

There is a cluster of four prehistoric farmsteads on the north-west slope of the hill. Pottery and stone tools from these settlements suggest that the four sites are at least roughly contemporary. The scale of the sites suggests that each is probably the farmstead of a family and these family farmsteads are clustered to form a sort of hamlet. The landscape surrounding the farmsteads is divided by contemporary walls into fields of various sizes. It is possible that some of the smaller fields within and adjacent to the farmsteads were used as small garden plots while the fields farther from the farmsteads may have been used to graze animals. Set within the fields, are many megalithic tombs and other ritual monuments. Some are contemporary with the farmsteads and some are earlier.

The chambered 'court' tomb (Cl. 153) may be the earliest monument on the hill (probably 4th millennium B.C.) and a key to the development of the hill as a major concentration of ritual monuments and settlement. It was excavated over four summer seasons and produced the remains of at least eighteen people along with animal bones, pot sherds, beads, arrowheads, various stone tools, quartz crystals and limpet shells. Like all megalithic tombs, this tomb was more than just a repository for the dead. It was probably also the focus of seasonal, community and family ritual over many generations. Items in the tomb, including the bones, may have been moved in and out of the tomb over time and treated more like saint's relics in the Christian tradition than as burials not to be disturbed.

The overall picture on Roughan Hill is of a flourishing farming community in the Final Neolithic/Early Bronze Age which had its beginnings farther back in the Neolithic. This pattern probably holds true for much of the south-east Burren and similar communities were probably located in the Ballyganner/Leamaneh and Poulnabrone Depression areas as well. The attraction of the south-east Burren to these early farmers appears to have been the light well-drained soils and gentle topography of this area. Another attraction of the area may have been its proximity to the Fergus river valley which was probably a more heavily forested environment at this time providing a nearby source of wild resources. In contrast, much of the west and north Burren appear to have been less densely settled at this time. In the west this appears to be due to the boggy terrain, while in the north the combination of steep bare mountains and valleys filled with heavier glacially-derived deposits appears to have discouraged widespread settlement.

20. Right, map. The wedge tombs, the farmstead settlements and most of the mound walls on Roughan Hill date from the Final Neolithic/Early Bronze Age. Earlier Neolithic monuments are the chambered 'court' tomb, possibly some of the unclassified tombs on the hill and the portal tomb to the south-west. The cairns and cists may be from either period.

21. Right, above. Millennia of rain combined with acid from the soil has eroded the limestone bedrock of the Burren, lowering it a little each year. Ancient walls, however, shelter the bedrock underneath them from the eroding forces. The result is a 'pedestal' of bedrock under ancient walls that is higher than the surrounding bedrock. In general, the higher the bedrock pedestal under a wall, the older the wall. A chronology of the walls on Roughan Hill has been established by excavating trenches across walls and measuring the underlying pedestal. Walls contemporary with the prehistoric farmsteads appear today as low grass-covered linear mounds, or 'mound walls'.

22. The chambered 'court' tomb (Cl. 153) during excavation. Over 5,000 bone fragments and complete human bones were recovered from the tomb. These are the remains of at least eighteen people, the majority were adults but a teenager, a young child and an infant were also present. Most of the adults died between the ages of 25-35 but there were some who lived past 45. It is difficult to determine sex with such fragmentary remains, but there were at least two females and six males. The females appear to have ranged in stature from 4'9" to 5'2" while the males appear to have ranged from 5'6" to 5'8".

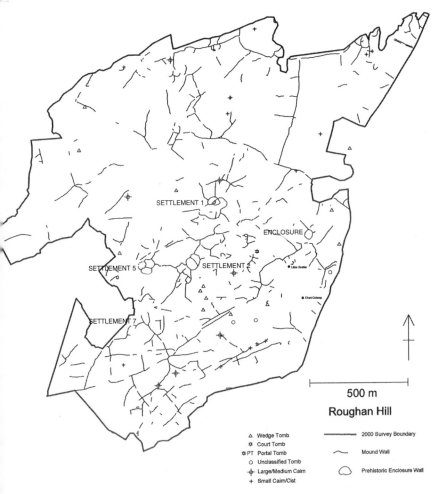

△ Wedge Tomb	——— 2000 Survey Boundary
✿ Court Tomb	
✿PT Portal Tomb	∿ Mound Wall
○ Unclassified Tomb	
✛ Large/Medium Cairn	◯ Prehistoric Enclosure Wall
✛ Small Cairn/Cist	

500 m

Roughan Hill

SETTLEMENT 1

ENCLOSURE

SETTLEMENT 5

SETTLEMENT 2

SETTLEMENT 7

Acknowledgements
Many thanks to the volunteers of Burren Archaeology Research who carried out most of the field work. Funding for various aspects of the project were provided by The Heritage Council and The Royal Irish Academy. As always, heartfelt thanks to Paul Keane who unfortunately passed away before we were able to finish the work on his land.

Dr. Carlton Jones received his Ph.D. from the University of Cambridge with a thesis on the Neolithic landscapes of Ireland. His work on Roughan Hill began in 1994 as part of his doctoral research and was later continued under the auspices of Burren Archaeology Research, an organisation set up for the purpose by himself and Alix Gilmer. He now lectures at the National University of Ireland, Galway. Further publications on Roughan Hill can be found in The Journal of the Royal Society of Antiquaries of Ireland *(1996),* The Journal of Irish Archaeology *(1998),* Archaeology Ireland *(1999) and* The Other Clare *(various issues). Finds from the excavations on Roughan Hill are on display in the Clare County Museum.*

Poets and the Burren

By Jessie Lendennie

Irish struggles for unique identity have often centered on the land; land gives life; shapes culture; defines ownership. We fight on and over the land; claiming territory; struggling over boundaries. The culture is no longer pagan but we have other ways of worshipping the land and the life that flows through it.

Much is written about the spirituality of landscape; particularly in Ireland during recent years. A combination of seemingly disparate factors have provoked deep questions: The weakening of church ties; essential spiritual needs not being met, set side by side with humanistic environmental concerns. Many people now want to go back and take another look at what land means to us. For writers here, the Burren landscape continually offers creative focus. It's unchanging timelessness refreshes what is essential to the spirit.

My first experience of the Burren was on a cold April day; a grey disorientating drizzle in the air. I was amazed and I was frightened. I had been living in New York and London for many years, used to streets leading places, buses running along routes, people moving from A to B on schedule, minding the clock. The sheer primeval feel of acres and acres of Burren stone is mind numbing even for those used to its immense unrelentingness. The difference in my perception now is in the gratitude I feel in being engulfed in an aura of timelessness. I now know from my years of living on the Burren's edge, the offer of peace and perspective; the way the stones feel on one's feet in early morning and late evening. The incredible summer flowering; the cool stone on a hot day; puzzling its origins, mind empty of all but the life of the earth.

No, it isn't difficult to see how this place inspires poets and writers of all kinds. Here is something unique, calling for a unique response. Almost a challenge. A reflective place; difficult to put one's own stamp on. **Anne Kennedy**, a long-time resident of Galway and frequent visitor to the Burren, celebrates a coming together of myth and place in her poem "Moby Dick in the Burren". The whale shaped rock, happened upon, becomes a symbol of striving and at the same time a way of understanding a life which eschews ambition.

"....Here history aspires
to the symmetry of myth
and Melville's mighty symbol
acquires accidental form
beached in the Burren
above the limestone sea,
intact, until flayed open
for secrets that Ahab never found"

(from The Dog Kubla Dreams my Life. Salmon Publishing 1994)

In the poetry of **Moya Cannon** myth is imbued with a reverence; we share her awe at the stones' seemingly magical transformation; our thirst for intellectual understanding forever unmet.

'Thirst in the Burren'

No ground or floor
is as kind to the human step
as the rain-cut flags
of these white hills.

Porous as skin,
limestone resounds sea-deep, time-deep
yet, in places, rainwater has worn it thin
as a fish's fin.

From the funnels and clefts
ferns arch their soft heads.

A headland full of water, dry as bone,
with only thirst as a diviner,
thirst of the inscrutable fern
and the human thirst
that beats upon a stone.

(from Oar, Salmon Publishing , 1988, 1993)

John O'Donohue's Burren inspiration runs throughout his work in both non-fiction and poetry. His poetic consciousness is linked directly to his birthplace in Co. Clare.

Selves

From where she is
he seems singular

clear as the sliver
longing of the moon
filling the memory
of an empty ruin,
still hidden, despite
the hunger of light
and night's dark preference
for burnt fragment.

He appears to be
relieved of the seeping
dross of nuance
no one but the stone
can name him now.

She grew somehow
haunted by the continuous
blue of his crevice voice

knew soon that a complete cry
even if he could make it
might leave nothing.

She rages, forgets
dreams of the ancestral
ocean coming
pouring over
the horizon.

(from Echoes of Memory, Salmon Publishing 1994,1997)

Poetry of the life of the land is a theme in **Knute Skinner's** work - his awareness of his own transience links the value he sees in quotidian things with the scale of Cliffs and sea. Through this perspective he reaches acceptance and peace.

A View from Lahinch

The Cliffs of Moher
can be viewed
three miles from here,
of rising rock.
The Atlantic sent them
shock on shock
till from the crags
Hags Head was hewed.
I move my hand
to wind the clock,
which, like my life,
must be renewed.

(from The Cold Irish Earth: Selected Poems, Salmon Publishing, 1996)

Frank Golden's poetry often marks the dark and starkly beautiful backdrop of land and stone; the spirit of who we are in relation to untamed forces; the self we share with landscape; unlimited in essence.

An Elegy for Colm Hogan
aged 4, for Michael, Ann & Donal

From the sheer crags of Ailwee Mountain
Past the deep woods of Ballyallaban
You can see the sturdy house
And spray of fields where Colm worked,
Taking his barrow of hay & silage to the cows
Walking the hazel & spindle lanes
His eyes unflinchingly holding
The blaze of the late winter sun.

His was a presence of light,
A sky-soul kindred with the air,
A presence also of delicate weight -
His hands as with his father's hands
In perpetual communion with the earth;

His heart as with his Mother's heart
Living in a union of love,
His smile as with his brother's smile
Reflecting the brightest of lives.

(from The Interior Act, Salmon Publishing, 1999

Linda McCarriston, whose visits here are always explorations of
land and spirit, sees the kinship between human expectation and
unrelenting forces which make up our love of the land, the sea,
the vast stone.

In Off the Cliffs of Moher

This is the wind they say makes people
mad here. Bare-legged after her bath
she is lying on the sofa by the window

as if watching a flock of birds at a feeder -
colour, ard or, flight. I have not been here
long enough to guess what such a wind

might do, season after season, to a woman,
to a man. But the sheep, I can see, all day
mill up and back among the tatters of the

stone pasture fences: restlessness, neglect
in the dooryards of before, and the grazing
ghosts the wind won't let leave home.

(from Little River: New and Selected Poems, Salmon Publishing, 2000)

Of course not all writers who live here have the Burren landscape
as subject; but then, again, living is a creative act and where we
live speaks for us as surely as words.

*Jessie Lendennie is the director of Salmon Publishing, one of Ireland's major
literary publishers. Since 1982 she has commissioned, edited and published over
two hundred books and twenty-six issues of The Salmon Literary Journal. Salmon
is known for its focus on new writers, and has the most representative list of
women poets in Ireland. Lendennie's own publications include a prose poem
entitled "Daughter" as well as "The Salmon Guide to Poetry Publishing in
Ireland" and "The Salmon Guide to Creative Writing in Ireland". Full
information about Salmon Publishing can be found on its extensive website
http://www.salmonpoetry.com*

Corcomroe:
a Mass at Dawn
By Maria Kerin

*A personal account of the Easter dawn mass
concelebrated by John O'Donohue, in Corcomroe Abbey,
Bellharbour, Co. Clare.*

Sometimes it's worth getting up early. My father,
with the responsibility of lighting the dawn fire,
was first to rise around 3:30 am on Easter Sunday
morning. He often met the "all nighters" partying or
talking politics in our kitchen. I usually opted for a
short nights' sleep. I wanted to wake to that
dreamlike excitement that was richer than
Christmas morning - being awakened by the Dawn
Mass.

This was no ordinary fire. It was the powerful
welcome to Corcomroe Abbey. The first sparks drew
the dedicated local farmers concerned with the
parking. The dawn procession began and we were
excited to be part of it, the expectation rising with
the continuous stream of car lights in the distance.

Darkness hid identities, making it an easy place to
lose yourself, only to be helped find yourself again.
Feeling introspective, despite the crowd forming
around you, led to a very intense experience. The
silence of the night hushed people and there was a
natural stillness in the air despite the gentle shuffle
across graves. For me, this athmosphere was also
rich with anticipation of something profound,
magical, spiritual.
The waiting was the best part.

In the stillness there came the "right" moment and
Fr. John O'Donohue drew us in to a sacred time
with his melodic voice and words of ancient
wisdom. Like the rocks themselves, solid yet

porous, filled with the past, but reflecting the light this man brought us through a rural celebration of the land and the light entertwined in a Catholic mass, the mass of the Resurrection. Easter Sunday dawn mass in Corcomroe Abbey, Bellharbour, became an enlightening ritual over the past ten years for those privileged to experience it.

Music from locals Chris Droney, Davy Spillane, Seán Tyrell and many others helped us to digest John's words on forgiveness, healing, and hope. Most significantly, he tried to help us face our dark sides. His books "Anam Cara" and "Eternal Echoes" reflect much of what John shared with us. I was always amazed that each year John's sermons seemed like they were written for me personally. The magic of it all was that most in the Abbey felt the same.

The Burren formed a strong theme in the mass. We felt the soil and were reminded of the sacred precious place we live in, that it should be valued and cared for. Holy seawater was sprinkled (liberally) over us to remind us of our source. Locals participated in the readings and as the dark slowly slipped away John would draw our attention to the brightening sky. On cue was the dawn chorus.

The light revealed the beauty of this 10th century Cistercian ruin and we became aware of all those around us. It can be all quite overpowering, to be suddenly surrounded by a thousand people. It was one of the rare times in my life as an artist that I experienced vision as a distraction: it broke the intimacy.

John celebrated the Eucharist of the mass in the main building and offered communion to all present. Chants from the Cistercian monks of Mount Saint Joseph's, Roscrea, gave us a taste of the former glory of this magnificent Abbey. Spirited jigs and reels marked the finale of this unique celebration. The smiles on everyone's faces reflected the openness and the gentleness of such a soulful occasion. There seemed to be something shared by everyone, given out so generously and

unconditionally during those two sacred hours. That takes a lot of love.

In 1990, on the first year of "the dawn mass" I was standing beside Henry, a retired farmer, who turned to me after touching the earth and said, "You're the lucky young one! If Mass was like this when I was growing up, I'd now be a different person". 10 years on, I am. Thank you John.

23. Dawn mass at Corcomroe Abbey. Photo, Nutan.

Maria Kerin grew up on a farm in Bellharbour, Co. Clare. After getting a Degree in Business Studies from University of Limerick, 1991, she went to study Fine Art at Portland Row, Dublin Institute of Technology. In 2000 Maria established Mrua Gallery, Bellharbour, the first artist run contemporary art gallery in Clare, exhibiting both local and foreign artists. This gallery and tea room is open from Easter to October. In the winters she concentrates on her own art and is a member of the Courthouse Studios, Ennistymon. For more information please contact mrua@indigo.ie

His wood is gleaned from the local coppices of hawthorn, blackthorn and ash. "Nature provides me with all the shapes I need for my designs in its own challenging way". Only natural materials are used. Seats are woven or wrapped using sisal or sea grass. The wood is sealed and finished with natural oils or waxes.

Gabriel is very much tied to function in his approach to design and craft and that, along with structural strength and aesthetics, is what matters most. At the end of the day 'the sign of one's hand' is a lasting pleasure.

Gabriel Casey
Working the Wood

Gabriel handcrafts furniture from seasoned local hard woods. He grew up in the Burren 'on a pocket of coldstone land, where the limestone meets the shale'. After a career in teaching, he left to pursue his passion, woodcraft. "I love wood and needed to use my hands. Returning to live in an area like this, which provides and nurtures, set the scene for my craft".

Each piece of furniture is individually crafted using traditional methods. His work includes rocking chairs, armchairs, dinning chairs, stools, cradles and tables of all sizes. But custom-built 'rockers' are a speciality. "A good rocking chair is the ultimate seat and not just a functional piece: it is a remarkable medical device in terms of its therapeutic value.

25. Gabriel's Workshop.
Photo, Ilsa Thielen.

27.1 *Above, different stages of the 'performance'.*

"Shining Cliffs"
Aughinish, Co Clare

A Light Performance by Carl Vetter

27th August 1995 from 22.15 p.m. to 22.50 p.m., performed along the cliffs on the SW coast of the peninsula.

27.2 *Left, final stage of the 'performance'.*

Looking from New Quay towards Aughinish at night, Carl Vetter noticed that 'the peninsula looked like a black stretched log' against a sky brightened by the lights of Galway across the bay.

He decided to 'light up' the different shaped caves in the cliffs – to produce a 'light performance', to paint the cliffs with light. After weeks of working out the kind of effect he wanted and how to achieve it, the performance took place before an audience watching from across the water.

Carl and his assistant Petra Taieb dropped balls of fire into the coves as they walked the cliffs from east to west. Seventeen fireballs glided down thin wires from the top of the cliffs to the shore where they vanished behind big rocks or into caves. The reflection of the flames left the cliffs bathed in a warm and continuously changing light.

(For Carl Vetter's biography see page 209)

27.3 *Below left and right, details of the different light sources.*

28. Wrapping erratic boulders at Mullaghmore, Co. Clare.

Deirdre O'Mahony
Wrap Paintings

29. Wrap #6 1999 acrylic/mud/pigment/linen. 238 by 214 cm collection of the artist.

Deirdre's 'wrap' paintings are part of a major body of work which relate specifically to the landscape of the Burren and are a major part of her work over the past eight years. These paintings take, as a starting point, the residual marks left after wrapping Burren boulders with canvas or linen and then rubbing their surface with soil or pigment. The resulting image or take becomes a template giving visual coherence to the different objectives of each piece. Some of the canvases are stretched and hard edged, others unstructured and fluid, the format of the work reinforcing the content.

O'Mahony's intention is to raise questions about her relationship with the Burren, in the context of dealing with complexities of both living with and maintaining this unique landscape.

Deirdre O'Mahony was born in Limerick, studied at the Regional Technical College, Galway and graduated from St Martin's School of Art, London in 1979. Solo exhibitions include ERRATICS (Guiness Hopstore) 1997, Wrap (Galway Art's Centre) 2000. She received an arts international Pollock/Krasner bursary in 1996 and an Art's Council bursary in 1997. Her work is in numerous private and public collections throughout the world. She is currently a full time lecturer in the painting department of the Galway and Mayo Institute of Technology.

Photographs, Veronica Nicholson.

30. Wrap #3. 1999 acrylic/pigment/canvas. 270 by 230cm by 8cm collection O'Mahony and Co Ltd.

31. Wrap #8 1999 acrylic/pigment/linen. 212 by 200 cm collection of the artist.

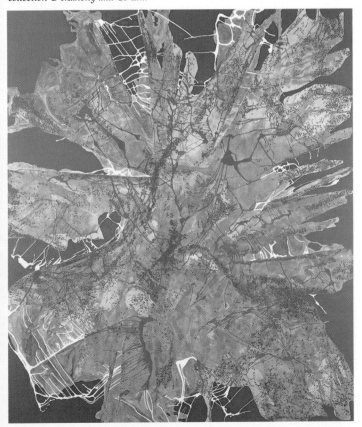

259

Obituaries

Michael Greene, 1957 - 2001

Michael Greene, Burren visionary, entrepreneur and sportsman, he died while playing football for his native Ballyvaughan. He was only 44. His achievements for a man in middle age were extraordinary. He had already founded what became the annual Burren Archaeological conference where at its first meeting the debate about Mullaghmore began. He established Ireland's first private Art College, involving the restoration of Newtown Castle, now of international renown and that, in turn, led him to found the Breton Law school for those interested in the association of Breton lawyers with contemporary legal systems. The idea to create a nature trail under the escarpment of Cappanawalla mountain was his as well.

He played a crucial role in the Ballyvaughan Development Association, steering this sensitive area away from inappropriate development and the creation of a proactive pioneering plan for the town, which has become a model for other communities. This generous passionate man left unfinished business too; plans to house the O'Loughlin genealogies, facsimiles and other Clare's writers, for example, as well as a centre for Burren contemporary art. Few have done so much. His loss is irreparable and the Burren will be poorer without him.

Cyril Ó'Céirín

Cyril Ó'Céirín, poet, artist, writer and scholar died on February 4th 1999. It was an untimely loss and a great shock to all of us who knew him. His work as a writer, poet and artist was not at all finished, yet looking back over his achievements, it is hard to believe that he managed to pack so much into his 64 years.

He was a secondary school teacher in Limerick for twenty years and the author of nine books. Three of these,

Wild and Free (O'Brien Press 1878) – a book on the lore and use of the wild harvest that became a popular classic, *Séadna* (Glendale 1989), a translation of the classic tale by An tAthair Peadar (Peter O'Leary) and the biographic dictionary *Women of Ireland* (Tír Eolas 1996) were in collaboration with his wife, Kit.

His poetry in Irish won several awards, including one from the Listowel Writers Week for the collection *Le hAer's Le Fuacht* which appeared in 1986. While his poetic vision made him a self styled "lone bird" amongst his contemporaries in terms of subject and style, his later work in English and his painting embraces the community of the Burren he had come to adopt and become a conscience for. In his last publication, *The Outlandish World of the Burren* (1998 Rathbane Publishing/Cló an Rátha Bháin, of which he was a founder), he demonstrated his considerable talent as an essayist.

As one of the original members of the Burren Action Group, he campaigned against the interpretative centre at Mullaghmore but sadly did not live to see the Group's final success.

Leo Swan

When I was asked to write this piece, my son. Dara had just been born. So I thought what would I tell him of the grandfather he would never know. Leo grew up in Co. Meath in the 1930's, where he began his brilliant career as a teacher at the age of nineteen. In 1960 he moved to Dublin to teach in Raheny and was able to indulge his passion for flying. After an evening course, he worked for the Flying Tigers in the US, Frankfurt Tripoli and London.

In the mid sixties Leo married and returned to Ireland with his young family to teach in Tallaght. His growing interest in archaeology led to an evening course and a masters degree at UCD and this new enthusiasm together with his skills as aviator led to his pioneering use of

aerial photography to analyse early historic sites. Over the years this has become ground-breaking work.

In later life Leo continued to pursue this interest through his publications, his college courses, summer schools and the field trips. He even established a museum at the Loreto Boys' School. And, after he took early retirement, he set up an archaeological consultancy, Arch-Tech Ltd.

Many people knew and liked Leo and will have their own memories of him. Indeed you could say his was a life fully lived. A man of many talents and interests, he was, above all, a good friend.

Rónán Swan

Patrick Sheeran

There's a game we used to play as kids. We'd toss a stone into a perfectly still surface of the lake and watch how far the ripple spread. The death of Patrick Sheeran, on 15th September 2001, the professor of Modern Irish literature, ecology and cinema, characteristically eclectic, sent ripples in all directions too. Some have yet to reach the shoreline.

I knew him as a colleague, friend and as godfather to my youngest daughter and as someone who shared his interest in all sorts of things but chiefly in what he would recognise as 'heterodox mysticism'. I recall an extraordinary outing. Pat was keen to test Yeats' idea that places where people had lived might retain spiritual 'traces' of their presence. We drove to a particular spot on the Burren – it was about 2 a.m. and if anyone had seen us they would have truly thought we were, truly, away with the fairies – and wandered around.

Suddenly we began to see tiny points of light all over the place for maybe 15 or 20 minutes. We were stunned. We compared notes and found that we'd had the same kind of experience. Drawing no conclusions, we headed home. Years later I discovered that the

spot we had chosen was the site of a long deserted village. We hardly ever talked of it again, but it forged a bond between us.

Pat Sheeran was a very special person – boyish, enthusiastic, bursting with ideas, touched with genuine brilliance. He could be kind, self-effacing and touchingly vulnerable. I was proud to think of him as a friend and I will miss him profoundly. May God's blessing keep him.

Jeff O'Connell

Pat Healy

Pat was born on the 20th March 1941 and raised to a life of farming in the hills around Bellharbour, as one of nine children. He began his education at school in Tullagh where his mother was the only teacher. Following in the family tradition, he was sent to St. Mary's as a boarder where he received his training in spiritual values, an education he continued at the Colombian Seminary at Dalgan Park. He was sent to the Philippines to work as a priest where he came to identify with the poor peasantry who where losing their land in the mountains to speculators.

When martial law was declared in 1972 he was detained in Camp Alagar for a short time. After his release he was appointed parish priest in a fishing village but by 1976 the military dictatorship was making his work impossible.

So in 1977 Pat came to Ireland with his wife and children. But he retained his links with the Philippines through his work with the Philipino-Irish campaign which was highlighting the injustices people where suffering there. But his great love became the Burren where he quarried Liscannor flag stones and learnt to be a stone mason, creating elegant paving and a unique style in outdoor stone furniture.

He died tragically on the 7th September 1997. He was laid to rest in Corcomroe Abbey.

Index

Acknowledgements for illustrations
1. Photo, Veronica Nicholson.
2. Drawing, Royal Irish Academy.
3. Photo, National Library of Ireland. 4. Photo, Anne Korff. 5. Photo,Veronica Nicholson. 6.,7.,8.,9., Photo, Brendan Dunford.
10.,11.,12., Photo, Nutan.
13. Photo, BAG. 14. Photo, Press 22.
15. Photo, Cilian Roden. 16. Drawing, Cilian Roden.
17.,18.,19., Paintings, Gordon D'Arcy. 23. Photo, Nutan. 24.,26. Photo, Gabriel Casey. 25. Photo, Ilse Thielen. 27. 1-3, Photo, Carl Vetter. 28.,29.,30.,31. Photo, Veronica Nicholson.

The opinions represented in this book are the sole responsibility of the individuals who expressed them and should not be taken to reflect either the views or the policy of the editors and publishers.

Ten Years On
pages 228-264
compiled by Anne Korff
edited by Richard Broad and Anne Korff